COMMUNICATION
REVOLUTION

Also by Robert W. McChesney

*The Political Economy of Media: Enduring Issues,
Emerging Dilemmas* (2008)

*Tragedy and Farce: How the American Media Sell Wars, Spin
Elections, and Destroy Democracy* (with John Nichols) (2005)

*The Problem of the Media: U.S. Communication Politics
in the 21st Century* (2004)

*Our Media, Not Theirs: The Democratic Struggle Against
Corporate Media* (with John Nichols) (2002)

It's the Media, Stupid! (with John Nichols) (2000)

*Rich Media, Poor Democracy: Communication Politics
in Dubious Times* (1999)

The Global Media: The New Missionaries of Corporate Capitalism
(with Edward S. Herman) (1997)

Corporate Media and the Threat to Democracy (1997)

*Telecommunications, Mass Media, and Democracy: The Battle
for the Control of U.S. Broadcasting, 1928–1935* (1993)

Edited Volumes

The Future of Media (with Russell Newman and Ben Scott)
(2005)

Our Unfree Press: 100 Years of Radical Media Criticism
(with Ben Scott) (2004)

*Capitalism and the Information Age: The Political Economy
of the Global Communication Revolution* (with Ellen Meiksins
Wood and John Bellamy Foster) (1998)

*Ruthless Criticism: New Perspectives in U.S. Communication
History* (with William Solomon) (1993)

COMMUNICATION REVOLUTION

Critical Junctures and the Future of Media

ROBERT W. McCHESNEY

THE NEW PRESS

NEW YORK
LONDON

Requests for permission to reproduce selections from this book
should be mailed to: Permissions Department, The New Press, 38
Greene Street, New York, NY 10013.

Published in the United States by The New Press, New York, 2007
Distributed by W. W. Norton & Company, Inc., New York

LIBRARY OF CONGRESS CATALOGING-IN-PUBLICATION DATA

McChesney, Robert Waterman, 1952–
    Communication revolution : critical junctures and the future of
media / Robert W. McChesney.
        p. cm.
    Includes bibliographical references and index.
    ISBN 978-1-59558-207-2 (hc.)
    1. Communication—History—21st century—Forecasts. I. Title.
P91.M25 2007
302.2309'0501—dc22   2007017387

The New Press was established in 1990 as a not-for-profit alternative
to the large, commercial publishing houses currently dominating the
book publishing industry. The New Press operates in the public interest rather than for private gain, and is committed to publishing, in
innovative ways, works of educational, cultural, and community value
that are often deemed insufficiently profitable.

www.thenewpress.com

Composition by Westchester Book Composition
This book was set in Palatino

Printed in the United States of America

10 9 8 7 6 5 4 3 2 1

Contents

Acknowledgments

The genesis for this book came in two talks I gave at the Annenberg School for Communication at the University of Pennsylvania in 2006. The second talk, in December, produced a paper, "The New Political Economy and the Rethinking of Journalism History," and was part of the conference titled "Back to the Future: Explorations in Communication and History." I want to thank the conference participants, especially Paul Starr, Michael Schudson, James Curran, Carolyn Marvin, John Durham Peters, and David Nord, for their assessment of some of the issues I take up in this book. I also want to thank Michael Delli Carpini and Barbie Zelizer for asking me to come to Penn, and for the extensive feedback from Penn faculty and grad students that each talk received.

I have been very fortunate to have received considerable help with this book, though I am obviously the responsible party for anything written herein. There is a world of talent in the next several paragraphs. I depend so much on the support and help of other people that I think at times I am more like the "producer" of a book than its author.

The following people helped me with specific points in the

text: John Anderson, Michael Schudson, Mark Cooper, Larry Grossberg, Jim Snider, Edward S. Herman, Pedro Cabán, Peter DiCola, Ben Scott, Toby Miller, Susan Douglas, Marvin Ammori, Christian Sandvig, Ed Baker, Jenny Toomey, Sundiata Cha-Jua, Ron Yates, Steve Helle, Jim Baughman, Allen Ruff, David Felix, Patrick Barrett, Tim Wu, Paul Buhle, Derek Seidman, Richard Du Boff, Amit M. Schejter, Jim Harper, Michael Greve, Randy Baker, Robin Hahnel, Craig Aaron, Sut Jhally, Geneva Overholser, James L. Gattuso, Sonia Livingstone, Ben Manski, Richard John, Stanley Aronowitz, and Scott Lovaas.

Derek Turner took time from his busy schedule to crunch numbers for me on a number of technical matters. Andrea Ray provided photocopying support. Kamilla Kovacs and Victor Pickard were both off-the-charts as research assistants. Without exception, for every request I made of them—dozens in a very short period of time—they responded almost immediately and exceeded my expectations. I am spoiled.

Rosalie Morales Kearns gave the entire manuscript a professional editing. Craig Aaron gave the edited manuscript a very hard proofreading and editing. Craig volunteered to do this over the weekend away from his duties as Communication Director for Free Press. Rosalie and Craig both worked under tremendous time constraints as a favor to me. I thank them both.

Here is the entering class for my Colleague Hall of Fame: Lance Bennett, Dan Schiller, Derek Turner, Vivek Chibber, John Bellamy Foster, Inger Stole, Larry Gross, André Schiffrin, Michael Delli Carpini, Victor Pickard, Ben Scott, John Nerone, Susan Douglas, Bruce Williams, Eric Klinenberg, Josh Silver, and John Nichols gave the manuscript a hard read and provided me with superb criticism. All of them went way above and beyond the call of duty in taking time from their demanding schedules to assist me with this book. Bennett, Delli Carpini, and Gross were quite encouraging throughout the process, which made it a lot easier to deal with the very strong (and appropriate) criticism the manuscript received. My four colleagues—Schiller, Nerone, Stole, and Williams[1]—and two brilliant Ph.D. candidates—Pickard and Scott—all put an extraordinary amount of time and energy into criticizing the manuscript, and helping me work through my basic arguments.

When I think of the "quality" of the rough draft I sent to each of these seventeen readers in January 2007, I cringe. To the extent this book does not make readers cringe, they get a good deal of the credit. They are true friends. Thank you.

For several years now I have had a visceral understanding that I would feel no more comfortable turning a manuscript over to a publisher before Jeff Cohen edited it anymore than I would feel comfortable marching up and down Fifth Avenue stark naked in January with the pages tied to my ankle. Jeff is simply the most extraordinary combination of talents. He is as knowledgeable about media as anyone I know, has razor-sharp political instincts, and is a truly gifted writer and editor. In some ways, his terrific book, *Cable News Confidential: My Misadventures in Corporate Media* (PoliPoint, 2006), was the inspiration for the style this book assumed. Jeff cleared time for me from his very busy schedule and turned this manuscript around on a dime.

Andy Hsiao at The New Press was encouraging and supportive from the first instance I mentioned the possibility of writing this book. He didn't cut me the same slack he gives Nichols, but I am glad to get the silver medal. André Schiffrin was every bit as supportive, and took the initiative to read and comment on the manuscript. I am lucky to have such a publisher. We are all lucky to have such a press. Doing this book took me away from a book I am writing with John Bellamy "Duke" Foster (also for The New Press) on global communication and monopoly capital, so I am thankful that Duke was so supportive. He had every right not to be.

---

1. Bruce Williams left Illinois for a position at the University of Virginia in 2006, but he will always be a colleague.

Along with Duke Foster, much of the thinking in this book was inspired by my close relationships with Inger Stole, Vivek Chibber, and John Nichols. I remember the exact moment I met each of the four of them, ranging from thirty-four to thirteen years ago, and almost from that first moment, they each entered my life as soul partners for the duration. The insights of these four, in one manner or another, are reflected on every page of this book. They are my co-pilots, and as often as not, my teachers.

Over the past four years I have been involved with the media reform group, Free Press (www.freepress.net), and that experience is a key component of this book. I owe everyone at that extraordinary organization immense thanks for their willingness to take this wayward college professor seriously. In particular I want to thank Kimberly Longey, the managing director, and Josh Silver, the executive director, who founded Free Press with John Nichols and me in late 2002. Kimberly and Josh have both taught me how to run a large and complex organization efficiently, while making certain it remains a political movement, not a bureaucracy. Josh, to whom I have spoken more over the past four years than anyone outside my immediate family, has given me a phenomenal education in political organizing, and has become a dear friend in the process. If the history of Free Press is ever written, let it be clear that Josh Silver was the guiding force behind it, and without him it would not exist.

This one's for Inger, Amy, Lucy, and Chippie; and, from Elrod, to the memory of Red and DJ. Gone, but never forgotten.

Urbana, Illinois
May 2007

Introduction

The communication revolution is something we are witnessing, something that is happening *to* us, something we are powerless to change. That is the conventional wisdom, anyway. It is the message in our media and in our classrooms.

To some the digital revolution with its myriad technologies is something extraordinary, almost magical. It is being executed by brilliant entrepreneurs and genius inventors, taking their cues and inspiration from that holiest of grails, the free market. It is giving us all sorts of power as users of media. We have the good fortune to have been born in this period, so we have front-row seats to this amazing digital revolution. But otherwise it is something over which we have no control, except as consumers. There are a few naysayers, of course, who regard the communication revolution as at best a mixed blessing; but they are just as likely to accept that it is a process over which they have no control. This crowd longs for the past rather than a different future. Either way, citizens are seen as powerless before this extraordinary force that is redefining our societies and our lives.

In this book, I argue that the conventional wisdom is wrong.

The truth is that the communication revolution, or better put, our communication system as a whole, is not primarily the result of geniuses and free markets. It is the result of structures and markets created and shaped by policies and extraordinary public subsidies. Those policies and subsidies are made in our name, though only rarely with our informed public consent. Whether the communication revolution will prove to be something truly magnificent—or something we may come to dread— is going to be determined to a significant extent by whether the crucial communication policies are made with the informed consent of the citizenry or behind closed doors. What we as citizens do—or don't do—in the coming decade will make all the difference. The future is in our hands.

If we elect to do nothing, to accept the conventional wisdom, crucial policy decisions will be made by powerful corporate interests and the politicians they own behind closed doors, and the system will be created to suit their needs. In my view, that may well lead to highly undesirable outcomes: the ongoing deterioration, even elimination, of journalism as we know it; the commercialization of every aspect of our cultures, including childhood; and the loss of a vision of public space or the common good. In time, many people will accept such an outcome as being as "natural" as the air we breathe. Corporate public relations will fan the flames of conventional wisdom, telling us this was the inevitable result of free markets and democratic values. As I will demonstrate in this book, that argument is dead wrong. It is patent propaganda.

In view of the extraordinary democratic potential of the new technologies, such an outcome would be both absurd and tragic. Not only doesn't it have to happen, but citizens across the land are organizing to create a different communication revolution, one that generates a media system that emphasizes democratic values over corporate profits.

The premise of this book is very simple. We have an unprecedented opportunity in the coming generation to create a communication system that will be a powerful impetus to a dramatically more egalitarian, humane, sustainable, and creative society, where justice and self-government are the order of the day. This window of opportunity—what I call a "critical juncture"—will not be open for long. We will be opposed by very powerful entrenched corporate and political interests. We will need all hands on deck to win the fight. In this historic moment, there is a particularly important role for communication scholars and students to play. This book is written for all Americans, but especially for my colleagues and students in our schools, colleges, and universities. This is a fight we cannot afford to lose.

At this point, I imagine some readers are already saying, "fat chance." The history of American media is one continual victory of powerful corporate interests over everyone else. Most see that state of affairs as inevitable: the American way. So we should just sit back, shut up, and shop.

In this book, I demonstrate that corporate rule over media was *not* inevitable in the past, and that there are grounds to believe that the corporate stranglehold over our media system is very much in jeopardy today. In just the past three years, organized citizens have won dramatic victories on a number of media policy fights—from media ownership rules and protecting public broadcasting to stopping government and corporate propaganda masquerading as news. Perhaps most important is the battle keeping the largest telephone and cable companies from privatizing the Internet. Such victories would have been unthinkable only a decade ago.

The movement for media reform is now entering a new phase of proactively creating policies that can truly democratize our media system. For example:

- creating the notion of super-fast ubiquitous broadband, wired and wireless, uncensored by corporate or government interests, as a birthright of all Americans;

- ownership policies to make it possible for competitive commercial media markets, so the idea of starting one's own outlet is again realistic;
- policies and subsidies to support a viable heterogeneous tier of noncommercial and nonprofit media, especially at the local level, with particular emphasis on policies promoting journalism;
- a media system that actually informs citizens about candidates at election time and does not turn over the job to asinine ads paid for by wealthy contributors;
- clear limitations on the penetration of commercialism into our media content, and a complete walling-off of childhood from advertising.

The result of policies like these—there are many more to be discussed and debated—will be a vibrant independent journalism, a dynamic civic society, and a healthy culture not driven by the needs of Wall Street and Madison Avenue.

These victories, this movement, these ideas, get virtually no coverage in the mainstream media. There are vested intellectual and commercial interests that are threatened by them. And in the end, any movement that radically transforms media into a more democratic force will be opposed by those in society who fear that genuine democracy might threaten their privileges. One of the purposes of this book is to explain this movement to citizens and scholars, and demonstrate the immense promise that it holds. This is not a theoretical or hypothetical argument; it is about real developments happening in community after community in the United States right now. It is about the stunning critical juncture we are entering where the *ancien regime* is dying, and it is very much up to us to determine what replaces it. Our awareness and activity can greatly increase the possibility that we have a communication revolution that serves democratic values, one that truly capitalizes upon the progressive and revolutionary promise of new technologies.

In what follows, I will make the case by chronicling key developments over the past two decades that led us to where we are today. In Chapter 1, I explain what I mean by the term "critical juncture," and I lay out my argument about the importance of critical junctures for understanding how media systems are established and changed. I also discuss how the field of communication developed in the United States as an academic discipline, and why scholars have such an important role to play in the critical juncture we're now entering.

In Chapter 2, I discuss the rise and fall of the subfield of the political economy of communication. This was a direct outgrowth of the political turbulence of the late 1960s and 1970s—another critical juncture—and was a key component of the "critical" school of communication research. I thought political economy could invigorate communication research, even redefine it, when I entered the field in the 1980s, but it failed to do so for reasons largely outside its control. However, this field was the immediate precursor to the policy-related research I believe is so crucial for communication scholars to pursue today.

In Chapter 3, I discuss the historical turn in communication policy research and the recognition of the considerable importance of critical junctures for understanding the emergence and nature of communication systems. This work played a key role in providing a vision—what I term the "five truths"—for the massive media reform movement that has emerged in recent years.

In Chapter 4, I chronicle that movement and assess the first steps communication scholars have taken to participate in this critical juncture. I outline some of the key pressing research areas for scholars to address, and offer an argument for why we now stand poised to make communication research the most dynamic and important social science research of our times.[1]

What we are seeing in the United States today is a rare phenomenon: citizens and scholars working together to enhance the quality of democracy and public life. For those of us in the field of communication, we are in the fortunate position to be in the middle of this process and, in doing so, we have an opportunity to reinvent our field. It is an opportunity we cannot let pass.

In this book, I make my case for how we should understand the communication revolution we are living in and the important decisions citizens confront in the coming years. Concurrently, I argue that the communication revolution requires the field of communication to fundamentally rethink its past, present, and future. It is an argument, or series of arguments, I have been pondering for many years in my research, public outreach, and teaching.

As I conceived of this book, I faced two vexing problems: First, can I write a book for a general readership that also addresses concerns specific to communication scholars, researchers, and students? This is something I have attempted to do in my previous books, but in no other book have I addressed the concerns of communication scholars as a central theme.

The entirety of the book should be of interest to communication scholars, teachers, and students. Even those sections of the book in Chapters 3 and 4 primarily addressing the popular media reform movements are important to them, and they are essential evidence for the case I am making about the significance of critical junctures and the need to rethink the field of communication.[2] One of the subplots in this book is the importance of scholars reaching out to broader audiences, without watering down the integrity or power of their research.

I believe the book will also appeal to readers with little interest in the academic field of communication. I do not believe writing a book that discusses the academic study of media must turn off the general public. All citizens have a stake in what happens with the field of communication because the outcome will affect us all. And I have been surprised over the past few years at how much concern there is in the general public about what is regarded as the inadequacies about communication research, and academic scholarship in general.

My second problem stared at me every time I looked in the mirror: what to do about myself. What role should I play in the narrative? When I began to write, the story seemed to flow naturally as a first-person narrative. But I did not want to write an autobiography or memoir, and this book can in no way be considered as such. The book is not about me, but about the issues addressed herein.

However, my argument grows directly out of my personal experiences after having spent nearly twenty-five years in the field of communication. I think that in recounting the development of the field over the past two-plus decades, a personal approach is necessary, even unavoidable. Communication is such a heterogeneous field that there is no single canon, no roundly accepted story, to explain the field. My colleagues who came through speech or traditional mass communication programs, or, as is often the case, through other fields like history or sociology or political science, had a very different experience than I did. They might regard my peculiar framing of the field as quite unlike their own. I think it would be impossible—or hugely time consuming—to accurately convey these other paths. So I acknowledge them but concentrate on my personal experience in the field and what I have learned.[3]

Regardless of our origins as scholars, or the paths we have traveled, I think we are all ending up pretty much in the same place. Because of that, I will use personal anecdotes to illustrate my points. I realize that anecdotes have limitations as evidence, but the experiences I recount play a significant role in the formulation of the argument I present here. In some respects, this book could be subtitled "the education of a wayward college professor."[4]

I also had to determine what role I play in the narrative as a scholar, and what role as an activist. My own research, which I discuss in Chapter 3, is central to my argument. And, more important, my own association with media policy activism is central to my discussion in Chapter 4. But I'm not trying to claim a "starring role" in these developments. Please let me make it clear: Everything of fundamental consequence I describe in this book, especially in Chapters 3 and 4, would have occurred even if I had never been born. These are profound structural developments in which I am participating.

In particular, as the co-founder and president of Free Press, the public interest group committed to establishing informed public participation in the core communication policy issues of our times, I have come to appreciate the importance of communication research as never before. This includes research in areas I knew little about heretofore, and research that I may have been dismissive toward in times past. I also have had the capacity to use resources I influence to draw communication scholarship into these public debates and deliberations. This book is intended as a necessary part of that process, because if the field of communication does not get engaged with the critical juncture we are in, I fear not only for the future of the field, but for the future of the Republic.

COMMUNICATION
REVOLUTION

1

Crisis in Communication, Crisis for Society

We are in the midst of a communication and information revolution. Of that there is no doubt. What is uncertain is what type of revolution this will be, how sweeping, and with what effects. Precisely how this communication revolution will unfold and what it will mean for our journalism, our culture, our politics, and our economics are not at all clear. In a generation or two we may speak of this era as a glorious new chapter in our history: democratizing our societies, revolutionizing our economies, lessening inequality and militarism, reversing environmental destruction, and generating an extraordinary outburst of culture and creativity. Or we may speak of it despondently, measuring what we have lost, or, for some, never had: our privacy, our humanity, our control over our own destiny, and our hope for the future. Or we may end up somewhere in between.

Where we end up, how our communication revolution unfolds, will be determined to a significant extent by a series of crucial policy decisions that will likely be made over the course of the coming decade or two. In this book, I will present a conceptual framework to help citizens understand why this is a moment when they must take media policy seriously. My argument is both familiar and original, theoretical and historical. It will also be empirical: Among other things, I will demonstrate that in the past decade there already has been an unprecedented increase in popular concern about media policies. This is no longer the secretive and mysterious domain of self-interested corporate executives, accountants, lawyers, politicians on the make, engineers, and techno-geeks. Media policy is becoming everybody's business. The more that continues, the more likely we will attain a progressive outcome to the communication revolution.

In my view, as much as any technological innovation, it is the democratization of media policymaking, and the democratization of politics in general, that will ultimately be seen as the truly revolutionary aspect of the communication revolution. I write this book for concerned citizens so they may better understand the choices that can generate the best possible outcome.

Let me put this another way: If fifteen or twenty years from now, the result of the communication revolution is merely technological wizardry or a testament to enhanced market opportunities for the world's most privileged people, it will have been a failure. If it is about hooking up affluent consumers to more choices, investors to more opportunities, and making it easier for them to bypass the wretched of the earth, it may prove to be a dubious contribution to the development of our species. At the very least it will be a missed opportunity, and I do not know how many more of those are coming down the pike. If in a generation social inequality has not begun to be dramatically reversed, democratic institutions are not considerably more vibrant, militarism and chauvinism have not been dealt a mighty blow, the environment has not been significantly repaired, then we will have had an unfulfilled communication revolution.

Communication has been at the heart of our species from our very emergence some 100,000 years ago, and communication is central to democratic theory and practice. New technologies are in the process of forming the central nervous system for our society in a manner unimaginable, even in the media-drenched late twentieth century. No previous communication revolution has held the promise of allowing us to radically transcend the structural communication limitations for effective self-government and human happiness that have existed throughout human history. But such a communication revolution will not occur because of a magical technology; it will only occur because organized people make it so.

I also address this book and this argument to my fellow scholars, especially those who work in communication or media studies, and to our students, both graduate and undergraduate, past, present, and future.[1] This is one constituency that has only begun to consider the nature of the historical moment we are entering, and whose very existence depends upon coming to terms with it. I believe that scholars have a crucial and indispensable role to play in the coming period, and that the best possible outcome for media policies is dependent upon their active involvement. We all have a stake in whether communication scholars and students grasp the potential of the times we are in. Moreover, I believe that the future of the field of communication rides on how well the field adapts to what I consider a moment of truth. We need a revolution, of sorts, in the way scholars conceptualize, study, and teach communication. I direct this book primarily at an American readership, though I suspect it may strike a chord with citizens and scholars in other nations.

This should be the moment in the sun for the field of communication at U.S. universities, as it has been for computer science. Indeed, in the not-too-distant past, that was what seemed to be on the horizon. The academic field of communication had enjoyed a certain increase in prominence in the generations following World War II. By the 1970s and into the 1980s, important epistemological, theoretical, and political debates were being raised, and the discipline was influenced by the vitality of intellectual life in those times. "I have no doubt that many communication scholars can hardly believe their luck," Nicholas Garnham wrote in the *Journal of Communication* in 1983. "After years on the margins of intellectual concern and academic power, we suddenly find ourselves center stage, with the spotlight of social relevance full upon us."[2]

Since the mid-1980s, and clearly by the 1990s, however, the dynamism has been extinguished. The field of communication matured and solidified in an institutional sense, and its place in the university firmament is for the most part secure. At the same time, the field has settled into a second-tier role in U.S. academic life, and there is too little research that is distinguished. We produce Ph.D.'s to work at the many dozens of doctoral programs that exist, but little of the work commands much interest or attention outside narrow confines of the field. Concurrently, the importance of information and communication has exploded with the digital revolution. What seemed to Garnham in 1983 like a symbiotic marriage has become a striking paradox.

Strictly speaking, these words concerning the state of U.S. communication studies are too harsh. There are scores of dedicated communication scholars in the midst of distinguished careers, and a handful of stars whose works are known outside the field and will transcend our times. But note that my general concern about the field's trajectory is not original or even especially unusual. "With the exception of a few works produced by a handful of notable scholars," a despondent longtime chair of a U.S. communication department wrote upon his retirement in 2000, "most of what passes for 'scholarly research' in media is pretty trivial."[3] Raymie McKerrow, the recent president of the National Communication Association, one of the three main U.S. organizations for media and communication scholars, wrote a scathing critique of the field's irrelevance in the NCA newsletter. McKerrow noted that "Criticism, at its best, is informed talk about matters of importance."[4] McKerrow called for "criticism as intervention," for the field to "become more familiar with and influential in public policy deliberations," and for the aggressive spawning of "public intellectuals."[5]

The 2001 annual conference of the International Communication Association, another of the main scholarly groups in the field, was titled, perhaps to convince itself, "Communication Research Matters." The conference was structured to promote the important work that media and communication scholars can do to assist the public with the fundamental issues of our age. Then, in 2004, the ICA annual conference was titled "Research in the Public Interest." Clearly this is a concern.

Perhaps the strongest and most important statement in this regard came in the presidential address at the 2005 ICA annual convention in New York City by Wolfgang Donsbach. Donsbach is an empirical scholar whose approach, research methodologies, and political values differ from my own, but here we stand on common ground. He brings both an international and historical perspective to the task. "While decades ago, we had too much politics and too little empirical research, today, within the paradigm of empirical research, we are shifting into a direction with too much petty number crunching and too little really important research questions, that is, research with state-of-the-art methodology and with validity but with little relevance and significance."[6] My concerns spread across the discipline and across methodologies and encompass a range of political perspectives. I would add only that the problem extends beyond the empirical scholars Donsbach is addressing in this comment.

I believe that the gaping chasm between the role of media and communication in our society and the current direction and structure of the field of communication in the United States has reached crisis stage, and that this crisis affects not only the professors, students, and administrators associated with these departments, but our entire society. There are, as economists like to put it, considerable "externalities." Our nation desperately needs engaged communication scholarship from a broad range of traditions and employing a diverse set of methodologies to address the issues before us. And to the extent this situation exists in other nations, it is a crisis there as well. Why? In a narrow sense, what happens in communication departments and universities eventually affects everyone. Ideas are important. (That is why the political right has devoted so much energy toward encouraging pro-conservative scholarship and right-wing media over the past three decades.)[7] If communication provides a substandard education to undergraduate and graduate students alike, we will see the consequences in poorer media and weaker civic institutions and public life.

But the problem is even greater than that. The digital revolution we are part of is raising fundamental questions about communication and how it affects economics, politics, culture, organizations, and interpersonal relationships. Some of the most important questions, I suspect, have not yet been asked, let alone answered. And most important of all are a series of core structural questions: How will the communication system of the coming era be organized, structured, and subsidized? How will decisions be made that determine these structures and policies? What values will be privileged? What will be the nature of accountability both for the communication system and for the policymaking process? If anything is certain, it is that the emerging communication system will go a long way toward shaping our economy, our politics, and, for lack of a better term, our way of life. It has become our central nervous system. Hence, if communication research tends to avoid these fundamental issues, then all the resources devoted to it will be of little use to the citizenry when it looks to experts for assistance and context in addressing core policy decisions surrounding media, culture, and communication. Indeed, if communication scholars do not actively engage with this moment, it may well undermine the ability of the public to participate effectively and lead to undesirable and undemocratic outcomes.

This is what NCA President McKerrow was getting at in his

2001 address. We in the field of communication all have a stake facing up to the situation we are in and moving aggressively to fill the breach. If the field of communication fails, the entire prospect of a more democratic communication system that promotes a more just and humane society will be compromised, if not terminated. The stakes are that high.

In this book, I argue that the way out of the doldrums, the way forward, is for communication scholars to recognize what millions of Americans are coming to understand: Our communication system and, to a lesser extent, our political economic system are now entering a *critical juncture*, a period in which the old institutions and mores are collapsing.

The notion of critical junctures explains how social change works; there have been relatively rare and brief periods in which dramatic changes were debated and enacted drawing from a broad palette of options, followed by long periods in which structural or institutional change was slow and difficult.[8] During a critical juncture, which usually lasts no more than one or two decades, the range of options for society is much greater than it is otherwise. The decisions made during such a period establish institutions and rules that likely put us on a course that will be difficult to change in any fundamental sense for decades or generations.

This notion of critical junctures is increasingly accepted in history and the social sciences. It has proven valuable for thinking broadly about society-wide fundamental social change, and also as a way to understand fundamental change within a specific sector, like media and communication. The two types of critical junctures are distinct, yet, as I will demonstrate, very closely related. Most of our major institutions in media are the result of such critical junctures, periods when policies could have gone in other directions, and, had they done so, put media and society on a different path.

As a result of my research, I have concluded that critical junctures in media and communication tend to occur when at least two if not all three of the following conditions hold:

- There is a revolutionary new communication technology that undermines the existing system;
- The content of the media system, especially the journalism, is increasingly discredited or seen as illegitimate; and
- There is a major political crisis—severe social disequilibrium—in which the existing order is no longer working and there are major movements for social reform.

In the past century, critical junctures in media and communication occurred three times: in the Progressive Era, when journalism was in deep crisis and the overall political system was in turmoil; in the 1930s, when the emergence of radio broadcasting combined with public antipathy to commercialism against the backdrop of the Depression; and in the 1960s and early 1970s, when popular social movements in the United States provoked radical critiques of the media as part of a broader social and political critique.

The result of the critical juncture in the Progressive Era was the emergence of professional journalism. The result of the critical juncture in the 1930s was the model of loosely regulated commercial broadcasting, which provided the model for subsequent electronic media technologies like FM radio, terrestrial television, and cable and satellite television. The result of the 1960s and 1970s critical juncture is less tangible for communication. In many respects the issues raised then were never resolved and they were buried by the neoliberal epoch that followed.

Today, we are in the midst of a profound critical juncture for communication. Two of the three conditions for a critical juncture are already in place: the digital revolution is overturning all existing media industries and business models; and journalism is at its lowest ebb since the Progressive Era. The third condition—the overall stability of the political and social system—is the great unknown. There are certainly grounds for suspecting that a critical juncture is imminent. Our overall political system is awash in institutionalized corruption and growing inequality. The economy is in turmoil, too, and it appears likely that we are entering a period of structural transformation to points unknown. U.S. global military dominance is wobbling with the disaster of the Iraq war, and the combination of empire and republic is difficult to maintain.[9] In January 2007, the *Bulletin of the Atomic Scientists* moved its symbolic doomsday clock to five minutes to midnight. For the first time ever, the editors stressed the role of not just nuclear weapons but of global climate change in the impending catastrophes facing humankind. This is becoming a political and social crisis of major proportions.[10]

What remains to be seen is to what extent the people engage with the structural crises our society is facing, or leave matters to elites. In the critical juncture of the 1960s and early 1970s, for example, elites were concerned by a "crisis of democracy." This crisis was created by previously apathetic, passive, and marginalized elements of the population—for example, minorities, women, students—becoming politically engaged and making demands upon the system.[11]

For communication scholars, all the long-standing presuppositions they were trained in, and that were taken for granted in our society, no longer hold. Both professional journalism and commercial broadcasting are in crisis and fundamental transformation. The communication system that emerges from this critical juncture will look little like the communication system of 2000 or 1990. Already the media system of the 1960s seems about as relevant to what lies before us as a discussion of the War of the Roses does to contemporary military strategists. Most important, we know that how the emerging communication system is structured will go a long way toward determining how our politics and economics, our way of life, will play out.

Although broader popular social movements are nascent, what's been striking is that this critical juncture has spawned the birth of an extraordinary media reform movement in the past few years. Hundreds of thousands, perhaps millions, of Americans have engaged with media policy issues in a manner that had been previously unthinkable. Politicians and regulators are discovering for the first time in their careers that what they do with regard to media is being watched closely by voters and citizens, and they are beginning to respond. What remains to be seen is whether there will be a broader resurgence of popular politics in the coming period. If there is, it will shift the emerging "media reform movement" into a much higher gear and the range of possible outcomes will increase dramatically. Such a boom in popular social movements would also combine with media reform to lead, at the least, to the sort of periodic reformation of institutions that happens every two or three generations in American history, and for which we are sadly overdue. Without such a broader popular political movement, there will still be a critical juncture in media and communication, only the outcomes will be more likely to serve the needs of dominant commercial and political interests, not the public.

Engaging with public policy issues from the vantage point of concerned citizens rather than from the perspective of owners and administrators opens new vistas for scholars, raising pressing new research questions and issues. In my mind, the evidence is clear that scholarship in the social sciences can be strengthened by being connected to real-life social movements and political affairs. In economics, for example, many of the great breakthroughs in theory were made by scholars with a direct engagement with the politics of their day, from Smith, Ricardo, J.S. Mill, and Marx to Marshall and Keynes. Even Milton Friedman is notable because his work was driven by pressing political concerns.[12] I think that this can be and should be true for communication as well.

Let me be clear on this point. My argument is not that communication scholars and students need to become full-time activists or must dedicate a portion of their time to public engagement with media issues. That is fine for some of us but not for everyone. My point is simply that the notion of being in a critical juncture, of recognizing the political moment we are in, should permeate all of our research agendas and our teaching. It needs to be embraced. Nor am I arguing that scholars should shape their research to reach predetermined outcomes, that they should place a political agenda ahead of the integrity of their scholarship. My argument is that during a critical juncture, scholars simply need to broaden their horizons and engage with the crucial political and social issues of the moment. Question presuppositions and abandon them; replace them, unless the weight of evidence justifies their maintenance. Dive in head-first equipped only with curiosity, democratic values, and research skills, and see what happens.

For those of us who study communication, this is an opportunity that few other scholars can ever experience. With recognition of the historically unusual, if not uncharted, waters we are in, communication studies can leapfrog over the barriers that have constrained it heretofore, and come to play a central role in social science research and education. It will not be an easy fight, for the barriers remain high, but it is the only way forward. Otherwise, our field loses much of its raison d'être, and the legitimacy of its claim to society's scarce resources.

It would be comforting to think that it is no big deal if communication programs continue to flounder, because other, more dynamic and established university programs can seize the initiative. Perhaps political science or economics or law schools or sociology or history could fill the void and provide searing insights into media and communication and their role in the emerging social order. Although media and communication issues have permeated many other fields to varying degrees, the results have not been satisfactory. Media research began in sociology in the United States and has existed on the distant margins of that field since it was largely abandoned over 50 years ago. But even allowing for the notable exceptions like Herbert Gans, William Gamson, and William Hoynes, media sociologists have not been able to establish much of a beachhead, and communication is arguably as weak today in the field as it has ever been.[13]

U.S. history programs in colleges and universities, which feature courses and research in a broad range of topics, have, to my knowledge, no courses in the history of journalism and precious few, if any, in the history of media. When Robert Darnton was the president of the American Historical Association, he used his 2000 presidential address to call for the field to make a "general attack on the problem of how societies made sense of events and transmitted information about them, something that might be called the history of communication."[14] The proposal fell on deaf ears, as far as I can tell, so strong is the institutional conservatism of the established disciplines.

In some respected disciplines, where media should be a central concern, it is virtually ignored altogether. Striking in this regard is political philosophy. One can read the brilliant work of political philosophers and theorists like John Rawls, Ronald Dworkin, Robert Dahl, and Amy Guttmann, among others, and find scarcely a word on the matter.[15] Book after book weighs in with detailed and thoughtful expositions on the necessary social conditions to promote democratic deliberation and viable self-government—often elaborating in detail upon the role of educational systems, the evils of censorship, the importance of free expression, and the best way to construct political parties and electoral systems. But the nature of the media system and how it is structured, and how that might affect the conditions for the informational needs of a democracy, are often nowhere to be found. It is a blind spot in their field. This work not only cannot reduce the weight on media studies' shoulders, it needs a thorough dousing in communication research to generate better answers to the important questions it is addressing.

Conversely, there is a range of important works being generated in fields other than communication that put considerable emphasis on the role of media in our polity and our culture. Some of these books, like the important works of Robert Putnam and Derek Bok, are by highly respected scholars and go directly to the basic caliber of our democracy.[16] Others sometimes make dramatic claims about media, in a manner that often makes communication scholars queasy.[17] These books vary in quality, and all have the virtue of attempting to make strong claims about media and society. But these books, including those by Putnam and Bok, all suffer from the weakness of their analysis of media. Were there a strong and vibrant literature in communication for these authors to draw upon, their books would be the better for it. They are not getting it in their home disciplines.

Some outstanding work is produced by scholars working in other fields, but they often work against the grain of their discipline. Usually a scholar with a strong interest in media and communication starts a career in some other field and then moves all or part of her appointment to a communication program to be surrounded by people with a grounding in media and an interest in her work, even if, or especially because, they have different disciplinary backgrounds. People like Lance Bennett, Susan Douglas, Stuart Ewen, Constance Penley, Mark Crispin Miller, Neil Postman, Michael Delli Carpini, Todd Gitlin, and Michael Schudson come immediately to mind, and there are scores of others. They do so for a reason. And noncommunication fields that do media research, but keep it within the narrow confines of their own field, tend to suffer for it. A colleague of mine from Illinois spoke to a group that was characterized as an elite team of media researchers at one of the leading business schools in the nation in 2006. He reported back to me with incredulity at their response to his research on

Internet policy. "This is all well and good," the senior faculty member, a former chief economist at the Federal Communications Commission, snorted, "but what does this have to do with how firms can make more money?" When my colleague, later in his presentation, mentioned that feminists had raised concerns about certain aspects of Internet policy, the audience members broke into laughter at what they regarded as the irrelevant and preposterous nature of such a claim.

The jury is now in on this matter: For communication research to be effective, it needs to be done in an interdisciplinary context, ideally a communication department, where scholars with different methodologies and research traditions interact with each other. It is in this environment that the best questions get asked and the flaws and oversights in the research are most readily exposed. And the field of communication must devote itself to addressing the central issues of its times squarely and courageously.

Media scholars are justifiably sensitive about the relative lack of importance accorded communication research at major U.S. research universities. At the University of Wisconsin-Madison, where I taught for a decade, despite the communication departments on that campus having a distinguished research record, it was seemingly regarded by the pooh-bahs in history, political science, and sociology as having roughly the same intellectual merit as, say, driver's education.[18] The immediate reaction of some communication scholars has been to erect the same type of intellectual barriers-to-entry as social scientists in other fields to justify and exalt the field's existence. This is the wrong direction. Although difficult terminology sometimes is necessary, the instances in which that is true are fewer than the instances when such terminology is presently employed. Former ICA president Donsbach also sees the downside of narrowing the field, following convention, and ramping up the disciplinary barricades: "With more personnel striving for professional distinction, the research questions become smaller and more remote all the time because everybody is going for (a) the ruling paradigms and (b) niches within these paradigms that have never before been subject to research."[19] In short, communication cannot escape its rut in academia by imitating the established fields. We have to boldly strike out in a popular and interdisciplinary manner that runs directly counter to the dominant trends in the academy. The times demand it. We have to be leaders.

In view of the perils of the academy, it would be comforting to think that intellectuals committed to communication research could bail out of the university system and do their work independently, perhaps holding down "day jobs" or incorporating their intellectual interests into nonacademic employment, like think tanks or public interest organizations. But this is not really an option, nor should it be. People outside the academy are going to have their judgment affected by the positions they are in, and, while that has positive aspects, it also compromises their vision. Societies need public intellectuals and need to provide them with some autonomy and insulation in the academy. As Harold Innis has argued, it is the hallmark of a liberal and democratic society to have an autonomous university sector, where scholars can provide critical analysis for the benefit of all of society.[20] More recently, John Michael has made a strong argument for the necessity of intellectuals for a democratic society.[21] Academics, accordingly, are granted tremendous privileges and occupational freedom compared to most people, and with that comes considerable responsibility. True liberals, in the best sense of the term, fight to defend this vision of the university even if they disagree with the nature of the scholarship. It is essential for a viable democratic culture. We can defend the tenure system only on the grounds that it protects the integrity and autonomy of intellectuals, so they can tell the truth and let the chips fall where they may. I am not naïve. I know this is an ideal, not a reality. But it is a struggle we can never abandon.

Let me be clear on this point, because it is complicated. I do not mean to posit university intellectuals as being "objective," because that clearly is not the case. They have their values and their perspectives, and those are unavoidable. But I would say that once one factors in their values—and their self-interest in the university system—university intellectuals can be more objective than those seeing the world from a more narrowly defined vantage point. Nor do I think academics or intellectuals are necessarily comfortable engaging with public life, especially if it puts them in an adversarial position to those in power. Noam Chomsky observes that the moments in which intellectuals have actually adopted dissident positions against the dominant institutions have been rare in U.S. history: "There are moments when a critical stance toward one's own society is (barely) tolerated; periods of popular ferment and struggle, the immediate aftermath of scandals and atrocities too extreme to suppress quickly. . . . But these moments are the exceptions in the history of intellectuals and academic social scientists. The usual stance is triumphalism about domestic power and providing the ideological support for it, meanwhile feathering one's own nest."[22]

A recent study by Carol Posgrove provides evidence of this phenomenon. She reveals that during the developing years of the civil rights movement, the support provided by many establishment academics and intellectuals was tepid.[23] Even so, it is in society's interest to create institutional space to protect and encourage as much autonomy and independence from dominant forces as possible. In the uncertainty that comes with a critical juncture, there will be more scholars willing to rise to the occasion. The goal should be to generate a critical mass, to build it into the occupational and intellectual culture.

In my view, therefore, the great threat to the notion of a liberal or democratic university today comes from neoliberalism, the notion that scholarship in the public interest is bunk and that research should properly assist the needs of the dominant economic interests and be supported through commercial auspices. This is a noxious and antidemocratic notion of higher education, the point of which is to eliminate independent and critical research and teaching.[24] As Christopher Lasch wrote in his final, glorious book, the main academic freedom battle on university campuses today is to arrest and roll back the increasing corporate-commercial penetration of higher education. It is inimical to the university tradition.[25] (This is not an issue that divides along left-right grounds. While I was at the University of Wisconsin-Madison, some of the faculty most concerned about this issue were regarded as political conservatives.) If universities increasingly become subservient to corporate interests, they are less likely to serve those groups or values, or address those issues disfavored by the commercial patrons. Nor is this entirely recent; it is a core tension in a capitalist society that neoliberalism merely brings to the fore. In the 1940s. Harold Innis went so far as to say, "The descent of the university into the market place reflects the lie in the soul of modern society."[26]

Why, exactly, is communication a second-tier program in American colleges and universities? How did we get to this point? Why didn't the field blast off as Garnham anticipated in 1983? The best reasons for the minor league status of communication include a variety of institutional factors within universities. Consider, for example, the field's belated arrival. It developed a generation or two later than the other leading social sciences, largely due to the rapid emergence of communication as a significant social factor in the first half of the twentieth century. Or consider that the emergence of communication on many campuses coincided with, and was fueled by, the emergence of TV as the central medium of U.S. society. This "contaminated" the study of media by association with the "popular" in the views of academics from across the political spectrum. I recall the words of my former colleague James Baughman, when he described the disdain he faced when he was explaining to his history faculty in grad school at Columbia in the 1970s that his dissertation was on television. As he put it, they thought anything to do with television earmarked a scholar as residing in the "toy department" of the university. But being "late to the table" hardly accounts for the field's current small portions, as the field of computer science attests. Likewise, the toy department of television, rock 'n' roll, and popular culture are now fair game for the most prestige-conscious of academics. So while these points offer some instruction, we need to look elsewhere.

A related explanation for the field's status is its heterogeneous antecedents. Modern communication has developed from English departments, speech programs, journalism schools, theater and drama departments, library schools, radio-TV departments, and film schools, and has been influenced by economics, political science, psychology, and sociology. Even engineering and mathematics programs have played a role, especially with the development of "information theory."[27] On some campuses, like the one I taught at for a decade in Madison, there are two or three departments devoted to communication and there is little rational explanation for which department does what.

This returns us to the subject of interdisciplinary work and its relative lack of status in the university. And this gets to one of the two core factors that explain the difficulties facing communication as it attempts to gain traction on college campuses: Rhetoric notwithstanding, interdisciplinary work is held in low regard in the academy, especially compared to more narrowly defined disciplines and fields. (The other factor is linkages to professional education and media industries, which I turn to below.) In this sense, the problem facing communication is the same one facing gender and ethnic studies programs. Ironically, to be done well, interdisciplinary work requires more training and education, and should be held in the highest regard.

The contemporary practice of communication research extends from cognitive, experimental, and survey research to rhetorical studies, cultural studies, ethnography, political economy, law, archival history, and much else. Methodologically it is a hodgepodge. (Other fields, like sociology, political science, and anthropology, have their own hodgepodge, it is true, but there the fields are large enough and established enough that the subfields as well as the broader disciplines are integrated into the academic firmament.) Many, perhaps most, communication scholars have as much in common with people in other fields as they do with people in their own. The lack of status is understandable. The notion of "communication" has all too often not provided enough critical mass to generate the gravitational power to hold the diverse methodologies and traditions together, except formally. This breeds the concern that the field can never generate the quality of research that a more defined discipline can, that communication lacks the necessary focus to establish itself as a distinct field. Hence it receives fewer resources and is taken less seriously.

Without a defining and unifying purpose, methodological diversity becomes a weakness instead of a strength. Communication departments often have some variety of quantitative scholars, psychologists, sociologists, cultural theorists, historians, legal and policy experts, political economists, and so on. They tend to keep to themselves, so the whole is less than the sum of the parts. To outsiders, the communication faculty specializing in history or law or economics or psychology may appear like people lucky to have a university job but not of sufficient quality to be employed in the history, law, economics, or psychology departments. Hence communication is classified as a minor-league field. I argue in this book that methodological diversity and interdisciplinary approaches can again become a great strength for communication studies—if it uses the notion of a critical juncture as a defining and unifying concept for the field. Communication can become the most desirable place for an intellectual to be on a college campus.

For that to occur it would be necessary to acknowledge the 800-pound gorilla in the back of the seminar room: prestige. For any number of reasons, the pursuit of prestige is an occupational hazard for people in academia, even for those who know just how asinine and counterproductive it can be. It is part and parcel of the greatest inherent problem with academics: the prevalence of elitism. And this all tends to work to encourage intellectual acquiescence to the status quo, because elitism in academia contributes to reinforcing and legitimating entrenched ideas.

There is no simple solution to this problem. The institutional pecking order is as well established in academia as the caste system is in India. Communication is a failure in the prestige game on U.S. campuses for the simple reason that aside from Penn, Stanford, and Northwestern, it barely exists at the Ivy League and other elite private university campuses. And at the crucial big three—Harvard, Yale, and Princeton—it only recently has begun to have a research presence at Harvard's Kennedy School of Government. Hence the ten leading programs in communication research consist mainly of schools that would rank in the second tier for the other social sciences. So when a dean has to decide between devoting resources to communication or, say, sociology, it tends to be the safe route to go with the latter. Barring other factors, it is a bureaucratic no-brainer.

More than once, I have had friends in other fields or on the margins of academia, close friends even, say in passing that they were advising this student or that student to get their degree in some other field, despite the student's interest in studying media, because they considered communication to be a lightweight discipline. They simply assumed I would agree with them, because they could not imagine that an intelligent person would think otherwise. Upon friendly interrogation, it was clear that these friends knew nothing about communication, and made assumptions based entirely on perceptions of prestige, the lack of a hoity-toity pedigree.

The second basic explanation for communication's second-tier status is its tendency to be seen as a professional school. Broadly speaking, the prestige of communication is undermined by its close association—past and present—with the media and communication industries. As communication research is often conducted in departments with course work devoted to professional training, its role in a liberal arts college is legitimately called into question. Communication appears as just a hepped-up form of vocational education, while the traditional social sciences sit atop Mount Olympus pondering the fate of the world. I recall, while teaching in Journalism and Mass Communication at Wisconsin, once speaking to the dean of the College of Letters and Sciences, in which our department resided. I implored the dean, a biologist, as I recall, to give us more teaching assistantships so we could support more graduate students (and improve our undergraduate instruction) and be more competitive in attracting the best talent to our campus. He responded that additional teaching assistantships were not necessary, because our graduate students should be able to land part-time jobs working on the local newspaper. It became clear he thought we mostly had professional students, when his college generated more Ph.D.'s in communication than all but a handful of universities in the world. And this was *our* dean.

There are very serious grounds for concern about the implications of the linkage of the media industries to communication departments for communication research. To the extent that a communication department is directly or indirectly dependent upon the support of the media industry, there will be distinct limits on the range and nature of what can be done. In the current era of cutbacks and retrenchment, there is even greater pressure from university administrators on communication departments to solicit commercial media and communication interests to bankroll an even greater portion of the field's expenses. This has been a source of considerable frustration for public interest groups working on media policy issues. "Communication and journalism departments are fearful of alienating the business contacts their students will need for internships and jobs," Jeff Chester wrote in his book *Digital Destiny*. "Practically everywhere there is a media studies program, media companies are pursued as donors. Consequently, academia has become largely incapable of addressing important questions concerning the media. Academics are one of the few groups in our society afforded both the time and independence to stake out policy issues. They should be weighing into the debate with independent analyses, research, and even advocacy."[28]

In these neoliberal times, this acquiescence to private power in the field of communication is simply accepted as an unavoidable fact, even by people who would openly disparage the situation were they not part of it. There is little doubt, however, that this is the most significant threat to communication actually engaging the imminent critical juncture and becoming a major-league discipline. (I imagine that if communication departments received enormous sums of money from media corporations and moguls, the field could march its way into academic high society, much like the robber barons joined the gentry in the Gilded Age, but that would require dollars instead of the pennies the field currently attracts.) At a practical level, too, business schools are far better-suited to conduct commercially sympathetic research, especially as communication is now a central business activity. Who needs departments predicated upon public service, democratic citizenship, the free flow of information, and professional principles like journalism when the whole idea is to maximize profit?

Despite the damage this has done to communication's stature, I am not arguing that the field should ignore or repudiate its connection to media industries, creators, and producers. To the contrary, we should embrace the connection. I believe that this connection can make our research and our teaching stronger. But we need to do so in the context of a critical juncture. We need to see our interests aligned with journalists, writers, creative people, media workers, and audiences, not just with big media owners and investors. Our interests are with the content producers, who often work with a public service ethos about communication, rather than investors whose interest in anything but profit is demonstrably negligible. What is striking about the current critical juncture is how strongly journalists and media workers feel alienated from the corporate system. I believe it is crucial that we establish and maintain close ties to the media professions and draw their perspectives into our work. Again, what is seen as a "weakness" in conventional academic hierarchical thinking—links to media practices—can and should be a strength.

Perhaps the better way to understand the current status of communication is not to ask why it is so weak relative to other social sciences on American universities. Instead, we may learn more by asking why communication exists at all as an academic discipline.[29] And when we ask the question this way, I think we return to the theme of this book, the importance of critical junctures. There was nothing intrinsic to U.S. communication that preordained its present configuration. What is striking when one looks at its history, broadly construed, is how the field of communication emerged and developed in the United States as a response to the three great twentieth-century critical junctures already mentioned. The field was birthed in the first critical juncture, crystallized in the second critical juncture, and was rejuvenated by the third critical juncture. Without critical junctures, there may not be much of a field at all.

The first critical juncture was during the late Gilded Age and Progressive Era, when U.S. journalism was increasingly the domain of large commercial interests operating in semicompetitive or monopolistic markets. Social critics ranging from Edward Bellamy to Henry Adams were highly critical of the corrupt and antidemocratic nature of U.S. journalism, owing to its private ownership and its reliance upon advertising.[30] Between 1900 and 1920 numerous muckrakers and social commentators wrote damning criticism of the antidemocratic nature of mainstream journalism. In many respects, this was the Golden Age of media criticism.[31] The depths of crisis for journalism came between 1910 and 1915. It was then that the newspaper magnate E.W. Scripps launched the adless pro-labor daily newspaper in Chicago, *Day Book*, and that Joseph Pulitzer considered leaving his newspapers as a public trust. Instead Pulitzer left $2 million to Columbia to endow its Journalism School upon his death in 1911.[32] In 1920, Upton Sinclair's *The Brass Check: A Study of American Journalism* was published. This breathtaking, 440-page account of the corruption of journalism by moneyed interests sold some 150,000 copies by the mid-1920s.[33] All but forgotten in the intervening years, it is a book that could well be the starting point for all assessments of journalism, if not contemporary media, in the United States. The topic of media control also became a part of progressive political organizing. The great progressive Robert La Follette devoted a chapter of his book on political philosophy to the crisis of the press. "Money power," he wrote, "controls the newspaper press . . . wherever news items bear in any way upon the control of government by business, the news is colored."[34]

It was as a response to the crisis in journalism that the revolutionary idea of professional journalism—the formal separation of the owner from the editorial function—emerged as the solution to the crisis. Citizens no longer needed to worry about private monopoly control over the news; trained professionals serving the public interest were in charge and had the power. It was in this period that schools of journalism were formed.

None existed before 1900; by 1920, the majority of major programs had been established, sometimes under strong pressure from leading newspaper publishers—desperate to reclaim legitimacy for their industry—over their state legislatures. At the University of Illinois, where I teach, the journalism department was formally authorized by the state legislature and is one of only two departments that the university cannot close by law. Research as an aspect of these programs did not begin for another generation or two. Some prominent academics, like Robert Park and John Dewey, were affected by the turmoil surrounding journalism and dabbled in media issues during the Progressive Era, but for the most part the field lay fallow into the 1930s. The tumult in society generated immense amounts of educated popular writing but did not establish much of a beachhead in the academy.

The first few decades of the twentieth century also saw the rise of advertising, public relations, the film industry, and radio broadcasting. The latter two would be instrumental in stimulating the rise of formal communication research in the 1930s, and during these years there was also a nonacademic communication critique emerging in response to all of them that was critical by nature. In the case of advertising, for example, by the 1920s and 1930s a large and militant consumer movement emerged that was highly critical of advertising and the consumer culture it spawned. It resulted in the formation of groups like Consumers Union.[35] Likewise, with the emergence of commercial radio broadcasting in the early 1930s, a feisty and heterogeneous broadcast reform movement emerged that was piercing in its criticism of the limitations of commercial radio for a democratic society.[36] Both of these movements were expressly dedicated to enacting political reform in Washington, D.C., and both generated a sophisticated critique of advertising and media that anticipated some of the best academic criticism made five or six decades later.

But it was the overlay of the world crisis of the 1930s and

1940s, with the Depression and the global rise of fascism, that provoked the critical juncture in communication above all else. This was a period in which the credibility of journalism was returning to its low ebb of the Progressive Era, and was increasingly seen as a politically reactionary force. William Allen White, renowned editor of the *Emporia Gazette*, addressed the issue of crisis in his 1939 presidential address to the American Society of Newspaper Editors: "We must not ignore the bald fact that in the last decade a considerable section of the American press, and in particular the American daily newspaper press, has been the object of bitter criticism in a wide section of American public opinion. In certain social areas a definite minority, sometimes perhaps a majority of our readers, distrust us, discredit us."[37]

When communication did make its grand splash in the academy in the late 1930s, it did so by looking at the very big issues, in the context of social crisis. There was the matter of democracy, and what it meant in the age of corporate capitalism and mass media. The master works of John Dewey and Walter Lippmann in the 1920s granted the topic sufficient gravitas, and made matters of communication central to debate in the leading intellectual circles in the nation.[38] There was the matter of propaganda, as it was employed not only by the Soviets and the fascist states, but also in the Western democracies as a routine matter of course. The question was, in whose interests was it and how would this propaganda be deployed? And there was the matter of media effects. How did the immersion of our society into a world of media affect us? All of these issues were linked, and they held the potential for a significantly critical approach to communication, with an eye to the reconstruction of society along more democratic lines.

The launching pad for communication research was not only at a few large, Big Ten universities, but also at the premier Ivy League universities like Princeton, Harvard, Yale, and Columbia. Dan Schiller has written brilliantly on this period, concentrating on the activities of Paul Lazarsfeld and Robert Merton.

Schiller notes that all the elements for a powerful radical critique of propaganda were in place in communication, aided and abetted by a relatively sympathetic political climate, and elites concerned and confused by the world they were entering. But the critical approach was nonetheless unwelcome by commercial media sponsors, university administrations, and the key foundations, especially Rockefeller, which bankrolled much of communication research during these years.[39] In the hands of Harold Lasswell, propaganda research was turned on its head: It went from being a critique of propaganda as a threat to self-government to a theoretically informed treatise on how elites could use propaganda to manage people in their own interests.[40] After World War II, the practice became commonplace, only it was no longer called propaganda.

By the late 1940s the critical impulse was effectively marginalized, if not purged, from U.S. communication studies. The opening created by the critical juncture disappeared, the progressive impulse of the New Deal replaced by the postwar American Century. Ironically, Lazarsfeld, who had framed communication research to be open to critical inquiry in the 1930s and early 1940s, became the icon of mainstream research.[41] The political climate was changing dramatically. The broad historical and intellectually informed sweep that informed the research of the 1930s and early 1940s was gradually replaced by an increasingly ahistorical approach that accepted the commercial basis of U.S. media and the capitalistic nature of U.S. society as proper and inviolable. Research became more closely tied to the needs of the dominant industry interests.[42] When the Hutchins Commission made its seminal study of the press and media in the immediate postwar years, it combined piercing criticism of commercial media with lame pleas for industry self-regulation as the solution.[43] Had the popular movements that opposed commercial broadcasting and advertising in the 1930s been more successful, the notion that commercial media were innately "American" might not have been regarded as a presupposition in the academy. Instead, the room for critical analysis and study was shrinking quickly.

The Cold War encouraged this anticritical process; indeed, it made it almost mandatory. Christopher Simpson and Timothy Glander, among others, have documented the close relationship of the "founding fathers" of mass communication research to the emerging U.S. national security state in the 1940s and 1950s.[44] In this environment, notions that commercial interests might use their control of media to disseminate propaganda fell from grace; propaganda became something done only by "totalitarian" states and governments. This was a stunning change in both rhetoric and analysis. (In the early 1930s, for example, the U.S. advertising industry hailed Adolf Hitler and Josef Goebbels as brilliant fellow propagandists. "Whatever Hitler has done," the trade publication *Printers' Ink* wrote in 1933, "he has depended almost entirely upon slogans made effective by reiteration, made general by American advertising methods." That wasn't all: "Hitler and his advertising man Goebbels issued slogans which the masses could grasp with their limited intelligence. . . . Adolf has some good lines, of present-day application to American advertisers."[45] Such candid commentary on the use of propaganda by powerful interests in democratic nations was soon relegated to the lunatic fringe, where, in many respects, it remains.) Propaganda became psychological warfare and then became mass communication.[46]

By midcentury the ideas that ownership and control over media were decisive and that media had large and important effects were applicable only to study of the Soviet Union and other communist nations. In the United States, structure was irrelevant or benign, the system served the interests of the people, and media had limited effects. Had the U.S. political climate in the 1940s veered leftward—not as absurd a notion as some might think—rather than to the right, the critical juncture may have led to a different outcome and critical communication scholarship may have survived and even flourished as a viable entity in U.S. universities.[47]

By the 1950s much of the enthusiasm among foundations for communication research had dried up, the critical juncture had passed, and the field lost its toehold in the Ivy League. Thereafter, the balance of power shifted to the large public research universities of the Midwest. Critical work was not entirely dead. Kenneth Burke and, a bit later, George Gerbner, James Carey, and Hanno Hardt, among others, would keep the flame alive; Dallas Smythe and Herbert I. Schiller almost singlehandedly put the field of political economy of communication on the map in the United States in the 1950s and 1960s. But as influential as their work was, the times did not foster a legion of collaborators. Smythe returned to his native Canada in the early 1960s to find more fertile soil for critical scholarship. Much critical work on media returned to its traditional status and was done by people outside the discipline, like the educator Paul Goodman and C. Wright Mills, a sociologist at Columbia, or outside the academy. In many ways Mills's work provided a superior framework for the critical evaluation of media, and I will discuss his influence upon subsequent critical work in communication in Chapter 2. Mills's *The Sociological Imagination* made a trenchant critique of the limitations of the sort of mainstream work that was ascending in the academy. Mills's untimely death at age forty-five in 1962 was a dark moment in the history of critical communication.[48]

The explosion of popular politics—civil rights, black power, antiwar, student, consumer, feminist, environmental—in the 1960s and early 1970s brought the third great critical juncture to communication. This was the foundation of the critical juncture—the broader upheaval—because it brought all social institutions under closer examination. There was a communication technological revolution of sorts, with the rise of satellite communication and cable television, which fomented visions of a decentralized and/or commercial-free television system.[49] In addition, the journalism of this era was under attack as inadequate, and consequently there was a mushrooming of "underground" newspapers and journalism reviews.[50] The 1968 Kerner Commission Report on the urban riots of the 1960s specifically cited the profound long-term consequences of racist and insensitive media as a core factor contributing to the uprising, raising grave concerns about the Fourth Estate in a manner that had not been seen in elite circles since the 1940s:

> The news media have failed to analyze and report adequately on racial problems in the United States and, as a related matter, to meet the Negro's legitimate expectations in journalism. By and large, news organizations have failed to communicate to both their black and white audiences a sense of the problems America faces and the sources of potential solutions. The media report and write from the standpoint of a white man's world. The ills of the ghetto, the difficulties of life there, the Negro's burning sense of grievance, are seldom conveyed. Slights and indignities are part of the Negro's daily life, and many of them come from what he now calls "the white press"—a press that repeatedly, if unconsciously, reflects the biases, the paternalism, the indifference of white America. This may be understandable, but it is not excusable in an institution that has the mission to inform and educate the whole of our society.[51]

(This was much more a global critical juncture for communication than the two earlier ones, and a main policy battle that emerged in this era was over the prospective New International Information Order [NIIO], the campaign by newly independent countries in the late 1960s and 1970s to have formal redress of the legacy wrought by colonial communication systems.[52] This intense global struggle dragged on and was of such magnitude that it led the United States and England finally to withdraw from UNESCO under protest in 1984 and 1985, respectively. That was more or less the final straw for the opening created by the critical juncture; thereafter the era of neoliberalism—profits *über alles*—was in full swing.)

The consequences for communication of this critical juncture remain unclear. On the one hand, the sanctity of the commercial media system and the practice of professional journalism were never in question to anywhere near the extent that they were during the earlier critical junctures. On the other hand, there were dramatic developments. Public broadcasting was established in 1967, and for a brief moment it held the potential to become a system far more independent and critical than what finally emerged.[53] In some respects the 1960s also crystallized a majoritarian view of the First Amendment, a potentially much more radical and democratic interpretation than had been generally countenanced. Justice Byron White's majority opinion in 1969's *Red Lion Broadcasting Co., Inc. v. Federal Communications Commission* held to broadcasting alone, but the logic and spirit opened the door at least a crack for a very different way to envisage the role of media in a free society:

> But the people as a whole retain their interest in free speech by radio and their collective right to have the medium function consistently with the ends and purposes of the First Amendment. It is the right of the viewers and listeners, not the right of the broadcasters, which is paramount. . . . It is the purpose of the First Amendment to preserve an uninhibited market-place of ideas in which truth will ultimately prevail, rather than to countenance monopolization of that market, whether it be by the Government itself or a private licensee. . . . It is the right of the public to receive suitable access to social, political, esthetic, moral, and other ideas and experiences which is crucial here. That right may not constitutionally be abridged either by Congress or by the FCC.[54]

As with the 1940s, had American politics gone in a different direction in the 1970s, this critical juncture may have paved the way for a dramatic reformulation of the communication system, along with other institutions in society. Instead, what can be said is that the late 1960s and early 1970s laid the foundation—in the form of unfinished business—for today's media reform movement, just as the Progressive Era critical juncture generated challenges that were taken up during the 1930s and early 1940s.

For the sake of our discussion, the most striking development of the third critical juncture was the birth of the "critical" approach to communication research, not only in the United States but across the world. The critical movement challenged the presuppositions of the mainstream paradigm and threw the field into a period of creative turmoil that would last into the 1980s. It was this critical movement that attracted me to the field of communication in 1983, and I will devote much of Chapter 2 to discussing its rise and fall.

Critical junctures and communication are joined at the hip, in the way communication structures and institutions are established in our society and also in the way we study them in our colleges and universities. In our most dynamic moments, critical junctures have given our field its identity and it can and must be that way again. But it will not happen without concerted and conscious effort to that end; there are powerful forces keeping the status quo in place.

One particular feature of this current critical juncture is aiding and abetting the transformation of communication study. The revolutionary nature of digital communication technologies is eliminating traditional divisions between media sectors, between media and telecommunication (e.g., telephony), and between mediated and interpersonal communication. The rise of the Internet exemplifies and encourages this border collapse, as it encompasses both one-to-one and traditional mass communication simultaneously. What does it matter if the origin is a newspaper or a cable TV station or a film studio when audiences receive their content online? What does it matter if the delivery system comes via a television network, a cable company, a telephone company, or an electric utility? What is the difference between telephony and media nowadays, as both deliver digital messages, some media, some interpersonal, increasingly an amalgam? When one factors in the radical increase in two-way communication, exemplified by MySpace, Facebook, and YouTube on the Web today, it is clear that this is a dramatically new world we are entering.

This is a radical change. Back in the 1980s, when I entered graduate school in a communication program, I never once set foot in the speech department on our campus. I didn't even know the names of any of the faculty or graduate students in that department. It might as well have been at a different university in a different state in a different century. I recall, too, how when I once mentioned to a friend that I was working on a Ph.D. in communication, he pulled out his telephone bill and started to ask me about some of the expenses. I remember laughing and later saying to a fellow grad student, "how absurd it is that someone would equate something as simplistic as telephones with the serious study of media just because they share the name communication." Well today, that "ignorant" friend looks a lot smarter than I did. All those walls are a-tumbling down.

In view of this, all programs in communication are forced to reconsider what exactly it is they are studying and teaching. Some universities, like the University of Illinois at Urbana-Champaign, where I teach, are considering the consolidation of their communication research under one roof, in recognition of what is happening and in anticipation of what is to come. Communication departments and schools across the country and even worldwide are quickly realizing that a comprehensive program mandates the inclusion of both mediated and non-mediated communication in the same unit. The borders between communication and library schools may some day crumble, and then the border between communication and other disciplines may be in play. But that is still down the road. The immediate requirement, the crucial next step, is to take advantage of the self-evaluation the digital revolution is demanding of the field, embrace the critical juncture we are in, and dedicate the field to being a leading participant in it. If we do, the future is bright.

In the balance of this book I will make this case. I do not wish to bend the stick too far in one direction to make the problem seem worse than it is. Since 2003 or 2004, there has actually been impressive movement in the field of communication to address the critical juncture we are in. But this movement is still in only a corner of the discipline—albeit at some of the leading research universities—and it is not at all clear if it will get the necessary support at those institutions or across the field. I am at most cautiously optimistic. There are powerful forces that push toward maintaining the status quo. These include university budgets; close relations for student employment with existing media firms; implicit pressures to lure corporate funders; professional commitment and institutional loyalty to existing research questions and models; deep-seated occupational practices that regard public outreach as problematic, and providing more risk than reward; and loyalty to presuppositions about the nature of our communication system and society that simply cannot survive examination. Merely reciting them can induce paralysis, so powerful are they. But as I have already argued, if there were ever a moment in the field's history to leap out of its marginal status, this is it. And it won't be here forever.

2

The Rise and Fall of the Political Economy of Communication

Like nearly the entire generation of scholars who would follow Smythe and Schiller to the political economy of communication, I was a product of the critical juncture of the 1960s and early 1970s. Opposition to the U.S. invasion of Vietnam galvanized many of us and made it clear that politics was a life-and-death matter. Just as much as the war forced a rethinking of what the United States stood for and its role in the world, it also imprinted the ravages of class inequality on our brains. This was a war fought disproportionately by the poor and working class, as student deferments and family influence kept more of the middle class and nearly all the upper-middle and upper class out of harm's way.[1] The defining social movements of the critical juncture arguably were the civil rights/black power movement and the feminist movement.[2] These movements signaled to me, and others like me (perhaps reflecting the conceit of youth as much as a sense of history) that the United States (and the world) was entering a qualitatively different era, and there would be no turning back. Our generation, especially those concerned with politics and social change, was immersed in these movements, and they have in many respects defined us ever since.[3]

For me a political moment of singular importance came on September 11, 1973, when the United States helped organize the overthrow of the Allende government in Chile. Allende, a socialist, had been democratically elected and had been committed to constitutional rule—to a fault, it turned out. (In fact, his commitment to constitutional rule far exceeded that of the Nixon administration, which promoted the coup against him.) I harbored the hope to that point that the stated U.S. goal of democracy over communism would lead the United States to tolerate, if not embrace, Allende's democratic government as precisely the alternative to authoritarianism. The U.S.-sponsored Pinochet regime was one of the bloodiest and most reprehensible dictatorships in recent history. For many of my generation this episode was deeply troubling and led to a serious questioning of the U.S. commitment to democracy and the ability of the world's peoples to peaceably govern themselves if the U.S. government was opposed to them.[4] This rude awakening led me to a significant interest in history, economics, media, and politics, as an undergraduate and beyond. The early to mid-1970s was a period of considerable intellectual frenzy on American campuses, by subsequent standards at least, and I was able to pursue all my interests to my heart's content with numerous similarly inclined students at the newly established Evergreen State College in Olympia, Washington.

Seven years after graduation, I entered graduate school at the School of Communications at the University of Washington; this was 1983, the same year Nicholas Garnham congratulated the field on its success and future prospects. My aim as an undergrad had been to study economics and to follow in the tradition of left economists like Paul Sweezy, Paul Baran, and Harry Magdoff. But when I discovered that economics was inhospitable to that approach, I went into publishing and reporting for several years in Seattle. As I passed my thirtieth birthday, I finally decided to enter graduate school, only now in communication. I confess I had little idea what that field stood for when I entered graduate school, except that I did not wish to leave Seattle. Having taken a couple of communication classes at the University of Washington in 1978, I determined I could study media there in an interdisciplinary and critical manner, drawing upon history, economics, sociology, and political theory. I was instantly attracted to the openness and flexibility of communication as a social science, its interdisciplinary nature, in comparison to economics. This interdisciplinarity remains one of the most attractive elements of the field, and the reason why it can adapt to the changing circumstances we face today.

At that time, Washington was a backwater program, immune from the growth of critical communication studies in Europe and at Illinois, my current home. In a way, being in the intellectual hinterlands was a blessing for me, because I could make my way without any pressure to follow the hot trends of the moment. But it also meant that cornerstone figures like Raymond Williams were largely unknown to the faculty, at least not taught, and the interesting work being done, especially in Britain, was unrecognized. The communication program was strong in traditional history, law, and international communication, and had some wonderful principled senior faculty, so I found the university open-minded to my pursuing a critical examination of media institutions. But I was pretty much on my own.

Although there was little indication of this in the Washington curriculum or the research of Washington faculty, I soon became aware that there had been a dramatic growth in "critical" scholarship in communication over the previous decade, owing to the critical juncture described earlier. As soon as I became aware of the critical school, I recognized that its identity was formed to no small extent by its opposition to the dominant "mainstream" or "administrative" communication researchers who had held sway since the 1940s and 1950s.[5] I found myself in the midst of an intellectual war zone.

In the eyes of the young critical scholars, "mainstream" communication research adhered to unquestioned, noncritical presuppositions that pointed the work inexorably in a particular direction, while never holding those presuppositions accountable. These presuppositions included a belief in the basic propriety of the U.S. political economy and the justness of the corporate media system. The notion that the media system could be changed or should be changed was simply unthinkable and never subject to open debate. It was no more likely that scholars would examine the merits of a commercial media system (or a capitalist economy) in a structural or categorical sense than they would devote research time to questioning whether the western United States would benefit if the Rocky Mountains did not exist.

To critical scholars, this adherence to uncritical assumptions was a thoroughgoing abrogation of intellectual responsibility; mainstream scholars seemed to be in bed with society's elites. Mainstream scholars, in contrast, saw themselves as realistic, value-neutral, or both. The problem showed up in the conclusions of even the best mainstream studies, when the authors provided weak analysis and lame recommendations that did not and could not ever escape the status quo assumptions built into the research. For even the most serious issues, with the most damning evidence, the solution often was reduced to further calls for more education, begging those in power to change their ways, or reforms that ignored the root cause of the problem.

To make matters worse, mainstream communication studies evinced a neutrality that was often dubious upon close inspection; compromises to power were built into its very terminology. It became accepted, for example, that public relations and advertising were forms of "persuasive" communication. That nonsensical designation—what communication isn't persuasive?—was said to be neutral and unbiased. To critical scholars, such a formulation was balderdash. In the 1930s, public relations and advertising were understood to be propaganda in the interests of business. The industries themselves acknowledged as much. But when a critical communication scholar dared to say that truth by the 1980s, she would likely be dismissed by mainstream scholars as being subjective, opinionated, biased, and incapable of fair, impartial research. To critical scholars, mainstream research had accommodated itself to the ideological needs of the powers-that-be and defined that accommodation as neutrality.

Critical scholars, on the other hand, saw their work as premised on rejecting the notion that what exists exists because it is natural and good. They began with a set of values and working assumptions and proceeded to make what Karl Marx famously termed "a ruthless criticism of all things existing. Ruthless in two senses: that it is not afraid of its own conclusions nor of conflict with the powers that be."[6] The range of inquiry for a critical scholar was not bounded by the needs of those who rule society, who benefit by the status quo, but by the range of what is determined to be socially possible. Almost by definition, then, critical scholarship will be in a tenuous position in a university or society at large. This vision of critical scholarship had an air of self-righteousness to it, which, whether justified or not, was taken as an insult by some mainstream scholars. In short, relations between critical and mainstream communication scholars were frosty when I entered the field. And if one wanted to have a successful career in the field of communication, one needed to be very careful treading in critical waters.

This point was made clear to me when I attended my very first academic conference, a graduate student "mini-conference" at the Annenberg School for Communication at the University of Southern California in April 1986. The day before I arrived to make my very first public presentation of my research, Herb Schiller had given an address to the conference, and then had to leave before I arrived. By the time the Washington legation appeared, the remaining faculty, all mainstream, could not have been more openly dismissive of what they regarded as Schiller's lack of rigor and evidence for his arguments. As one who had read and admired Schiller's work, I was surprised by the dismissive response, the refusal to engage with Schiller's arguments on any substantive basis whatsoever.

Then, as fate would have it, that same night Noam Chomsky gave a lecture on media and U.S. foreign policy at USC, which nearly all the conference participants attended. It was the first time I had ever seen Chomsky speak. Chomsky was then at the peak of his media analysis, and he gave the most brilliant and riveting lecture I have ever witnessed. In the question and answer period, Chomsky addressed a wide range of topics and to each of them he gave a detailed, thoughtful, and sometimes astonishing answer. I do not use these adjectives lightly. Afterward, I was buzzing for hours, my mind racing, and I recall conversations deep into the night with some of the other grad students. The next morning when the conference reconvened, I anticipated a lively analysis of Chomsky's lecture; even those who did not share his political values would want to discuss his provocative arguments, in which media played such a central role. Instead, the assembled faculty all dismissed Chomsky categorically as a conspiracy nut who was unfamiliar with the "real" research on media that they were doing. No actual hard criticism was leveled, just insinuation. No student dared to raise a dissenting voice, including me. I was flabbergasted.

(I had the same experience on other occasions in subsequent years, before mainstream faculty understood where my sympathies rested. I remember in particular attending a presentation by Edward Herman of his media analysis at a conference in 1990, and then having drinks with a bunch of fellow professors and graduate students afterward. The conversation was dominated by a senior professor from Stanford, by all accounts one of the "stars" in communication research in the United States, who dismissed Herman's research as "horseshit." I quietly sipped my drink, knowing that Herman was doing some of the best news media analysis in the business. Seven years later I would have the privilege of writing a book on global media with Herman.)[7]

That afternoon at the closing session of the USC mini-conference, the Annenberg director laid out his vision for the field of communication using elaborate diagrams on a blackboard. It was a complex mapping, but the research was, as I recall, largely quantitative, and decidedly in the social science mainstream. I remember looking at this chart and seeing no mention of communication history and law, or international communication, or democratic political theory, and certainly no mention of political economy or cultural studies. All of these areas I imagine were farmed out to other disciplines; communication was a quantitative social science that could go toe-to-toe with any other social science in the academy. But for this vision to hold, the embarrassing relatives had to be stashed in the back room. Needless to say, this was a vision for the field that was entirely foreign to me. What on earth was I doing there?

An undercurrent to the critical–mainstream split in communication at the time was the Cold War. The dominant thinking was that there was a polarity in the world: democracy and capitalism on one side, government-run dictatorships on the other side. You were either with us or against us. In the realm of media, this translated into a presupposition that the basic option facing humanity was a commercial and independent media system or a government-run media system that lacked independence. This was maddening for most critical scholars, like myself, who had no interest in emulating communist societies and who held the highest regard for democratic practices and civil liberties. Whatever the benefits of communist regimes may have been with regard to education or health care, their media systems and their records concerning civil liberties were indefensible. We wanted a new course, independent of corporate or state control. We came out of the New Left, which was decidedly hostile to one-party states. But in the Cold War climate it was difficult to make the position hold; opposition to the status quo was often translated into support for foreign government attacks on individual liberties. The problem was accentuated by our opposition to U.S. imperial activities overseas; we found ourselves in the seemingly ambiguous position of defending the autonomy and self-determination of nations that sometimes engaged in media and political practices we would have deplored had our own government done them. The core principle was that other nations needed autonomy from U.S. meddling to be free, and that supporting this autonomy was our first duty as Americans. To unsympathetic eyes, the principle was lost and it appeared that critical scholars were too comfortable with tyranny, as long as it came from the left.

This was a real problem. I recall a conversation with a fellow Ph.D. student at Washington. He had been a practicing journalist for many years and then, while in grad school, spent considerable time in Nicaragua, where he became enamored with Nicaragua's Sandinista revolution. As a journalist, he was familiar with how the United States was breaking all sorts of laws—domestic and international—to overthrow the popular Nicaraguan government. We were discussing Nicaragua's upcoming 1984 elections, and he dismissed them as "bourgeois lotteries," the sole purpose of which was to take power from the many and deliver it to the few who were in the pocket of the United States. He implied that he would have no problem with Nicaragua adopting a government more along the lines of Cuba to lock in and protect the advances of the revolution. I recoiled at his comment. I understood there were real problems that third world nations faced holding elections when the world's superpower was dedicated to subverting the process, but I thought the idea of condoning, even embracing, authoritarian rule to protect a people's revolution a contradiction.[8]

The sense from many mainstream communication scholars was that critical scholars were carrying water for communist regimes and certainly had little sympathy for basic democratic principles and civil liberties. I recall a 1989 conversation with a senior colleague specializing in international communication at Madison—with whom I was on good terms—when I expressed my admiration for Habermas, because his work pointed toward building media systems independent of both corporate and state domination. He was pleasantly surprised that someone on the left actually was opposed to state-controlled media; it seemed the thought had never quite occurred to him before.

The next year, at the 1990 International Communication Association convention in Dublin, Ireland, this issue boiled over. I was talking with one of my senior Madison colleagues when a prominent mainstream scholar from Indiana approached us and began to chat about the conference. "I can hardly wait to see Herb Schiller's session," she informed us. "I want to see how he justifies his advocacy for the communist regimes all these years now that they have been overthrown." My colleague nodded approvingly. This provided a moment of truth for me. I knew that Schiller was a true democrat who was no bagman for communism, but I was a powerless assistant professor standing next to two prominent senior scholars in the field, including a senior member of my own faculty. I could see my career flashing before my eyes. But, for the first time, I spoke up and defended Schiller from the charges. My uninvited input threw a wet blanket on the conversation, and I am not sure what it did for my career. If nothing else, it was the last time I was privy to those sorts of candid conversations.

The mainstream–critical split was not the only civil war in communication research in the 1980s. The critical movement itself, such as it was, began to unravel. In the late 1960s and 1970s there was a certain unity to emerging critical communication

scholarship, at least in the English-speaking world. This scholarship developed as part and parcel of the broad global resurgence of interest in left-wing political theory in the academy.
There was considerable interest in the theoretical works of
Antonio Gramsci and Louis Althusser and their adherents.[9]
Theory was going to guide the practice of popular political
movements, and the experience from those movements would
improve the theory. The Frankfurt School authors—Theodor
Adorno, Max Horkheimer, Herbert Marcuse—were also widely
read.[10] Much of this work addressed issues of ideology and culture, so it spawned the vibrant wave of critical communication
study. Raymond Williams was a guiding figure, along with
continental scholars like Armand Mattelart.[11]

Marxism was very much in vogue, and all of the figures
mentioned in the preceding paragraph, including Williams,
regarded themselves as Marxists, or at least did not run away
from the designation. The critical communication movement
wrapped itself in Marxism in Britain in the 1970s, where it took
off first and then became very influential for people like myself
in the United States. Marx and Marxism were held up as the alternative to the dominant approaches to communication research in Britain and the United States.[12] At this moment in
history, the late 1960s and 1970s, being a Marxist in the West, in
the context of the New Left, was not seen as being a supporter
of one-party dictatorships. Marx inspired young critics of the
communist regimes of Eastern Europe as much as their supporters, perhaps more so. This was a period in which there was
a renaissance of interest in reading Marx systematically, and I
had read most of his core works as an undergraduate in the
early and mid-1970s. I read the work chronologically after having been immersed in European history, Hegelian philosophy,
and classical political economy. It was an exhilarating experience. Ironically, in view of the way Marxism in the past generation has become equated with vulgar reductionist materialism,
even anti-intellectualism, in the 1970s a commitment to reading

Marx required a young scholar to read widely, even intensively, in history, economics, and philosophy or feel ill-equipped to be taken seriously. In my case, it meant that I also felt compelled to study neoclassical and mainstream economics, so I could understand capitalism from a capitalist perspective. Economics was my undergraduate major.

Marx had singular importance during these years for critical communication scholars, as he did for radical young social scientists everywhere. As Edward S. Herman has noted, there were two Karl Marxes. One was the socialist activist and enlightenment optimist. It is this aspect of Marx's life that most people are familiar with, and in that light he was (and is) either inspiring or repugnant depending upon one's attitude toward radical anticapitalist social change. In my view, Marx's importance in the 1970s as well as today is not particularly great in this area; the socialist movement in the sense Marx understood it ran its course nearly a century ago. Beyond a few very broad principles, he does not have a lot to say to us—in fact, very little—about the process of making social change and what a postcapitalist society would look like. Then, after several decades of communism, I think the New Left had it right: The path forward involves a dramatic transformation of existing social and economic relations, but what that means and how we get there are very much unclear and in need of discussion, study, and experimentation.[13] Open-mindedness and humility are the only requirements.

If anything is certain to me—and this was a premise of the New Left—a commitment to democracy is foundational. Not a phony "democratic centralism," but the genuine article, with civil liberties and institutional structures to protect and promote popular political participation. This includes, at the center, a notion of democratic media. In my view, a self-governing people would be unlikely to decide to have an economic system that generates so much waste and inequality as the current system provides, but I am willing to live with the results of a democratic forum. Regrettably this is not a discussion those sitting atop the social structure and benefiting from the status quo wish to encourage—for self-evident reasons—and it is one few American scholars are encouraged to pursue.

Because Marx did not leave a blueprint to answer these pressing matters—what thinker has?—does not mean scholars should throw Marx under the bus. We should not ignore what Herman characterizes as the second Karl Marx, an "exceptionally intelligent and learned observer of capitalism."[14] As an observer of capitalism, Marx proved to be an indispensable resource for scholars in communication—not merely for those who shared Marx's commitment to socialism, but for all who were and are committed to understanding how the system works. As a scholar Marx was as rigorous as anyone. His arguments were supported by evidence and testable. Because Marx has been, in effect, banished from communication studies in the United States except as some sort of cartoon figure, allow me to digress to explain his influence on this formative period in critical communication research, and what value he has for communication today. In my view, it remains considerable.

Most important, Marx emphasized that capitalism was based on the pursuit of profit, or what is called the capital accumulation process. This is the starting point to grasping the extraordinary economic growth of the past few centuries. Understanding how the profit system works, how it plays out, and its economic and social effects is also the starting point for any analysis of a capitalist society. Accumulation provided a way to distinguish capitalism from feudalism and previous social systems, and to understand the basis for socialism—presented as the logical postcapitalist alternative.

Accumulation means that capitalists are always seeking profits wherever they can find them. Much of media history is the colonization of existing noncommercial cultural practices or the creation of new ones by capital—turning culture into a commodity. (And as we will see in Chapter 3, much of the new media history is chronicling public and organized opposition to this colonization.) Accumulation guides us to an understanding of the U.S. commercial media system, where everything is directed at maximizing profits, and everything else is pretty much public relations. After Marx died, Engels spent years explaining that Marx never meant for accumulation to be a vulgar determinant of everything, in some crude mechanical sense, as if that obviated the need for detailed scholarly inquiry.[15] And that point was self-evident in any of the histories Marx wrote himself. The point is simply that under capitalism the accumulation process is an extraordinarily powerful force, and social science that gets too far away from it will tend to be less likely to provide compelling explanations of social phenomena.

By understanding the centrality of accumulation in a capitalist society, one gains insights into major aspects of life in the modern world. By examining accumulation, Marx's work highlighted that the system did not work toward equilibrium as much as it had deep-seated internal tensions—"contradictions"—that pushed the system toward crises. What was rational for the individual capitalist to do—say, withhold investment when the climate does not appear promising for profits—produces highly irrational results when done by many capitalists. It virtually forces other capitalists to do the same or risk their capital. The point Marx emphasized is that a system where the economy is in private hands, run for self-interested reasons, will always be in conflict with the needs and potential of a highly integrated social system.

Accumulation also leads businesses to constantly attempt to pay labor as little as possible. The more workers get, the less profit capitalists make; a capitalist who pays workers more than necessary will be at a severe competitive disadvantage. Hence class inequality—yes, class struggle—is built right into the DNA of the system. Class is an ever-present fact in a capitalist society. No matter how wealthy the society, only a very small fraction of the society will be able to live off the labor of others, and they will enjoy privileges unthinkable to the preponderance of the population. I need only ask my students how many of them would like to have enough money so they did not have to work for others for a living to see how well the class cue is ingrained. It literally can be taken as evidence of insanity that a person would prefer to be poor than to be a millionaire. But capitalism is the most sophisticated class system ever, and the importance and centrality of class tends to be obfuscated. This may well serve the interests of those who benefit by the status quo, but it is a central problem for scholars. Ignoring the problem does not make it go away; it only makes it worse.

Likewise, accumulation disregards environmental damage. No sane capitalist can factor environmental costs into her operations because her competitors will not. The environment tends to be a classic "externality"; much of conventional economic growth and development fails to take into consideration the true cost of this activity to society.[16] (Recent research by John Bellamy Foster demonstrates convincingly that Marx actually was not the gung-ho, damn-the-torpedoes "industrialize-at-all-costs" figure he has been made to be, but rather had a remarkably sophisticated understanding of the relationship of humans and nature.)[17] As we teeter closer to possible extinction as a species, such a blindness approaches social suicide. The 2006 British official commission on climate change chaired by the economist Sir Nicholas Stern stated that climate change "is the greatest and widest-ranging market failure ever seen."[18] Yet the power of accumulation is such that the possibility of reform appears quite weak.[19] As Fredric Jameson is reported to have said, it is easier for people to think of the end of our species than it is to think of the end of capitalism. Maybe rodents and cockroaches will have "free markets" after we are gone.

Marx's analysis also provided a basis for understanding both the nature of the state and the range and nature of political debate in capitalist societies. The state was not a neutral body, obviously, nor did it represent the will of the majority of the people in democratic societies. There is a systematic bias toward favoring those with capital, and it is generally out in the open, built into the system. In current times it is presented as the need to promote economic growth, efficiency, and create jobs. Once one understands capitalism as a class system, it means there is a direct conflict, or at least serious tension, with the premises of democratic governance. It is worth recalling that prior to capitalism nearly all notions of democracy equated democracy with communism or one-class societies. As Aristotle put it, "Democracy is when the indigent, and not the men of property, are the rulers." Moreover, Aristotle noted that "if liberty and equality are chiefly to be found in democracy, they will be best attained when all persons alike share in the government to the utmost."[20]

This tension provides the starting point for a political economic analysis of governance in capitalist democracies. But this does not mean that capitalist societies cannot be reformed under popular pressure to establish public policies that substantively address inequality and ecological crisis—only that the core problem is built into accumulation and will be present as long as the society remains capitalist. It is not a level playing field. In rare historical moments, with extraordinarily well-organized working-class movements, like Sweden under the socialist governments in the postwar generations, capitalist societies can go a long way toward ameliorating the ravages of accumulation. But as the Swedes have discovered, maintaining those victories is difficult when control over society's wealth is in private hands. Marx's political economy opened the door to viewing the state in general terms as an agency of upper-class interests, but, specifically, as an institution that is fought over by all of society on a playing field sloped in favor of those with capital. (This is of particular value as a framework for understanding the policy debates we will turn to in Chapters 3 and 4.)

Likewise, the pressure to maximize profit in a competitive environment is a constant spur to technological innovation. That is why there has been more technological change in any recent decade than there had been in any two or three centuries prior to capitalism. Marx also provided the basis for understanding social conflicts over technology; they are deployed to serve the interests of capital, not workers or society as a whole. In particular, Marx showed a keen interest in the importance of revolutionary transportation and communication technologies—like the railroad and the telegraph—to the development of capitalism and to the development of socialism. Communication technology was not a dependent variable of accumulation; it had considerable independent effect upon society in its own right.[21] It is worth noting that in *The Communist Manifesto*, Marx and Engels highlight the nationalization and nonprofit management of communication (i.e., telegraph and post office) and transportation systems as one of their core demands, and as a requirement for the progressive development of society.[22]

And, finally, for present purposes, accumulation knows no national borders; hence Marx understood capitalism as a global system from its very beginning. This understanding infuses all of his work. He wrote about the importance of imperialism and the slave trade to the very foundation of capitalism, and how the accumulation process moved inexorably toward increased global integration—and conflict.

As valuable as understanding accumulation can be in a general sense, these are not meant to be iron laws that explain everything, immune to change. Accumulation is crucial to understanding capitalist society, but it opened the analysis of capitalism, it did not end it. Just as important for Marx was the notion of "historical specificity."[23] This meant that when analyzing a society a scholar needed to avoid timeless criteria and understand a society in its own terms. Other factors need to be brought into the analysis to gain an understanding suitable for action. So it has been that capitalist societies are always in the process of remaking themselves, and often the differences between them internationally and across time are so striking that only a few generalities can apply to all of them. It became fairly clear to me, for example, that the nature of capitalism in the United States in the first half of the nineteenth century was radically different from the capitalism that came to dominate a century later.[24] This principle of historical specificity was especially important for political economists of communication, because the nature of communication systems tended to change dramatically every generation or two in capitalist societies; analysis needed to be grounded in concrete historical terms to have any value. In short, reading Marx seriously meant having a deep respect for the richness and significance of history.

None of the points made above are necessarily radical or socialist ideas. Nor are they metaphysical. They must be tested and debated. Perhaps one of the most eloquent presentations of Marx's notion of accumulation in recent times was made by the liberal economist Robert Heilbroner.[25] He was no socialist revolutionary, and no Marxist, but he clearly explained the value of understanding Marx's vision of accumulation if one wants to grasp the role of economics in capitalist societies.

There are three specific areas where Marx's thought stimulated the greatest immediate currency in critical communication research in the 1970s and thereafter. Marx wrote of the cultural implications of the capital accumulation process, where profit is all that is sacred, life is reduced to the "cash nexus," and everything else is subject to its whims. Such a society is aflutter with radical cultural change, as capital and commercialism spread into every nook and cranny of social life, and noncommercial values and institutions must accept their secondary status, embrace or at least adapt to the market, or prepare to be crushed. As Marx and Engels famously wrote: "All that is solid melts into air."[26]

This remains the indispensable starting point for cultural analysis; its truth blares at us across all aspects of our lives, as we are awash in commercialism. It is why Neil Postman loved to note the irony that the most radical figures in the United States were the businessmen who cast tradition aside in their mad hunt for profit.

Second, Marx also highlighted another manner in which commercialism permeates our lives under capitalism, what he termed "commodity fetishism." A capitalist society, centered around commodity production, gives seemingly magical personalities to the products that are manufactured, sold, and bought in our daily lives. This fetish, which is typically expressed in brand names and advertising slogans, transforms social relations between people into relations between things. With labor power itself put up for sale, the processes of human labor that produced commodities are ripped from our conscious minds, leaving only the categories of the market to define the value of these goods—and the qualities of our lives. The resulting social alienation is a form of universal "forgetting" that later Marxist philosophers (most notably Georg Lukács) called "reification."[27]

Third, Marx's social analysis was predicated on always keeping a close eye on material relations, the many who pulled the wagon and those few who sat on it. With this in mind, Marx always cast a skeptical eye at the proclamations of those in power—those riding on the wagon—when they spoke on behalf of all society. Marx was skeptical toward intellectuals on similar grounds. This is the basis for Marx's well-known critique of ideology, and one of the main entrees for a political economic critique of the media. As Engels and he wrote in *The German Ideology*, "The ideas of the ruling class are in every epoch the ruling ideas: i.e., the class which is the ruling material force of society is at the same time its ruling intellectual force." What is usually forgotten is the sentence that comes next: "The class which has the means of material production at its disposal, consequently also controls the means of mental production, so that the ideas of those who lack the means of mental production are on the whole subject to it."[28] Hence the ideas of an age are not preordained to reflect the view of the dominant class, but they are struggled over on a playing field sloped to the advantage of elite interests.

There is one additional aspect of Marx's career that bears directly upon communication and that became widely known in the 1970s, but that few people are familiar with today: his extraordinary career as a practicing journalist. Marx devoted a large part of his life to journalism. He and Engels wrote more than 800 newspaper articles and published in some of the most important newspapers of their day. Marx's most important journalistic period was from 1842 to 1849, when he was an editor and fighting journalist in Germany, forced to confront issues of censorship and press freedom. He was arrested numerous times for his journalistic activities. This was Marx's principal occupation from 1842 until 1849, ending with his departure for London in 1849 at the age of thirty-one, following the defeat of the 1848 revolutions. This did not end Marx's relation to journalism, however. Marx wrote for ten years (1851–61) for the *New York Daily Tribune* (or *New York Tribune*), one of the leading newspapers in the United States, with a circulation as high as 250,000 during this period. It was the paper of Horace Greeley (founder and publisher) and Charles Dana (managing editor). Marx authored 356 articles as European correspondent for the *Tribune* and co-authored 12 with Engels.

Marx was among the greatest journalists of the nineteenth century. As Charles Blitzer has noted: "If a preoccupation with the social and economic background of politics, and a determination to uncover the real motives that lie behind the words of politicians and governments are the hallmarks of modern political journalism, Karl Marx may properly be said to be its father."[29]

His journalistic accomplishments are even more impressive considering that he lived in poverty and lacked high connections. As Blitzer writes:

> The mystery of how Marx was able to produce such distinguished work under such inauspicious circumstances can perhaps partially be solved by suggesting that at least some of the apparent handicaps under which he labored were in fact advantages. Thus, for example, it may be argued that Marx's very real isolation from the obvious and conventional sources of news compelled him to look elsewhere for material. In so doing, he turned to such published—but seldom exploited—sources as commercial statistics, official reports, treaties, and parliamentary debates. This gave to his articles a depth and a solidity that were not to be found in the writings of those who relied upon court gossip and political chit-chat. Similarly, the fact that while Marx was writing for the *Tribune* he was also regularly engaged in scholarly research, although obviously inconvenient for him, was unquestionably a source of strength rather than of weakness.

Blitzer concludes, "If a preoccupation with the social and economic background of politics, and a determination to uncover the real motives that lie behind the words of politicians and governments are the hallmarks of modern political journalism, Karl Marx may properly be said to be its father."[30] Marx's practice of independent and critical inquiry provides a sense of what quality journalistic practice might look like; interestingly, it looks very similar to the journalism practiced by I.F. Stone in the middle of the twentieth century.[31]

Marx had constant run-ins with the authorities over his journalism, which led him to write continually on the subject of the fundamental importance of a free press.[32] He opposed state censorship categorically. Concurrently, Marx was aware from the outset that the existence of a free press under the regime of private property was in jeopardy as a result of its being turned into a business. "The first freedom of the press consists in it not being a trade. . . . But is the press true to its nature, does it act according to the nobility of its nature, is it free, if it is degraded to a trade? The writer, to be sure, must earn a living in order to exist and be able to write, but he must in no way exist and write in order to earn a living."[33]

In another article Marx wrote,

The French press is not *too* free, it is not free enough. It is not subject to intellectual censorship, to be sure, but subject to a material censorship, the high security deposit. This affects the press materially, because it pulls the press out of its true sphere into the sphere of big business speculations. In addition, big business speculations need big cities. Hence the French press is concentrated in a few points, and when material force is thus concentrated, does it not work demonically, as intellectual force does not?[34]

In Marx's journalism we see already the basis for a critical approach to understanding the "press," and in much of his work, valuable insights for the critical study of media.

Marx, of course, did not leave a rich and detailed criticism of media in his body of work. Most of the issues that concern us he never asked or barely imagined. He died a generation or two before media made their decisive move into the central nervous system of modern societies.[35] For most of the issues the field has been concerned with, Marx's work provided an important broad context, a way of thinking critically, but not much more. Marx cannot be used to answer debates in communication, but he can be used to clarify our questions and point us in fruitful directions. Marx, as Ed Herman pointed out, should be a familiar figure for communication scholars regardless of their political leanings.

Marx's influence in critical communication research declined sharply as the 1970s evolved into the 1980s. Marx barely plays a role at all in the political economy of communication, as it developed in the United States after the 1970s. By the time I came into the academy, citing Marx, unless it was to dismiss him, was something one had to be very careful about doing, for fear of being dismissed as an ideologue.[36] And when he was cited, even by adherents, I often could not reconcile what was being stated with what I knew from my own readings. The heavily theoretical debates around "Marxism" struck me as decontextualized and sometimes pretentious, almost scholastic or Talmudic by nature. I can understand why what some of what was passed off as Marxism held little appeal even to critical scholars by the 1980s.

In the 1970s, however, there was a clear unity among critical communication scholars, and they were all strongly influenced by Marx. One need only read the cultural studies icon Stuart Hall's classic 1977 essay, "Culture, the Media, and the 'Ideological Effect'" to see the guiding influence of Marx, when what later split off as political economy and cultural studies were still combined in the same project.[37] In the midst of the critical juncture, it was a triumphant moment. Around that time, surveying the recent and dramatic emergence of the broad critical tradition in communication research, Hall wrote, "What cannot be doubted is the profound theoretical revolution which it has already accomplished."[38] As James Curran put it, in this period the main critical approaches that would soon diverge "had a lot in common. Both worked within a neo-Marxist model of society; both perceived a connection, whether weak or strong, between economic interests and ideological representations; and both portrayed media as serving dominant rather than universal societal interests."[39] "The structure of ownership and control," Hall wrote, "is a necessary starting point."[40]

By the early 1980s, as popular political movements petered

out and neoliberalism ascended, the unity in critical scholar-ship strained and eventually shattered. On the one side came the post-structuralists and the postmodernists, often engaging in high theory with a decreasing interest in capitalism, social-ism, or organized social change; on the other side were those more concerned with conventional politics, as frustrating as that was, often emphasizing the importance of criticizing capi-talism and asserting the continuing importance of class analy-sis as an organizing concept. With the decline of popular left politics, Marx declined in importance on both sides of the di-vide, especially the former.[41]

This split played itself out in communication departments as well throughout the 1980s. Some sense of this growing di-vide between postmodern-influenced cultural studies and po-litical economy can be seen in critical communication anthologies published during this period. In the 1970s and into the 1980s, several exceptionally important and influential edited collections of critical communication research were pub-lished, and it is striking that these volumes included material from both political economists and cultural studies scholars. The material weaved together comfortably, even seamlessly. The critical ties that bound them were at that time much stronger than the tensions that would soon provoke a civil war.[42] Such volumes continued into the late 1980s and even the early 1990s, but the marriage was forced and the books had much less impact.[43] A sense of the full state of divorce came in the volume produced from the well-attended "cultural studies" conference held at the University of Illinois in 1990.[44]

As for myself, I was never big on high theory, and I had little attraction to postmodernism. When it made sense to me it was sometimes provocative and sometimes self-evident; and too much of the time it made no sense to me at all.[45] I liked low-orbiting theory that was grounded in politics and could make sense to people outside a seminar room. So for me it was a no-brainer to move toward the political economy school, such as it was. But the split happened gradually, over a good ten to fifteen years, and during this span of time there was considerable confusion and antagonism. By the early 1990s there was a series of debates between the two sides—they were more like shoot-outs—most famously the encounters between Nicholas Garnham and Lawrence Grossberg.[46] In many respects there was much greater ferocity to these debates than to the mainstream–critical divide, if only because the two sides actually wanted to lay claim to being the advance army of critical work and democratic politics. At any rate, by this time the divorce was final. No anthologies attempted to link the wings of critical research into a coherent whole, and the unifying term "critical" fell from usage. Several individual scholars worked hard to draw from elements of both the political economy and cultural studies traditions in their research, and some, like Toby Miller, Janice Peck, Janet Wasko, Larry Grossberg, Jim Wittebols, Eileen Meehan, and Vinny Mosco succeeded, but they were going against the grain.[47]

So, pretty much on my own at Washington in the mid-1980s, I gravitated to the subfield of the political economy of communication. I began to devour the work of Brits like Garnham,[48] James Curran,[49] Peter Golding,[50] and Graham Murdock.[51] This was the gold standard; the four of them and their British cohort staked out the parameters for political economic analysis of communication. Golding and Murdock often wrote together, and their seminal 1973 essay in the *Socialist Review* effectively introduced the notion of the political economy of communication to the world at large.[52] I examined the emerging U.S. tradition, too, starting with Schiller and Dallas Smythe and the younger generation of scholars like Vinny Mosco, Dan Schiller, Oscar Gandy, Eileen Meehan, Manjunath Pendakur, Stuart Ewen, Eileen Mahoney, Sut Jhally, and Janet Wasko.[53] One of the truly important works of the political economy tradition was a pathbreaking and underrecognized collection called *The*

Political Economy of Information, edited by Mosco and Wasko and published in 1988.[54]

This struck me as my home, where I belonged in the field. Political economy of communication even had a de facto professional organization, the Union for Democratic Communications. I soon heard about George Gerbner, and how he was creating a protected zone for critical work with a political economic emphasis at Penn. As editor of the *Journal of Communication,* Gerbner did what he could to turn the field in that direction. Nearly one-third of the articles in his special edition on the future of the field in the *JOC* in 1983 grew out of the political economic tradition.[55] Come to think of it, in the early 1980s it seemed like the political economy of communication was a dynamic and up-and-coming field; it did not have the pizzazz of cultural studies, but it was alive and kicking.

Smythe and Schiller unquestionably were the dominant senior figures associated with the political economy of communication in North America.[56] Smythe was a native of Canada who earned his Ph.D. in economics at Berkeley and went on to become the first chief economist at the U.S. Federal Communications Commission in the 1940s. While at the FCC, Smythe was the primary author of the "Blue Book," the public interest standard for commercial broadcasters that was arguably the most progressive regulation in U.S. broadcasting history.[57] In 1948, he joined the faculty in the newly formed Institute of Communications Research at the University of Illinois. Smythe immediately launched the first formal classes in the political economy of communication—not only in the United States, but possibly the world—and gave the field a toehold in the United States. Before returning to Canada in the 1960s, where he had considerable influence over Canadian political economy of communication, Smythe established himself as one of the foremost figures in U.S. media studies and plowed a wide path for others to follow behind.

During his fifteen years at Illinois, Smythe wrote papers on a broad range of topics, including how commercialism is the defining feature of U.S. television; how U.S. broadcast regulation and policy debates were distorted to serve corporate interests; the commercialization of the electoral process; and the elements of propaganda in the U.S. media system. He wrote reports or testified on policy debates surrounding the development of public broadcasting, pay television, satellite communication, and the telephone monopoly of AT&T.[58] His landmark work from this era addressed telecommunications economics and policymaking, and here too, Smythe was decades ahead of his time in recognizing the need to fuse telecommunications with media in communication research.[59]

After returning to Canada, Smythe remained highly influential. In the 1970s and 1980s he redefined the study of commercial media, challenging the mainstream perspective that the primary relationship within media was that between media and the audience. Smythe argued that the core relationship, at least for broadcast media, was between the broadcaster and the advertiser. The product of value that was being produced, therefore, was in fact the audience, which was then sold to advertisers. Smythe then argued that the audience was in fact being exploited as it labored on behalf of the media company. His pacesetting work on the "audience commodity" has become central to the political economic tradition and debates in the United States.[60]

Herbert Schiller was a trained economist, too, who became Smythe's colleague at Illinois before moving to the University of California at San Diego in 1970. He is the single person most commonly identified with the political economy of communication, and in his long and storied career his work covered a broad range of issues.[61] Like Smythe, Schiller looked at communication as an important component of corporate power. His first book, *Mass Communications and American Empire*, argued that communication and culture were an indispensable and growing part of the U.S. global economic, political, and military agenda. It became the work that defined the debate on media or cultural imperialism for the next generation. To provide some sense of what a departure this was from thinking at the time, Schiller could find no publisher for the book among university or commercial presses, and had to rely upon a small publishing house that specialized in out-of-print economics classics, and was managed by an old friend.[62] Schiller wrote several more books in his career. His greatest work, in my opinion, was 1989's *Culture, Inc.*, published just before his seventieth birthday, in which he made a compelling argument about the excessive commercialization of culture and everyday life in the United States and its antidemocratic implications. The book includes, among other things, a superb analysis of the commercialization of the First Amendment, one of the best critiques of the "audience has all the power" argument, and a discussion of the privatization and commercialization of information and data services and how this pertains to communication.[63]

Together Smythe and Schiller made the crucial and original argument that communication was becoming a central component of capitalist accumulation, with significant and striking implications for both communication and capitalism. They viewed communication and information—journalism, entertainment, libraries, museums, telecommunication—as a totality. Smythe and Schiller were making a historically specific argument about contemporary capitalism, one that had strong implications for politics. In many respects, these can be regarded as the founding observations upon which the political economy of communication is based. It was an argument made not just to communication scholars, but to political and social theorists and scholars in general, whom they believed undervalued the importance and role of communication.[64]

Smythe and Schiller were products of the great critical juncture of the 1930s and 1940s. They waded through the dark years of the 1950s and then dove headfirst into the tumult of the 1960s and 1970s. Although Smythe left for Canada in the early 1960s, he had helped lay the groundwork by participating actively in political discussions in Congress and in as many public forums as possible about satellite communication and other policy issues. By the late 1960s, Schiller began to forge contacts with the progressive FCC commissioner Nicholas Johnson and with media reformers connected with the civil rights and antiwar movements. Smythe and Schiller's influence can be seen on a whole range of progressive reforms that emerged in that period: policies encouraging minority employment in the telecommunication and broadcasting industries; issues around concentration of ownership and cross-ownership (from blocking the ITT/ABC merger to pushing the "FinSyn" rules that prevented vertical integration in the television industry); and of course extending the earlier tradition of concern with the rights of viewers. Schiller is best known for his active role in publicizing and supporting efforts for a New World Information & Communication Order though UNESCO in the 1970s and 1980s.[65]

Finally, Smythe and Schiller both worked tirelessly to spawn a new generation of communication scholars working in the political economy tradition. Most of the next generation of scholars, which came of age in the 1970s and 1980s, had relationships with one or both of them. I was at the end of that generation and both of them embraced me and my research with open arms. They set the bar very high for those who followed.

Although Smythe and Schiller were the founders of the field, Ed Herman and Noam Chomsky played every bit as large a role for me and for many others who studied the political economy of communication. Herman was an economist who taught at the Wharton School of Finance at Penn, and he occasionally taught media courses at the university's Annenberg School. He was well aware of the field and close to Schiller. Chomsky was a linguist at MIT. Although I believe that linguistics belongs in the broader domain of communication studies, there wasn't much overlap between Chomsky's revolutionary research in linguistics and his prodigious analysis of media and politics.

Herman has made foundational contributions to the political economy of communication. He employed public good theory and microeconomic analysis to provide the basis for a critical assessment of media markets, one that did not presuppose profit-seeking media as inexorably "giving the people what they want."[66] Herman's work gave me increased respect for how the liberal tradition in mainstream economics could be used to great effect in understanding media industries.

Most important, along with Chomsky, Herman developed the "propaganda model" to explain the pro-elite and antidemocratic bias built into U.S. news media coverage of public affairs. The propaganda model uses five filters—media ownership, advertising, sourcing, flak, and anticommunist ideology—to explain how very similar stories get radically different press treatment depending on their relationship to U.S. elite interests. Stories that serve elite interests, like the Soviet downing of Korean Airlines flight 007 in 1983, receive extensive coverage and the treatment is full of outrage and sympathy for the victims; stories that go against U.S. elite interests, like the U.S.-allied death squads that murdered tens of thousands of civilians in Central America in the 1980s, barely rate a mention. The U.S. role is downplayed, and the victims are regarded with suspicion.[67] The system works not through any form of conspiracy; it is a "guided market" system where core values are internalized so that the story selection process seems natural and proper. Herman updated the propaganda model in the 1990s to account for the collapse of the Soviet Union.[68] The propaganda model remains a useful reference point for critical assessments of the news media, and, as I discuss at the end of this chapter, is one of the signal contributions of the political economy of communication.

Herman earned his Ph.D. in economics at the University of California at Berkeley, which was a locus for critical and institutional approaches to economics during the middle decades of the twentieth century. The most important figure at Berkeley was Robert A. Brady, who in the 1930s conducted pacesetting research on the relationship of business to policymaking. Brady compared the situation in Nazi Germany and fascist Italy with the United States, and saw parallels in the use of media, public relations, and advertising to control public opinion.[69] In this sense his work dovetails the outer limits of what communication scholars like Paul Lazarsfeld were broaching at the same time. As Dan Schiller demonstrates, Brady's work was influential on Smythe and Herbert Schiller.[70]

Noam Chomsky is the scholar who revolutionized the study of linguistics and ranks among the most prominent U.S. intellectuals of the past hundred years. Beginning in the 1960s, Chomsky began a parallel career as a social critic and activist, and soon he was arguably the most well-known and respected radical critic of U.S. foreign policy in the world. In the course of developing his criticism of international politics, Chomsky began to critique U.S. news media coverage of foreign affairs, which he found highly propagandistic on behalf of elite interests. It was this work that led to his collaboration with Herman and the development of the propaganda model in the late 1980s. Chomsky's contributions to the political economy of communication go beyond his collaboration with Herman. His own writings in the 1980s, most notably 1989's *Necessary Illusions*, developed a rich media critique that pursued the tension between capitalist and democratic societies.[71] Chomsky, more than any other figure, argued that the United States was far from being a genuine democracy, and that the media system played a major role in cementing inegalitarian class relations. His work drew from a critical reading of mainstream scholarship and a rich understanding of the classical and Anglo-American democratic traditions.

Chomsky's courage in forcefully critiquing communist countries while refusing to budge from his democratic, egalitarian, and radical principles influenced me a great deal. His commitment to rationalism, to evidence, to clear thinking, and his refusal to hold any sacred cows was intoxicating. Chomsky also, for the power and the principled nature of his critique, was remarkably open-minded and pragmatic about the process of making social change. His work with Herman became the prism through which my critique of news media, and much else, would be developed.

As impressive as this tradition was, even in its most dynamic phase there were only a relatively small number of scholars working in the area, and many important areas were unaddressed. The political economy of communication seemed like a great idea, but it was an idea still crystallizing. Therefore, I read widely in a number of other disciplines. In time, by the early 1990s, I cobbled together my own vision of what the political economy of communication entailed. When I read Vinny Mosco's admirable *The Political Economy of Communication* upon its publication in 1996—arguably the first systematic effort to define the subfield—I realized there really was no consensus about the core issues and readings; everyone was cobbling just like I was.[72]

In addition to the work being done inside the subfield, my understanding of the political economy of communication drew from a handful of intellectual traditions, only a little of which was found within the field of communication. In just about everything I taught, and in the formation of all my arguments in all of my research, these traditions have played a foundational role. They are:

1. The *Monthly Review* political economy of Baran, Sweezy, and Magdoff;
2. The political sociology of C. Wright Mills and Habermas;
3. The work on technology and communication of Innis, McLuhan, and Postman;

4. The First Amendment and democratic theoretical work of Alexander Meiklejohn;
5. The political theory of C.B. Macpherson.

In each of these traditions there were a number of scholars who influenced me, but I will mention the signature figures herein.

First, there was the *Monthly Review* political economy of Paul Baran, Paul Sweezy, and Harry Magdoff, which highlighted the nature and importance of monopoly and corporations in modern capitalism. Sweezy, arguably the most original and brilliant U.S. Marxist economist of the twentieth century, expanded upon Thorstein Veblen's work, and also drew from Marx and the left Keynesian tradition to produce the definitive treatment of modern corporate or "monopoly" capitalism.[73] He also studied under Harold Laski and Joseph Schumpeter. This school of work is called the *Monthly Review* tradition after the magazine Sweezy founded in 1949 with Leo Huberman, and later co-edited with Harry Magdoff.[74]

The centerpiece of the *Monthly Review* tradition has been its critique of contemporary capitalism, or what Baran and Sweezy term "monopoly capitalism," because it is dominated by large corporations working in oligopolistic markets. This historically specific understanding of modern capitalism provided me with a framework to understand the broad pressure behind the critical junctures of the Progressive Era and the 1930s and 1940s. The *Monthly Review* tradition never tried to show how existing capitalism conforms to analysis or made by Marx in 1867 or Lenin in 1914. Rather, the object is to understand how contemporary capitalism works based on its actual behavior using tools provided by Marx, Veblen, Keynes, Steindl, Kalecki, and Hansen, among others.[75] Unlike too many mainstream economists, the *Monthly Review* tradition does not assume that the market is neutral or benevolent, that class inequality is natural, and that capitalism is ahistorical. And unlike too much of both Marxist and mainstream economics, the *Monthly Review* analysis includes a refreshing integration of the actual real-world capitalism of finance and corporate behavior into its theory. It is an empirically driven analysis, which I found complemented much of my neoclassical education in economics.

Baran and Sweezy's core argument is that monopoly capitalism has a strong tendency toward economic stagnation. Unlike neoclassical theory, which argues that the system tends toward full employment if the market is left to its own devices, Baran and Sweezy argue that the system tends toward crisis and depression. They laid this out in a book titled *Monopoly Capital*, published in 1966.[76] In fact, while there is a good deal of debate over the merits of the *Monthly Review* position, their fundamental argument has proven valuable and provides a superior context for understanding economic policymaking in our times.

What makes Sweezy's work, expecially that co-authored with Baran, so important for media studies is that it explains why advertising is so prominent in modern capitalism, after being a negligible undertaking in the previous century of American private enterprise. (Baran, too, had linkages to the antecedents of critical communication. Before immigrating to the United States, he had been characterized as the "economist of the Frankfurt School.") In a capitalism dominated by large corporations operating in oligopolistic markets, advertising becomes a necessary, even mandatory, competitive weapon. Firms no longer produce as much as they can to sell at a market price over which they have no control. They produce only as much as they can sell at prices that permit them satisfactory profit, and they have considerable influence over pricing. Advertising, and marketing more generally, is the means to that end, especially since it does not require cutthroat price competition. Sweezy's framework for understanding advertising, largely confirmed in neoclassical economic treatments of the subject, also explains why the content of advertising tends to be so spurious, if not fraudulent. For advertising to tell the truth—our products are largely interchangeable with the competition and we do not compete vigorously in pricing—would be highly counterproductive. Indeed, the great paradox of advertising is that the more products are alike, the more they have to advertise to convince consumers they are different.

As the U.S. media system is subsidized to a large extent by some hundreds of billions of dollars of advertising annually, Sweezy's work highlights the close material connection of the commercial media to the broader economy. Sweezy's work on advertising remains the starting point for all political economic studies of the subject. When Raymond Williams wrote his famous essay on advertising as magic, the influence of Baran and Sweezy was unmistakable.[77] Nevertheless, the field of communication, which devotes considerable resources to teaching advertising, is mostly ignorant of the political economic approach to advertising, to its considerable detriment.[78] Scholars of advertising, along with those who address the matter only tangentially, too often have an ideologically loaded notion of advertising as a benevolent institution providing a "service" to consumers. Indeed, one study showed that advertising and communication textbooks often don't even acknowledge that advertising is a core business expense solely intended to enhance profits.[79]

Finally, in his last two decades, Sweezy, along with his fellow *Monthly Review* editor Harry Magdoff, was among those who pioneered in analyzing the striking shift of U.S. and global capitalism toward a system where financial speculation and debt were growing at exponential rates and altering the nature of the system altogether. This process is called financialization. While permitting the system to grow and avoid stagnation, this increase in speculation and debt also introduced extraordinary instability, which may define the coming generation much like the Depression defined the 1930s. This growth of finance and debt was possible, to some extent, because of dramatic changes in communication technology that globalized markets and made possible all sorts of speculation. Again, as with advertising, Sweezy and Magdoff's work pointed to crucial ways that communication was hardwired into the political economy.

The second tradition that influenced me was the work of C. Wright Mills and Jurgen Habermas, which I found closely related.[80] Mills's work drew attention to the importance of the public sphere and provided a searing critique of the problem of depoliticization in the United States. When I entered graduate school in 1983, I considered this the single most important issue for social scientists to address in the United States; it remains almost as important to me today. Like Mills, I found the fingerprints of the media all over the deplorable state of our political culture. I found Mills's *The Power Elite* to be one of the most extraordinary books I had ever read.[81] Although written in the 1950s, its critique resonated with much of what I saw in 1980s America, and what I see today.

In some ways Mills pointed to the issues that Jurgen Habermas would later trigger with the translation of *The Structural Transformation of the Public Sphere*, and I consider Habermas to be making a similar argument. In the book, Habermas paralleled Mills's critique of modern Western liberal democracies. His argument made communication a central component of democracy, the structural/institutional basis for communication of paramount importance, and regarded both business and government domination of media as problematic for democracy.[82] A central problem in the political economy of communication had been the matter of determining a more democratic media system than that provided by the market. The problem has been that much more vexing because the "really existing alternative" to capitalism and commercial media for much of the twentieth century—the communist systems in Eastern Europe and Asia—were singularly unattractive from a democratic perspective.[83] Habermas's notion of the public sphere, a place where citizens interact that is controlled by neither business nor the state, has provided an operating principle for democratic media. Following this logic, the policy trajectory of much political economic research in communication, certainly my own, has been to establish a well-funded nonprofit, noncommercial, heterogeneous communication sector that is decentralized and controlled in a democratic fashion. Habermas's formulation was absolutely crucial in moving the debate in media studies away from the dominant notion that there were two—and only two—ways to organize media: the free, private media of democracy or the state-controlled media of authoritarian societies.[84]

Third, Harold Innis, Marshall McLuhan, and Neil Postman each provided provocative critiques of society oriented around media technology.[85] The Canadian economist Innis wrote long studies on the importance of communication systems and technologies in the course of human history.[86] His approach was historical and sociological, locating communication in relation to social and political development. Innis argued that communication technologies were of paramount importance in understanding human development, and that they had profound biases. His work went far beyond traditional political economy and was influential most notably on James Carey, one of the founders of U.S. cultural studies.[87] Marshall McLuhan was also an acolyte of Innis, though this Canadian English professor altered Innis's arguments and disseminated them widely. He is best known for his notion that the "medium is the message," that media are changing the very way we think and that human societies operate. His work was very influential on innumerable thinkers, including Postman.[88] Innis and McLuhan both, perhaps due to their nation of origin, did not share the embrace of U.S. mainstream academic satisfaction with the commercial media status quo, and they were more than willing to greet the imperial claims of U.S. scholars with skepticism. Their work opened the door for far more critical takes on communication, technology, and society. Postman's work, especially *Amusing Ourselves to Death*, had the same effect.[89] It created space for critical work.

Since media and communication sectors were generally defined by a specific technology—for example, press, telegraph, film, radio, TV, cable, and so on—I found that this work provided an important entrée to the issues that concerned me, like depoliticization. I was immediately hostile to anything that smacked of technological determinism, but I was also convinced that media technologies did have significant impact, what Marxists liked to call "relative autonomy." Fundamental media technologies, which often emerged in a critical juncture, tended to be "path dependent," meaning that once society opted for them, it was very difficult to switch to a different technology, even if that new technology was superior. Media technologies had unintended consequences. Today, it strikes me as quite plausible that the electronic media avalanche that people, especially children, are experiencing is having considerable effects upon them, for better or worse.[90] These effects are so closely intertwined with the commercialism that drives media in the United States that it is not always possible to disentangle the technological effect, but that does not mean there isn't one. A great deal more research is needed.

Fourth, there was the work of Alexander Meiklejohn. It is hard for me to exaggerate the importance of his work upon my thinking as a graduate student through today. It is ironic that when I first read Meiklejohn in grad school, I thought he was at best naïve. I can't recall the exact piece I was assigned, but Meiklejohn was discussing the genius of the town meeting, and how this exemplified the way politics worked in the United States. I thought he was crazy. Didn't Meiklejohn know we live in a capitalist society? My professor, Don Pember, was unimpressed with my knee-jerk response; for my preliminary examination, he assigned me all of Meiklejohn's writings on the First Amendment. I was blown away. In the 1980s it was commonly presented that the First Amendment was this ahistorical commandment that commercial media were protected from any government regulation, except in broadcasting, regardless of the content that these media firms produced. Meiklejohn challenged that perspective and skewered it:

> First, let it be noted that, by those words [the text of the First Amendment], Congress is not debarred from all action upon freedom of speech. Legislation which abridges that freedom is forbidden, but not legislation to enlarge and enrich it. The freedom of mind which befits members of a self-governing society is not a given and fixed part of human nature. It can be increased and established by learning, by teaching, by the unhindered flow of accurate information, by giving men health and vigor and security, by bringing them together in activities of communication and mutual understanding. And the federal legislature is not forbidden to engage in that positive enterprise of cultivating the general intelligence upon which the success of self-government so obviously depends. On the contrary, in that positive field the Congress of the United States has a heavy and basic responsibility to promote the freedom of speech.[91]

Meiklejohn opened up a new, progressive way to envision the First Amendment as a policy prescription for a self-governing society, not as protective legislation for investors in communication industries. The First Amendment is not meant to sanctify the marketplace of ideas; it is meant to ensure to every citizen "the fullest possible participation" in the working through of social problems. As he wrote: "When a free man is voting, it is not enough that the truth is known by someone else, by some scholar or administrator or legislator. The voters must have it, all of them. The primary purpose of the First Amendment is, then, that all the citizens shall, so far as possible, understand the issues which bear upon our common life. That is why no idea, no opinion, no doubt, no belief, no counterbelief, no relevant information, may be kept from them."[92]

Meiklejohn was highly skeptical toward the commercialization of the press, and was opposed to commercial broadcasting in the 1930s. He highlighted the tension between the need for a press system to draw citizens into public life as informed participants and a press system set up to maximize profit for investors. His thinking pointed toward radical solutions, and in some ways, became impractical in a world where nearly all of media was conducted for profit. But it inspired me, and others, to think big, and to fight for an understanding of the First Amendment and freedom of the press that served self-government first and foremost.

In the postwar era, elements of Meiklejohn's thinking gained considerable currency and influenced several Supreme Court decisions, including the famous *Red Lion* decision discussed in Chapter 1. Jerome Barron was probably his most accomplished acolyte. Barron's seminal 1967 piece in the *Harvard Law Review* built upon Meiklejohn and in effect made a case for the need for a political economy of media, if the First Amendment's freedom of the press clause was going to be effective.[93] Barron actually went before the Supreme Court in 1974 and argued, in effect, that the *Red Lion* interpretation of the First Amendment as belonging to the public first and the owners second should be extended from broadcasting to newspapers in the famous *Miami Herald v. Tornillo* case. Barron lost the case in a dramatic 9–0 vote. In my mind, Meiklejohn and Barron were pioneers, decades ahead of their time, whose work may again enjoy a moment in the sun.

Finally, the work of Meiklejohn combined with the work of people like John Kenneth Galbraith pointed to a progressive strain in liberal thought that I found very helpful, indeed indispensable, as I grappled with the relationship of media to democracy. I pretty quickly determined that a political economy of communication that used Marxist or radical texts as the gospel and dismissed liberalism categorically was wrongheaded and seriously flawed. The work of C.B. Macpherson was especially influential on me.[94] Macpherson was a political philosopher— another Canadian—who was centrally concerned with the relationship of capitalism to democracy, or inegalitarian economics with egalitarian politics. He termed this the problem of liberal democracy, and he was, in effect, a political economist of democracy.[95] He was also concerned with what he regarded as the deterioration of the best of the liberal tradition under capitalist auspices. His research was based on rigorous analysis of the main thinkers in the Anglo-American tradition, including the U.S. "Founding Fathers." Perhaps most important, Macpherson's work paved the way for understanding why contemporary U.S.-style democracy is necessarily weak, and depoliticization is necessarily rampant. He argued that a corporate capitalist democracy can be stable only if decisions are made by the few with only superficial mass participation, and if liberal values wilt on the vine. In this sense, depoliticization, demoralization, and cynicism are rational responses by the bulk of the citizenry to their actual amount of power.[96] Macpherson's work did not address media directly, but his framework has proven useful as it offered a critical and materialist critique of Western capitalist political cultures.[97]

Macpherson pointed out the paternalism and elitism in elements of liberalism, the notion that enlightened intellectuals are the proper rulers of the world. Few have done a better job of showing the strain of contempt for genuine democracy that exists within aspects of liberalism, and how such liberals truly fear popular rule. It is this brand of liberalism that both the left and conservative populists harpoon. But what Macpherson also highlighted was the progressive and humanistic impulse of liberalism. I found this notion of liberalism extremely attractive and worth fighting for. He argued that modern capitalism was forcing liberalism to a moment of truth, where it had to decide which of its values it wished to preserve and promote, those of a flawed corporate system or those promoting its democratic ideals. I could not agree more.[98]

This was my foundation, but another question remained: What exactly was the subfield of political economy of communication about? What did it do that no other subfield or discipline did? I remember answering this question in my very first Association for Education in Journalism and Mass Communication (AEJMC) conference paper in 1986, and this is what I wrote, more or less.[99] (I cite myself not to brag about my vision but rather, as you will see, to highlight in the next chapter what is conspicuously absent, or underemphasized.) If there was no consensus of what the core readings and issues were for the political economy of communication, I have found that most of my peers were comfortable with this characterization, or some derivation thereof. Political economy of communication has two main components. First, it addressed *in a critical manner* how the media system interacted with and affected the overall disposition of power in society. Did the media, on balance, serve as a progressive force to draw the masses into political debate as informed and effective participants, or did the media system as a whole tend to reinforce elite rule and inegalitarian social relations? This was a topic of concern for more than political economists—in fact it drives much of communication research, especially cultural studies—but it was always central to the political economic tradition. It requires a certain command of history and political theory. Simultaneously, and of necessity, this required looking at how the media and communication systems were integrated into the economy. This required some facility with economics.

Now what I meant by "in a critical manner" gets to the nub of the matter. There are many different measures one could use, and over time the one I emphasized rested upon the provision of journalism, or, more broadly, the information necessary for self-government and effective freedom. (As we know well today, much of our political education comes from entertainment and nonjournalistic media, but even those media rely upon journalism to be effective.) In my view, the media system, with particular emphasis upon journalism, needed to provide several services to meet the communication requirements of a free and self-governing people. The media system needed to keep a ruthless check on people who were in power or who wished to be in power, whether in the public or private sector. The media system had to be a watchdog. It had to be capable of ferreting out truth from lies, so liars could not prevaricate endlessly, shamelessly, and without consequence. And the media system had to provide a range of informed opinion on the crucial social and political issues of the day, as well as be the advance scout to locate problems on the horizon.

Not all media had to do all of these things, but in combination a healthy media system would make these services available to the great bulk of the citizenry and not discriminate against people based on race, class, or gender. If it fulfilled these criteria, the media system would be a democratic force in society. Now if one looks at the list closely, these are all classical liberal criteria; when applied to other nations or to history, they are not especially controversial. These are right out of the Hutchins Commission playbook. But when such criteria were applied to the United States, or the U.S. role in the world, without pulling punches, the results were generally unflattering, and the critique was regarded as radical. And it was radical, because the logic of the critique suggested that structural reform of the media system and society were necessary if we were serious about democracy.

In addition, what this first area of the political economy of communication suggested was that the relationship of media to society was not a one-way flow. Not only did democracy require viable media and journalism to prosper; so, too, did media and journalism require healthy democracy and strong popular politics to survive and be effective as progressive institutions. It was a close and symbiotic relationship.

The second area in the political economy of communication tradition was largely its exclusive domain: an evaluation of how market structures, advertising support, labor relations, profit motivation, technologies, and government policies shaped media industries, journalistic practices, occupational sociology, and the nature and content of the news and entertainment. This required a certain mastery of microeconomics, history, journalism, and policy studies at a minimum. While some legal scholars, political scientists, and economists were interested in these questions too, they rarely were interested in the critical implications for society as a whole. They were content to accept the status quo as an unalterable given. And when one accepts the status quo as an unalterable given, it doesn't take long before it starts to seem benevolent. Political economy by definition was a critical enterprise. The combination of these two elements of political economy of communication gave the field its distinction and dynamism. Political economy also tended to attract people on the left, like myself, who were skeptical about the faith generally demonstrated toward the market and the U.S. government, especially in its foreign policy. I imagine that it would have been a fairly uncomfortable place for someone without left politics.[100]

In the field of political economy writ large, a nonsocialist and pro-capitalist school of thought was a long-standing tradition, one that engaged in a productive dialogue with those on the left who adopted a critical stance toward the market. Indeed, the genius of the market was not a totem for worship so much as an area for study among the first century of economists. During critical junctures, like the 1930s and 1940s, there has been dialogue between the left and those not on the left over fundamental issues. This has sometimes produced great insights, the classic example being Joseph Schumpeter's *Capitalism, Socialism and Democracy*.[101] His work also forced left political economists to rethink their positions and tighten their arguments; he was instrumental in shaping Sweezy's arguments about monopoly capitalism. Regrettably, economists withdrew from political economy by the second half of the twentieth century, and in many cases much earlier, when they removed the market from critical examination.[102] No such dialogue emerged in the critical juncture of the 1960s and 1970s, at least in the political economy of communication.

There was an explicitly pro-capitalist variant of political economy of communication that emerged in the 1970s, but it was more akin to the market theology of Milton Friedman than the rigorous debate, examination, and ultimate defense of the market system provided by Schumpeter. This parallel "mainstream" political economy of communication consisted of a core group of economists, political scientists, and lawyers who saw the new technologies of the late 1960s and 1970s as a reason to call into question the existing regulatory system, especially in telecommunication. These were scholars influenced by Ronald Coase, as well as the "Chicago School" of neoliberal economics, and their research was founded on the idea that markets and the profit motive are superior regulators and are used insufficiently in the realm of communication.[103] For all their mastery of mainstream economic theory or regulatory statutes, these scholars tended to know little about journalism, culture, or democratic theory. There was almost no dialogue between these scholars and those in the political economy of communication tradition; they were living in parallel universes with very different assumptions, perspectives, and views on the critical juncture of their times.

The pro-market scholars began an annual conference in 1972 called the Telecommunications Policy Research Conference with funding from the federal government, foundations, and industry. Business interest played a prominent role in the TPRC from the beginning. The purpose of the TPRC, as Bruce Owen put it in his history of the conference, was to address "the enormous gap between the implications of academic research and the actual state of communication policy in the United States." They were not interested in drawing the public into policy debates or assessing the democratic implications of commercial media; they were talking directly to elites about how to make communication a more viable business. The agenda of the TPRC was "deregulation," and Owen proudly notes that the TPRC played a role in seeing that "communications was undoubtedly the first of the major regulatory fields to be thus reformed, and has progressed the most."[104] A guiding intellectual figure for the TPRC was Ithiel de Sola Pool.[105] Arguably the person who has pushed this approach and agenda the most with regard to media policy issues has been Benjamin Compaine.[106]

To be accurate, the TPRC did invite the participation of critical scholars by the 1980s, and, as I discuss in Chapter 4, the public interest scholars have become regular and important participants, albeit a minority, in recent years.[107] But there was precious little dialogue between the two sides that pushed either one to question its presuppositions. They were talking past each other, to very different audiences, and with different goals. This was a lost opportunity. While the two traditions occasionally intersected, they rarely interacted. Consequently, the subfield of the political economy of communication was the almost exclusive province of the Left.

Make no mistake, this lack of a pro-market presence in political economy of communication, and political economy in general, was regrettable for both sides of the divide and much lamented by my students over the years. What always struck me was the number of pro-capitalist students majoring in economics or business who would take my classes, with its introduction to Marx's notion of accumulation and Sweezy's economics, and then come up to me and thank me for the exposure to this work. A typical comment was as follows: "This is the first time I have heard some discussion of how a capitalist economy actually works, and that what I am studying in economics or business makes any sense to me in a social, political or historical sense."

These students only rarely changed their political views, but they were almost always pleased to get this perspective. Apparently, this is a common phenomenon. "One can study economics for years without understanding the market system," the Yale political scientist Charles Lindblom writes. "I graduated from college without understanding it. If my instructors understood it, they did not take the trouble to explain its structure. They taught about trees rather than forest." It was easy to see why: "Mainstream economics still stumbles because the market's dazzling benefits half blind it to the defects. . . . One does not see much intellectual interchange on the market system between economists, most of whom admire it, and those scholars of history, literature, and philosophy who . . . judge its consequences for values like freedom, rationality and morality."[108]

Nor, due to the frosty relations I described above, was there much dialogue between political economists of communication and "mainstream" communication scholars in the 1980s, as far as I could see. Perhaps it is wishful thinking to imagine that critical and so-called mainstream voices might have had a fruitful dialogue, but I think that the prospect was not (and is not) impossible. In my view, critical scholarship was predicated not on socialist principles, but rather on liberal and democratic principles. It was committed to political enfranchisement, freedom of speech, intellectual inquiry, and social justice. These are also mainstream liberal values. If scholarship is done right, it requires scholars to question, interrogate, and possibly alter their own assumptions on a regular basis, and to take seriously opposing ideas. As Aristotle put it, "It is the mark of an educated mind to be able to entertain a thought without accepting it."[109] If conclusions were locked in by the presuppositions— which were off-limits to criticism—it made for flawed scholarship regardless of the scholar's values or politics.[110] But such dialogue was rare, especially when not in the midst of a critical juncture.[111]

The inability of the political economy of communication to gain traction, to command the respect of its adversaries, during the critical juncture of the late 1960s and early 1970s put it in a precarious position by the 1980s. Political economists of communication saw our work as part of a broader intellectual and political movement for social justice and peace. When social activism outside the academy was strong, it energized the research and gave it meaning. The politics in society as a whole provoked important and pressing research questions. There was an implicit understanding that the research could contribute to social change. There was always a legitimate concern that research could turn into cheerleading, but healthy debate, rigorous standards, and the actual events taking place on the ground would serve to keep the research credible, original, and focused.

The problem for the political economy of communication (and critical work more broadly) came in the 1980s, when it was clear that the social movements of the 1960s and 1970s had collapsed. Instead of having an army of supporters off campus, critical scholars were all alone and very lonely. Political economists of communication appeared to unsympathetic observers as absurdly out of touch with reality, and the research was increasingly stigmatized as more of an ideological exercise than a branch of scholarship. The dynamism in the official culture was all on the right, and anyone on a college campus in the mid-1980s could not help but be aware of the changes. I recall that in 1985 a student put signs up on the University of Washington campus bulletin boards inviting anyone on campus to a gathering of people interested in progressive politics. I attended the meeting of roughly twenty people, only to discover that, at age thirty-two, I was the second-youngest person in the room.

The prospects for progressive social change could not have been much bleaker, and all hands were on deck simply trying to maintain the status quo from further right-wing attacks. In this context all critical work, especially political economy of communication research, began to lose its moorings. If social change for the better was unlikely or impossible, what exactly were we trying to accomplish with our work? The work then turned to providing a critique of the status quo with a vague goal of eventually down the road contributing to an enlightening of students and citizens who will rise up in rage against the machine. Even the most brilliant work of the late 1980s, say Herman and Chomsky's *Manufacturing Consent*, allowed little hope that changing the media system or the society as a whole was a plausible goal. We were simply learning how the system worked for intellectual self-defense. We were speaking truth to power, but we had no illusions that we were in any position to contest that power.

To put it another way, nearly every work in political economy of communication provided extensive critique of the status quo with no plausible sense of how to change it. Many books seemed to end, almost as an afterthought, with the same short refrain: "The point of this research has been to alert citizens and fellow scholars to a major problem in our society, with the hope that sometime, in the future, probably way down the road, if at all, it might have some effect; but by the way I wrote this, I understand it probably won't." Obviously I reduced the refrain to the nearly absurd, but you get the point.

This defeatism was reinforced by the ideological as well as political success of neoliberalism and the defensive posture of liberalism and the left in this period. It got worse in the early 1990s. The collapse of communism, even though no one I was associated with on the left was at all a supporter of these regimes, seemed to cement the notion, as Margaret Thatcher put it, that *There Is No Alternative*. In my view, one barely heard at the time, it demonstrated only the bankruptcy and absurdity of nondemocratic socialism. (As the Hungarian socialist Gyula Hegyi put it in 2006, in a message to the successful left-wing governments in Latin America: "Believe me, *compañeros*, there is no democratic socialism without democracy—and the kind of socialism that exists without democracy could kill your dreams for the future.")[112]

But left/liberal decline was widespread: In Nicaragua, the Sandinistas lost the election in 1990; in Europe, social democracy was on the defensive; and in the former communist states, it seemed like Milton Friedman had become a virtual folk hero. The milquetoast Democratic Party was running from its New Deal and Great Society legacy and announcing its commitment to "deregulation." Markets worked, and even if they had some flaws, any alternative that involved the state was worse. Everywhere one turned, free markets and rhetoric extolling their virtues were ascendant; popular politics was in retreat. Even some critical scholars seemed to internalize the notion that unfettered markets promoted efficiency, growth, and possibly even a certain measure of justice, while governments were bureaucratic enemies of progress. One went so far as to characterize the market as "an expansive popular system."[113] Stuart Hall's classic 1977 critique of markets as providing a misleading yet ideologically powerful gloss of voluntarism and equality over the class inequality and exploitation that is the basis of capitalist societies was fading rapidly from view, especially in cultural studies.[114]

This was the "end of history." At the extreme end of the spectrum, cultural studies figures nominally on the left, like John Fiske, became prominent by producing book after book implying, if not stating baldly, that the concern with the commercial structure of media industries was overblown; indeed commercial media markets arguably were superior to alternatives because they seemingly gave the people what they wanted, certainly more than the nanny-state alternative.[115] Fiske had moved from a radical critique of television in the 1970s as an important and complex instrument of class domination, not unlike Hall's description of the market, to a position a decade later where television and corporate media in general had become a much more level playing field, a "semiotic democracy," with indeterminate outcomes.[116] By the early 1990s, as Susan Douglas puts it, cultural studies and critical communication were in the thrall of the "high Fiskean moment."[117] Fiske contended people had the power to "decode" commercial media messages in a resistant and subversive manner, so actual ownership and control over the media system was much less important than political economists thought, if not irrelevant.[118] Fiske came to symbolize the rapprochement of a strain of cultural studies with commercial media and, with that, the abandonment of a pressing concern for traditional political organizing more generally.[119] Structural change was pretty much out of the question.[120]

Pessimism barely captures the mood. I recall a conversation with Paul Sweezy in 1994, when he was eighty-three years old. I asked Sweezy how the current period compared to the last era of darkness, the 1950s, when socialists could barely get academic employment and harassment by the state was commonplace. Sweezy told me he had just written a new foreword to a book of his from 1956, and upon rereading the original book he was surprised by how much more optimistic he had been in 1956 than he was in the 1990s. In his view, the situation had never been bleaker.

Terry Eagleton brilliantly captured the dilemma of critical scholars over the collapse of the prospects for progressive social change by the early 1990s:

> Imagine a radical movement which had suffered an emphatic defeat. So emphatic, in fact, that it seemed unlikely to resurrect for the length of a lifetime, if even then. The defeat I have in mind is not just the kind of rebuff with which the political left is depressingly familiar, but a repulse so definitive that it seemed to discredit the very paradigms with which such politics had traditionally worked. It would now be less a matter of hotly contesting these notions than of contemplating them with something of the mild antiquarian

interest with which one might regard Ptolemaic cosmology or the scholasticism of Duns Scotus. . . . The historical basis of this belief would be that political movements which were at once mass, central and productive had temporarily gone out of business.[121]

People on the left and the right seemed to accept that the media system was inexorably attached to corporate capitalism, and that corporate media and the corporate system together would make leftward change unthinkable for the vast majority of Americans. And if social change was unthinkable for the vast majority of Americans, it is only a matter of time that it is unthinkable for the rest of us, too. We were battening down the hatches. But at a certain point, once the hatches are battened, the question for critical scholars becomes, what next?

This was a question some elements of cultural studies could address with greater ease, as it moved toward postmodernism and other variants of less explicitly politicized work.[122] Moreover, such variants of cultural studies were able to gain prominence by this time in higher-status fields like English and anthropology. For critical scholars doing political economic work the matter was far trickier, and regrettably the results were not always optimal. I could see the dilemma with my own dwindling number of students in this period, their difficulty in locating research projects on contemporary issues that were compelling. Most found their footing, as I did, by making a historical turn, as I discuss in Chapter 3. At its weakest, the research for some of the others was almost circular. It would start with the assumption that the media system reinforced some bad element of the status quo—such as militarism, inequality, corruption, racism—and then it would demonstrate this by observing some phenomena and generally citing like-minded authors as evidence. The conclusions restated the assumptions. If one disagreed with the assumptions, the research was unconvincing and of little value. In other cases my students might produce a case study to glorify some lost cause social movement or alternative medium, many times in some locale like Bolivia or Central America. It was hard to avoid the classic putdown that critical scholars once made toward mainstream work: "So what?" At any rate, political economy had lost its "mojo," and the dynamism that marked the field into the 1980s was a thing of the past.

Although the end of a critical juncture combined with the dreary political climate provides the context for the predicament that faced the political economy of communication, there were specific factors as well. For starters, critical work in general made university administrators ill at ease, regardless of their personal political convictions, so it was disparaged and discouraged, both subtly and, at times, directly. It was research that did not bring in much money, had little upside for the university as an institution, and tended to threaten or antagonize existing or prospective major funders (and politicians, a key concern for a state university). Therefore political economy of communication was always on thin ice due to its willingness to ask the sorts of questions that antagonized people in power.

More specifically, it directly undermined the two lifelines mainstream communication researchers and administrators were grasping onto to defend and expand their turf. First, the very nature of political economy made it an uncomfortable component of a department seeking robust ties with industry; and to the extent professional training was seen as being synonymous with being pro-industry, political economy of communication was no help there either. Second, it was also a thorn in the side of those communication scholars and administrators eager to ramp up the social science disciplinary credentials of the field. Political economy of communication was historical and multidisciplinary. It often asked questions that could not be answered by quantitative methods (although it had far more need and use for quantitative research than most people realized).

There were few classes and fewer jobs in the political economy of communication as the 1990s dragged on. As it was, by the 1990s there were only a handful of jobs in U.S. universities set aside for such people, and matters may have only grown worse since then. Most political economy scholars in media studies would get hired for some other reason—for example, to teach newswriting or new media—and do their research without tremendous encouragement. I was hired at Wisconsin in 1988 to fill a position teaching advertising.[123]

Nor were there divisions in ICA, NCA, or AEJMC—the professional organizations devoted to political economy—or journals to publish research. This had a reinforcing effect. Those graduate students even exposed to political economy were not blind. They saw that it was not a viable career option, at least in the United States, and some shifted to research that has more prospects for publication and employment down the road. Since the borders between political economy and neighboring fields were fluid, scholars leaned toward areas with more stature. In sum, by the 1990s the political economy of communication was a nonstarter in American communication departments.

This was a reality I did not want to accept. I long had been convinced that the future of communication as a discipline depended upon the emergence of political economy as a cornerstone of the field. Political economy would not answer all the questions the field entertained—far from it—but it would provide a foundation for the entire discipline. In addition to becoming a cornerstone such that every department would have faculty and students working in the area, it would infuse all the other research in the field, providing the field with momentum, context, and vision. That was a role political economy played to some degree in communication studies in other nations.

I would sometimes meet quantitative media scholars from Europe with a rich understanding of communication history and policies, and I hoped it could assume that role here. But by the 1990s, it was obvious that had failed. By then I was happy simply to see what little political economic work existed in the field survive.

One might think, then, that this would have been a renaissance moment for mainstream research. And the mainstream social science component of communication research did find a stable niche, albeit not a particularly significant one. But even mainstream and traditional communication research was limited by the neoliberal paradigm, with its assumption of infallible markets and the impossibility and undesirability of social change. If any unit was going to cash in on the Information Age, it would likely be business schools. In this context, the overall field of communication was unable to escape its second-tier status in U.S. universities. This was a grand irony—in the Information Age, those scholars expressly commissioned to study communication and information floundered.

It was no surprise that finger-pointing went on between political economists and cultural studies scholars arguing over who was more responsible for the dreadful state of affairs. In one sense, there were important issues at play that deserved to be debated. But these debates were a response to the defeated position of the left and the depoliticization of society. In retrospect there was a lot about these debates that reminded me of the proverbial left-wing firing squad: Everyone get in a circle and shoot. I confess to participating in these fights on a few occasions in the 1990s. But once the possibility of participating in actual movements for social change emerged, these debates seemed like gigantic time-wasters. There were even more absurd critiques of specific methodologies—usually quantitative methods—as being innately mainstream or counterprogressive.[124] This all took a toll. When the *Journal of Communication* published its follow-up special edition on the state of the field in

1993, a mere three of the twenty essays were by political economists, and only a couple more by critical scholars sympathetic to
political economy.[125] And the *JOC* was edited by George Gerbner, who had been the mentor and benefactor of scholars working in the political economic tradition. A mainstream journal
edited by any other prominent member of the field might have
excised political economy altogether.

Starved of resources, with precious little institutional support,
and in a hostile political environment, the political economy of
communication produced a surprising amount of important and
high-quality research. Although Smythe died at the beginning of
the 1990s and Schiller left us at the beginning of the next decade,
Mattelart[126] and the four Brits—Garnham,[127] Curran,[128] Golding,[129] and Murdock[130]—have remained productive, and the situation in Britain was arguably no better for political economy of
communication by then than in the United States. The second
generation of U.S. scholars who came of age in the 1970s and
1980s proved highly productive and have done original work in
a broad range of areas.[131] The real crisis facing the field is that because of the enormous constraints it has not spawned a significant "third generation" of self-identified political economists of
communication who are pushing the project forward and breaking substantial new ground.

Even in the darkest moments in the 1990s, what kept me
connected to political economy of communication was the
power of its critique, its capacity to coherently explain what
was going on in a manner that made sense and squared with
the evidence. I found myself turning to inspirational pieces by
Noam Chomsky, and Paul Baran's lovely "The Commitment
of the Intellectual" to get me through those times.[132] Their
simple point was always to tell the truth and let the chips fall
where they may. Even if political economy could not show me
the way forward, explain exactly how to change the situation,
or tell me what button to push to get immediate social change,
it could explain the media better than any other tradition.

Nowhere was the power of political economy of communication more evident than in its critique of journalism; indeed, during the 1990s, perhaps the most striking development was the emergence of the political economic critique of journalism as a widely recognized key to understanding the relationship of media and politics, not only on the left or on campus, but eventually in broad segments of society.

Recall that in the 1960s and 1970s, even in a critical juncture, professional journalism was riding high in the United States. Our news media were seen as effective at keeping our leaders in check and allowing citizens to have the power to govern their own lives. Bookstores were filled with tomes by heroic journalists discussing the great work they had done vanquishing the powerful and protecting the Republic. There was clear dissent to this generated by the New Left and the social movements of the 1960s, but surprisingly little compared to the uproar surrounding media in the 1930s or the Progressive Era, or today. As the 1970s ended, the field of sociology produced four notable books that dissected professional journalism, by Mark Fishman, Gaye Tuchman, Herbert Gans, and Todd Gitlin.[133] This outstanding research dramatically advanced the hard process of examining American journalism critically. But it tended to accept the dominant institutional arrangements as a given. The institutions were unassailable, and the work tended to concentrate upon newsroom organization, professional practices, and the implications for content.

Soon thereafter, Ben Bagdikian's *The Media Monopoly*, published in 1983, and Herman and Chomsky's *Manufacturing Consent*, published in 1988, advanced this critique to draw in the political economic framework of analysis.[134] The two books fundamentally changed the way the news media were regarded, not only in the political economy of communication subfield and among activists in the United States, but eventually to a much broader public.[135] Bagdikian's work is often cited for quantifying the extent of concentrated media ownership in the

United States, but it did far more than that, as I discuss in the next chapter. It also began the crucial process of linking up the development of professional journalism to the manner in which the newspaper industry was restructured in the early part of the twentieth century. It pointed to an immediate future where journalism would get considerably worse, and the best aspects of professionalism would get demolished by corporate pressures.

Manufacturing Consent took the step of linking up a structural explanation of news media content with an argument about how news tended to serve elite interests in the United States and was often significantly propagandistic and antidemocratic. The work highlighted the important role media play in politics in general, and for popular and progressive political movements specifically. This work, and the research it inspired, demolished the notion that professionalism in journalism was neutral, objective, or democratic. It also highlighted the way commercial imperatives shaped the news directly and indirectly, through influencing how the professional code emerged.

When this work came out it was heretical and largely dismissed in the field of communication and the world of journalism. In particular, Herman and Chomsky's bold claim—that elite U.S. journalism provided propaganda to serve elites—was rejected categorically. Routinely, with but one or two exceptions that I can recall, I would hear my colleagues dismiss Chomsky as providing a "conspiracy theory" or say Chomsky regarded journalists and the masses as "dupes."[136] My colleagues in cultural studies were every bit as dismissive. I recall one sniffing that she would not bother to read *Manufacturing Consent* because Chomsky had such an undeveloped theoretical appreciation of ideology. It was obvious none of them had read Chomsky and Herman's work or planned to do so. I remember when Chomsky came to speak in Madison in 1990. The sponsors were asked to find someone who would go on stage with Chomsky, interrogate him after his speech, and defend the honor of mainstream journalism. Despite all the trashing of Chomsky I heard over coffee in the mailroom, none of my colleagues were willing to go toe-to-toe with him on stage. The sponsors became desperate, and finally located a professor in something like anthropology to go on stage and serve as Chomsky's adversary. But she was a postmodernist, and after talking to her for ten minutes and not having any idea what she was talking about, the sponsors decided they would let Chomsky have the floor to himself.[137]

I had this same problem at the time in my classes. I would do long examinations of journalism, and we would conclude many weeks of work (which included long discussions of the dominant notions of news as well as the conservative critique of the "left-wing" bias in the news) by reading *Manufacturing Consent*. In this particular context, the argument was especially powerful. To balance the power of Herman and Chomsky, I always tried to find the best criticism of their work I could locate. I read every review of their book I could find.[138] But everything I used, even by authors I respected, made weak criticism, often employing straw men characterizations, and looked lame by comparison. Students wondered if I was stacking the deck to make the radical argument look good—when in fact I was desperate to find a reasoned critique of it that could stand up to a hard reading. I could not.[139] The mainstream critique of Herman and Chomsky was to dismiss their arguments categorically.

It's stunning today how our understanding of journalism has changed. The corruption of journalism, the decline of investigative reporting, the degeneration of political reporting and international journalism, the collapse of local journalism are now roundly acknowledged by all but the owners of large media firms and their hired guns. *Washington Post* editors Len Downie and Robert Kaiser wrote a critique of journalism in 2002 that was nothing short of devastating in its evaluation of how commercial pressures are destroying the profession.[140]

The 2006 Report from the Project for Excellence in Journalism observes, "At many old-media companies, though not all, the decades-long battle at the top between idealists and account-ants is now over. The idealists have lost." The same report gave an accounting of the state of journalism worth citing at length:

> Most local radio stations, our content study this year finds, offer virtually nothing in the way of reporters in the field. On local TV news, fewer and fewer stories feature correspon-dents, and the range of topics that get full treatment is nar-rowing even more to crime and accidents, plus weather, traffic and sports. On the Web, the Internet-only sites that have tried to produce original content (among them Slate and Salon) have struggled financially, while those thriving finan-cially rely almost entirely on the work of others. Among blogs, there is little of what journalists would call reporting (our study this year finds reporting in just 5% of postings). Even in bigger newsrooms, journalists report that specializa-tion is eroding as more reporters are recast into generalists.
>
> In some cities, the numbers alone tell the story. There are roughly half as many reporters covering metropolitan Philadelphia, for instance, as in 1980. The number of news-paper reporters there has fallen from 500 to 220. The pattern at the suburban papers around the city has been similar, though not as extreme. The local TV stations, with the excep-tion of Fox, have cut back on traditional news coverage. The five AM radio stations that used to cover news have been re-duced to two.

As recently as 1990, the *Philadelphia Inquirer* had forty-six re-porters covering the city. Today it has twenty-four.[141]

In February 2007, the *Washington Post* published an article on the state of international coverage in the American news

media by veteran foreign correspondent Pamela Constable.
She wrote:

> Instead of stepping up coverage of international affairs,
> American newspapers and television networks are steadily
> cutting back. The [Boston] *Globe*, which stunned the journal-
> ism world last month by announcing that it would shut down
> its last three foreign bureaus, is the most recent example.
>
> Between 2002 and 2006, the number of foreign-based
> newspaper correspondents shrank from 188 to 141 (exclud-
> ing the *Wall Street Journal*, which publishes Asian and Euro-
> pean editions). The *Baltimore Sun*, which had correspondents
> from Mexico to Beijing when I went to work there in 1978,
> now has none. *Newsday*, which once had half a dozen foreign
> bureaus, is about to shut down its last one, in Pakistan. Only
> four U.S. papers—the *Journal*, the *Los Angeles Times*, the *New
> York Times* and the *Washington Post*—still keep a stable of for-
> eign correspondents.
>
> Although more than 80 percent of the public obtains most
> of its foreign and national news from TV, the major net-
> works are also closing down foreign bureaus, concentrating
> their resources on a few big stories such as Iraq.
>
> In the 1980s, American TV networks each maintained
> about 15 foreign bureaus; today they have six or fewer. ABC
> has shut down its offices in Moscow, Paris and Tokyo; NBC
> closed bureaus in Beijing, Cairo and Johannesburg. Aside
> from a one-person ABC bureau in Nairobi, there are no net-
> work bureaus left at all in Africa, India or South America—
> regions that are home to more than 2 billion people.[142]

Working journalists routinely tell me that the Bagdikian critique is not radical enough—it fails to grasp how completely
commercialism has gutted journalism over the past two decades. Linda Foley, the head of the Newspaper Guild, the
union for print journalists, states that the number-one concern

of her members, by far, is how commercial pressure is destroying their craft. In December 2006, working journalists across the nation held a national day of protest to draw attention to the corporate demolition of journalism.[143] In the 1980s journalists tended to be the strongest defenders of the status quo. That is ancient history.

So thorough is the recognition that the existing corporate system is destroying journalism, that the acclaimed scholar Michael Schudson—who has been a singular critic of Chomsky, Herman, and Bagdikian, and who for years has argued that things are not so bad in the media—is concerned about Wall Street's negative impact on journalism. He wrote in 2007: "While all media matter, some matter more than others, and for the sake of democracy, print still counts most, especially print that devotes resources to gathering news. Network TV matters, cable TV matters, but when it comes to original investigation and reporting, newspapers are overwhelmingly the most important media. Wall Street, whose collective devotion to an informed citizenry is nil, seems determined to eviscerate newspapers."[144]

In 2002 and 2003 the news media largely abrogated their duty by uncritically publishing administration lies and exaggerations that were instrumental in taking this nation to an unnecessary, illegal, and disastrous war.[145] So indefensible was the press coverage that both the *New York Times* and *Washington Post* issued apologies. In 2007, the former *Des Moines Register* editorial page editor Gilbert Cranberg took an arguably unprecedented step of demanding a formal public inquiry into the failure of the news media in reporting the buildup to the Iraq invasion.[146] The Herman and Chomsky critique, the Bagdikian critique, and the considerable work that was influenced by them, increasingly provided the basis for understanding what was going on. By contrast, the dominant books in the 1970s extolling the genius of our news media or focusing on the newsroom as the center of power in determining the news seemed like historical artifacts from a bygone era. Those communication departments that continue to pump up the notion of our valiant and courageous and democratic journalism, our feisty Fourth Estate, quickly have devolved from court critics to courtiers to court jesters.

In short, nowhere has the power of political economy of communication been more evident than in its critique of journalism. In the present critical juncture, this critique has paved the way for policy research in the contemporary period. As I discuss in Chapter 4, it is the only critique that points the way to imagining democratic solutions to the crisis at hand. Political economic criticism is no longer academic. I can understand why a young scholar in the late 1980s or 1990s would abandon political economy, but I think its day in the sun may well be returning. It is now often called media policy studies and it is not exactly the same as the political economic tradition of the 1970s and 1980s. It has adapted to the specific conditions of our times and is responding to dramatically different objective conditions—a new critical juncture.

3

The Historical Turn, Critical Junctures, and "Five Truths"

Many scholars who came to communication studies with political economic concerns dealt with the crisis in the subfield by turning toward historical research. That certainly was my path. The political economy of communication was always closely linked to history. Political economists and critical communication scholars in general sometimes conducted historical studies of alternative and independent media, or studied how social movements incorporated media, emphasizing the labor, socialist, feminist, immigrant, or African American press. This research permitted political economists and historians to get at social and political issues of importance. (For these reasons, I considered writing a history of *Monthly Review* for my dissertation.) More important, nearly every political economic research project had a historical dimension, and contemporary analysis always regarded "the present as history," as Lukács famously put it. One of the finest books generated by the political economic tradition in the 1970s and 1980s, Dan Schiller's *Objectivity and the News*, was a historical case study.[1] When I was in graduate school I took roughly half my courses in the history department; I always felt at home there. Little did I know at the time that historical research would reinvigorate and transform political economy and, more important, shine a bright light toward a future path for the entire field.

Several factors accounted for the appeal of history to the political economy of communication. As mentioned, contemporary issues that concerned political economists invariably had historical antecedents. History provided an opportunity to be less abstract and more concrete, and to avoid the circular nature of theoretical musings. In addition, a political economist could marshal evidence and make arguments in historical research that would be taken seriously by other scholars and historians. It seemed that structural and radical analyses of history were ideologically less threatening, and the evidence would be more soberly appraised. Political economists did not need to water down their arguments to get taken seriously; they simply needed to make tight arguments and provide hard evidence.

There were important institutional reasons for the historical turn as well. Whereas political economy was a marginal enterprise in communication programs, there was a fairly strong history tradition. Most Ph.D. programs had at least one historian on the faculty, and one of the trade associations, the AEJMC, even had a history division. There was even a smaller trade association, the American Journalism Historians Association, which held annual conferences and published a journal. Many of these historians had little interest in political economy, but as far as I could tell, they welcomed political economists who conducted historical research. Several general communication journals periodically ran historical research. In addition, there was the enormous field of history itself, with its myriad journals and conferences. There was nothing like that for political economy.

All of this was running through my mind while I was in grad school. My M.A. thesis was political economic and historical: I looked at the relationship of sports and mass media in the 1920s in the context of monopoly capitalism. But it drew entirely from secondary sources, and the thesis is justifiably gathering dust on a University of Washington library shelf somewhere in Seattle. When I began my Ph.D. course work, I didn't know how to proceed.

My epiphany came in the spring of 1986 when I read Ben Bagdikian's *The Media Monopoly*. In some respects, the book was similar to what I had been reading in grad school for a few years, another book chronicling the weaknesses of the journalism produced in the commercial media system. I had grown frustrated during those classes by the constant critique that did not have the courage to follow the logic to its conclusion: The system is responsible, so the system must be changed. Instead, it seemed like whatever the criticism, the assumption always was that the commercial media system was innately democratic and quintessentially American. Freedom of the press meant the freedom of capitalists to make as much money as possible in the media business, for better or worse. We were left with trying to improve professional journalism or hoping the media firms would be guilt-tripped into some form of meaningful self-regulation. It struck me as delusional. But that is how entrenched these ideas were at the time. To think otherwise was pretty much off-limits.

Badgikian was different. He made the same critique about the negative implications of private, monopoly control over the news, but he made it better. He showed how absolutely destructive this kind of journalism was for generating informed self-government. His book made it clear that a viable journalism was not simply an optional accessory for a democratic society, but a mandatory foundation, one that a self-governing people had a duty to see existed. He demonstrated how the media system was not natural or based upon a "free market," but was made corruptly by politicians to benefit the big media owners. And Bagdikian deconstructed professional journalism to reveal how, instead of protecting the public interest, it also had inbred biases that served the commercial and political interests of media owners.

As I read Bagdikian, a series of questions came to mind. Why aren't people discussing this? Why isn't the effect that bad journalism has on our politics being discussed in our politics? Why aren't the cozy deals between media owners and politicians a national scandal? When, exactly, did Americans approve of the idea that a handful of corporations selling advertising were the proper stewards of the media or that it was inappropriate to ever question their power? I knew enough even then to understand that at the time of the Founders, there was no sense of professional journalism, media corporations, or modern advertising. So no way could it be said that the Founders authorized or signed off on the mess Bagdikian was describing. But if not them, then who? When in American history had this debate taken place? When had the American people ratified the corporate media system as the proper one for the United States? When, exactly, was this matter settled, apparently for all time?

It was roundly acknowledged that other nations had debates about who should control the media and how the media should be structured, but in America no such debates were necessary or had taken place. The reason offered for this exceptionalism was the strength and popular embrace of the market by Americans. That just did not make sense to me. Did people's DNA undergo a metamorphosis when they crossed the Canadian border or got off a boat? I could not believe it would square with the historical record.

So that led me on a search to find such a debate in U.S. history over how the media should be owned and controlled. In retrospect, I actually did a lousy search because I determined that the only such debate took place with the emergence of radio broadcasting in the 1920s and early 1930s. In fact, had I looked closer or known what to look for, I would have seen that there were numerous important media policy debates throughout U.S. history. They were all unexamined, underexamined, or studied without much sense of what was at stake. I easily gravitated to radio broadcasting because the evidence of organized opposition to commercial radio broadcasting was all around me as I hit the stacks of the wonderful University of Washington library. It was like going fishing in a lake where no one had ever fished before, and you could grab as many fish as you wanted with your hands.

Everywhere I turned, I found evidence of extensive organized opposition to commercial broadcasting from educators, labor, religious groups, journalists, civil libertarians, and farmers. The criticism these citizens made of commercial broadcasting could have been made by Ben Bagdikian or any contemporary media critic. It was scintillating. As I kept photocopying news stories, tracking down books, articles, and conference proceedings from the period, and camping out in the interlibrary loan office, the documentary record became a mountain in my apartment. Amazingly, no one had ever written a history of this movement before. I found my dissertation. Indeed, I found my intellectual calling.[2]

Immediately, I had to answer the obvious question. The history of radio broadcasting in the 1920s and 1930s had received a good deal of historical treatment in the United States. For a long time, Erik Barnouw's extensive three-volume history of U.S. broadcasting had been the only game in town; but by the 1970s other scholars had written books or dissertations on the topic and on this period.[3] Some had hinted at aspects of what I had uncovered, but none had put it all together—and most were clueless.[4] It seemed like even when staring at the documentary evidence suggesting the contrary, scholars accepted the claim that commercial broadcasting was the natural American system. After all, the reasoning went, commercial broadcasting did prevail in the end, so it must have been the system the American people wanted. And people sure like radio and TV, right? Even critical scholars seemed to accept this assumption.

I quickly grasped that by ignoring the ideological presuppositions that U.S. media were by definition corporate and commercial (and embraced by Americans without hesitation except for

the usual disgruntled fringe elements), I was able to look at the
same material as other scholars and see patterns no one had noticed before. And I was able to locate reams of material no one
had ever even looked at before. The real mother lode came when
I got to the archives and found file drawer after file drawer of
records from politicians and broadcast reform organizations.
This again points to the need for communication studies to remain a distinct field. As difficult as it was for this question
to emerge in communication studies, it almost certainly never
would have been asked in a traditional history program. It was
reading Bagdikian, after all, that put me on this path.

I determined that there was in fact a serious debate over
whether the United States should adopt commercial broadcasting in the early 1930s. Few people thought at the time that
corporate-owned, advertising-supported broadcasting was the
natural American system. That came later, when the PR went
into fifth gear after the system was consolidated. Commercial
broadcasting certainly was not regarded as inherently democratic. (As the BBC put it at the time, the claim by capitalist
broadcasters that commercial broadcasting was democratic
was "outside our comprehension" and, as the BBC politely put
it, "clearly springs from a peculiarly American conception of
democracy.")[5] In the early 1930s, citizens from across the political spectrum—probably as many Republicans as Democrats—
made compelling arguments that the commercial broadcasting
system produced results that were inimical to the needs of
a democratic society, and that the policymaking process in
Washington was grotesquely corrupt and served the interests
of powerful media owners. And although the reformers lost—I
will not keep you in suspense—they failed primarily because
of the corruption of the process, not because the American people opted for commercial broadcasting.

I argued that this battle over the control and structure of radio broadcasting was the last great battle over media in the

United States. Thereafter, with FM radio, terrestrial television, and cable and satellite television, policymakers always assumed that corporations would rule media to maximize profits from advertising and this was the desire of the public, the confirmed "American way." The public played no role in the process. The wealth of evidence I gathered made my argument difficult to ignore or dispute. It came to be accepted, though not all necessarily agreed with my precise interpretation or my conclusion that this was a debate that needed to be reopened.

Like many young scholars, out of my enthusiasm I probably exaggerated the importance of my research, and I certainly could have used more context. I was all too unfamiliar with other relevant chapters in U.S. communication policy history at the time, and lost much nuance and many connections that could have been made. The research and subsequent book appeared at a difficult time, the late 1980s and early 1990s. It went entirely against the neoliberal logic that suggested markets were the only democratic manner to regulate anything, including media. This argument was supercharged by the digital revolution. Already by 1992, people like George Gilder were arguing that the Internet eliminated the rationale for any regulation of media. Instead, he argued, it should simply be left to corporate interests to do with as they please, and the market would sort out matters with its inherent genius.[6] This would be Newt Gingrich's mantra on Capitol Hill, and, truth be told, the rhetoric came from Democrats as well as Republicans. From this perspective, my research was irrelevant, a throwback to a bygone era of spectrum scarcity with no significance for the digital world where markets were freed up to work their magic.

To my delight, both Dallas Smythe and Herb Schiller were thrilled by the research and encouraged me. (Smythe politely advised me in a long letter written in 1991, less than a year before he died, to do a good deal more research on the period leading up to the 1920s and 1930s, but I paid little attention at the time because I was trying to finish the book.) Political economists understood what was at stake, though the issue of re-opening the public debate over our media system seemed mostly hypothetical.[7] The prospects of organizing a public campaign around who controlled the media seemed hallucinogenic in the early 1990s. My book veered somewhat near the "so what" zone that plagued political economy in neoliberal times. In the early 1990s, it looked like the rest of the world was on a fast track to open-armed embrace of the market, too.

Shortly after the book came out in 1993, I gave a copy to Vivek Chibber, a close friend then getting a Ph.D. in sociology in Madison. (He is now on the sociology faculty at New York University.)[8] Chibber devoured the book, and we went to lunch to discuss it. "Of course, what you are providing is a case study of a critical juncture," he commented. I had no idea what a critical juncture was, but the way Vivek said it made it sound like a staple in social science. I didn't want to sound like an idiot, so I played along. "Uh, yeah, of course." I later talked with Vivek at some length about the notion of a critical juncture and read up on the matter in the citations he provided.[9]

I reconsidered my research and determined that the struggle over radio broadcasting qualified as a critical juncture because it met two of the three criteria I laid out in Chapter 1: Broadcasting was a revolutionary communication technology that did not conform to existing business or regulatory patterns; and there was an immediate crisis in the nature of the content of radio broadcasting. While some opponents of the status quo disliked what they regarded as the class bias of commercial radio, there was widespread, nearly universal dislike of advertising on radio before people became accustomed to it and accepted it as a necessary evil. The antipathy toward radio advertising was something everyone acknowledged at the time. One of the reasons the commercial broadcasters were so dead set against any form of noncommercial broadcasting in the early 1930s is that they were convinced no one would listen to their stations if there was quality noncommercial broadcasting available on the dial. It was these two factors that spawned the birth of the broadcast reform movement I chronicled in my book.

The third factor—the need for a period of broad social turmoil—doomed the reform effort. Although the 1930s are associated with radical politics and sweeping reform, the fight over radio was completed by 1934, before this was much of a factor. My hunch—purely speculative, of course—is that had radio developed five to ten years later, and the policy fights had fallen at the end of the 1930s, the political climate might have been much more supportive of the reform efforts. The Congress of Industrial Organizations (CIO), for example, was far more hostile to commercial broadcasting than the American Federation of Labor had ever been. But by the time the CIO was formed in the late 1930s, the topic of who owned and controlled radio broadcasting was off the table. As the CIO understood well, once control over broadcasting was lost to the commercial system, labor's job of winning progressive political fights became vastly more difficult.

I began to rethink communication history. I now considered whether it was my blindness, my own presuppositions, that led me to believe I had stumbled across the one important critical juncture in American communication history. Maybe there were others. If so, what were they? Were there common threads connecting them? I began to see everything in a new light, and I was drawn to episodes I had never paid much attention to before. I found many other policy fights in American history over media and communication, other struggles involving the public, and scholars had been examining them to varying degrees. Some may have even risen to the level of a critical juncture.

For starters, it became clear that I needed to pay a great deal more attention to the generation immediately preceding the

1920s and 1930s. I reread Dallas Smythe's 1991 letter to me, in which he provided chapter and verse of crucial policy developments between 1890 and 1920. It was during that era, as Dan Schiller's research demonstrated, that there was a major battle over how to structure the telephone system, which ended up with the regulated AT&T monopoly. It was by no means a predetermined outcome.[10] I recalled the work of my Ph.D. supervisor, William Ames, about the newspaper industry in Jacksonian times: He repeatedly told me it produced arguably the greatest journalism in American history, generating a vibrant democracy in the northern states, thanks to explicit public subsidies.[11] Hmmmm, maybe these subsidies were the result of debates and public involvement in media policymaking?

I thought of the book written by a fellow Washington grad student, Linda Lawson, about the debate surrounding the Newspaper Act of 1912. At the time, I thought she had picked the most boring dissertation topic imaginable. I then realized she had written a history of the exact moment journalism was in its greatest crisis of legitimacy and it had boiled over into the political arena.[12] I thought of Richard Du Boff's research on the emergence of the telegraph in the nineteenth century. Here again, a revolutionary new communication technology was met with a fierce battle over how it could best be developed and organized.[13] And I thought of Richard Kielbowicz's work on the post office, and the crucial role it played in establishing the press system in the first century of the Republic. There were significant public debates on the matter at the time.[14] There was also work on the fights over the control and structure of satellite communication and cable television from the 1950s to the 1970s. This long record of public debate had been far more extensive and radical than I had imagined.[15]

Again, back in the 1980s I thought all this stuff was inconsequential, almost antiquarian, and of little value to contemporary scholars. Now, with the prism of critical junctures, it became work of immediate, even breathtaking, importance. With the passage of time, by the mid-1990s, I began to see that my own formative period, the 1960s and early 1970s, had been a critical juncture too. There were great lessons to be learned, linkages to be made. And there were enormous holes in our history that needed to be filled. We knew very little about too much of our communication and political history. We had not been asking the right questions. And there was the entire question of looking at similar movements and critical junctures in other nations. Suddenly I confronted a situation where I knew much less about communication than I thought, but I knew much more about what I needed to learn.

At the same time, my book began to gain some attention among nonacademics. "You mean it didn't have to be this way?" people would say to me. "It could have been different?" By the mid-1990s, I was repeatedly being asked to speak in public on media politics. Almost always, I was asked to talk about what lessons the 1930s broadcast reform movement held for citizens today in the United States. The parallels jumped out at a lot of people. People were concerned about lousy journalism, the Republican attack on public broadcasting, massive media mergers, and the secrecy surrounding the passage of the 1996 Telecommunications Act. There was a growing recognition that the deep flaws in our journalism and our media system were a barrier to viable democracy and progressive social change.

I recall being invited to present a lecture on my historical research at the University of California at San Diego in 1995. Before the talk an official for the foundation sponsoring the event told me how much he admired my work. I still remember what he said: "I think we are going through a similar moment to the early 1930s with the Internet today. We cannot afford to blow it this time. Our goal should be to make it impossible for you to write a postmortem for this era like you did the early 1930s."

Those words stuck with me. What was the point of my research? What obligation did I have to participate in the media politics of the moment? Could I simply return to the archives and sit out the current events, waiting to write my history of the period after the fact? It was like the dilemma of a photojournalist watching a heinous crime taking place: Do you put down the camera and try to stop the crime, or do you film it and then get professional rewards for capturing a close-up? Put that way, it was not a difficult decision to make.

Whether I liked it or not, people were demanding I address the contemporary situation. And I discovered quickly enough that I liked it. As a result I wrote many short pieces for periodicals like *The Nation, The Progressive, Mother Jones,* and *In These Times.*[16] I wrote op-eds in scores of newspapers and centrist publications like *Current* and *The New Republic.*[17] I quietly abandoned the extensive plans for further historical research I had developed, and wrote a book on global media with Ed Herman and a pamphlet on the media crisis, both published in 1997.[18] Then in 1999, I published the book that had the greatest impact of anything I have written, *Rich Media, Poor Democracy.* My work was centered around the deplorable state of media and the corrupt policymaking process that made it possible. Although this work was inspired by history, it was pure political economy of communication.

There was clearly popular reception for these ideas, far more than might have been the case a decade or so earlier. In the second half of the 1990s, media was becoming a political issue, especially on the left. For the previous two decades the political right had made its critique of "left-wing" media a centerpiece of its campaign to assume political power. This had the desired effect of making journalism adopt a distinct double standard whereby Republicans were treated more charitably in the media than Democrats, because journalists were petrified of being called liberals. The claim that the media were biased in favor of liberals was promulgated so widely and so loudly that it became the official opposition to the status quo, and even some liberals thought it held more than a grain of truth. The argument was fraught with contradictions when analyzed closely, and it never really gained much legitimacy among scholars, despite the millions of dollars spent promoting it by well-funded right-wing think tanks. The claim of left-wing media bias was collapsing among moderates and liberals by the late 1990s, and a good deal of my work, and that of other media critics, was focused on debunking the claim. It was some of the most important work critical scholars did in this period and into the new decade.[19]

Evidence of the new interest in addressing media as a political issue was all around. *The Nation* and *The Progressive* began to run articles and special issues on the media crisis. Don Hazen and the Independent Media Institute organized two large "media and democracy" conferences in San Francisco in 1996 and in New York City in 1997 to draw attention to the problem. Mark Crispin Miller formed the Project on Media Ownership, and put his ample talents toward publicizing the extent of media consolidation in a series of special issues on media ownership in *The Nation*.[20] Former TV journalist Danny Schechter, the "News Dissector," was a one-man army calling for the formation of a media democracy movement along the lines of the student movement in the 1960s.[21]

In 1996, George Gerbner launched his ambitious Cultural Environment Movement (CEM) to capitalize upon popular concerns and to make media a public issue. Gerbner, as usual, was a visionary; his idea was simply too far ahead of its time to succeed. The next year the Rainbow Coalition and Operation PUSH held a major conference in Chicago to address concerns about media consolidation and the lack of journalism from inside the African American community. Rev. Jesse Jackson emphasized that the broadcast system was set up—and the monopoly licenses were doled out—during the era of Jim Crow, and African Americans were systematically excluded from the process. The

National Organization for Women, which had been active in media issues since its inception, stayed in the game. The media watch group Fairness & Accuracy In Reporting (FAIR) monitored the mainstream media with its magazine *Extra!* and radio program *CounterSpin*. Something was happening here.

But I do not wish to exaggerate what was being done then. For all the newfound interest and concern in media as an issue that required political attention, the activity was still pretty much on the fringes. When the 1996 Telecom Act passed, there was close to zero public participation. Three or four years later, Congress was still pretty much the property of the corporate media lobbies and it was next to impossible to get any traction for media reform ideas. It was still unclear what reform proposals exactly should be enacted to improve the situation. Select members of Congress like Michigan's John Conyers and Vermont's Bernie Sanders in the House, and Minnesota's Paul Wellstone in the Senate understood the issues, but they could not get it moving in Washington. And in the field of communication, the issue of media reform registered a big zero on the Richter scale.

It was around this time, in the mid-1990s, that John Nichols moved to Madison to become the editorial page editor for the afternoon daily newspaper, the *Capital Times*, and we became fast friends. We shared a passion for politics, a love of journalism, and a concern about media and democracy. Nichols had a command of politics, past and present, that was encyclopedic and, as far as I could tell, unrivaled. We began to collaborate and in the next decade we would write a good twenty articles—primarily in *The Nation*—and three books, all on media politics.[22] Our major argument from the beginning was that there needed to be an organized campaign to make media ownership, public broadcasting, and media policies a political issue with popular participation. We needed to expand the range of policy options in Washington beyond the corporate-sanctioned agenda, and the only way to do that was to generate grassroots heat on legislators. From the response we got to our writings and our talks, we sensed that the soil was fertile. We needed to do aggressive outreach to the already organized groups—labor, civil rights, feminist, environmental, educators, peace activists, health care—that were getting screwed over by the media but that had no conception that the media policy was an issue they needed to work on. Unless such a campaign was undertaken, we would never get anywhere. After all, the forces on the other side had all the money and owned all the politicians. As Saul Alinksy put it, we needed organized people to defeat organized money. By the end of the 1990s, we were pounding that theme like a broken record. It was the logical conclusion of both my research and, by now, my participation in the events of the times. But it was easier said than done.

There was a community of public interest advocates working on media policy issues in Washington during this period, most notably the Media Access Project, Action for Children's Television, Consumers Union, the Consumer Federation of America, the United Church of Christ, the Benton Foundation, and the Center for Media Education. The work on media policy by groups like these had blossomed in the 1960s and 1970s, when the space created by popular social movements gave public interest groups increased leverage over the FCC and Congress to enact proactive reforms, especially around issues of promoting community media and minority ownership. In particular, by the 1970s the feminist critique of how media represented women and gender roles attracted considerable interest in the importance of media and the need to change media. (Most of this critique remains all too relevant today and drives significant elements of the current media reform movement.)[23]

Some new groups, like Mark Lloyd's People for Better TV, Jeff Chester's Center for Digital Democracy (in 2000), and John

Stauber and Shelden Rampton's Center for Media and Democracy joined the fray—but only one or two of them had more than a few people working full-time on the issues. The main public interest players in Washington were Gene Kimmelman, Mark Cooper, Andy Schwartzman, Jeff Chester, and Mark Lloyd, and they were probably outspent by corporate media lobbies by a factor of a thousand to one. I recall speaking to one of them in 1997. He explained how dire the situation facing the public interest community was at the time and for the foreseeable future. "To be frank, we operate under the assumption that we are going to be battling hostile Republican majorities in Congress for the next generation." When one factors in that these groups and activists got little or no press coverage for their issues, so they had almost no way to generate public awareness or support, it is astonishing they accomplished as much as they did. They were in defensive mode and were losing ground. Nichols and I argued that a radical change in strategy and tactics, and a drastic increase in resources to the movement were necessary to get the increased public concern about media channeled into an effective political force.

Perhaps it would be unfair to say the field of communication was oblivious to what was going on in the country, but it seemed that way to me. There was an impressive "Habermasian turn" in the 1990s among political theorists, and this generated some important work in critical race theory and among feminist scholars, but it would be a while longer before this had much influence on media activism off-campus.[24] Postmodernists in communication professed their allegiance to the oppressed of the world, but this new wave of media activism rarely was on their radars.[25] There was work done on policy in a number of communication departments, but it was mostly reduced to the "legitimate" range of debate in Washington.

I recall speaking at the Annenberg School at the University of Pennsylvania only a week or two after the passage of the

1996 Telecommunications Act. When I criticized the Telecom Act categorically, and characterized it as a testament to corruption, it seemed like the air went out of the room. One of the most prominent faculty members present took the legislation very seriously and apparently was quite familiar with aspects of it. She never considered the idea that it did not accurately reflect the proper range of debate, and I could see from her response that I might as well have been speaking in Aramaic. This is no knock on Penn. I suspect that the response to my comments would have been similar in a group of communication policy experts on any campus in the nation in 1996.

The crisis in journalism was getting a smattering of attention in journalism schools, but not much. A handful of journalists and scholars—often prominent former journalists themselves—had written damning critiques of developments in the profession, but the critiques were very much on the margins.[26] The dominant effort to deal with the crisis in newsrooms in the 1990s was the civic (or public) journalism movement. This was an effort to get journalists to reconstruct their professional practices to draw the public into civic life. It was probably the most tangible consequence of the "Habermasian turn" I mentioned above. Civic journalism was promoted most aggressively by Jay Rosen at New York University and caused a good deal of useful debate at the time.[27] Because the critique did not chastise the commercial system or media owners, it hoped to be able to gain traction as a neutral and nonthreatening reform campaign. But because it failed to address the commercial assault on journalism, it did not fully grasp the powerful forces it was up against and proved mostly ineffectual.

One other major development was taking place in the 1990s and transforming the world of media and communication: the Internet, which I use as a term to capture the entirety of the digital communication revolution. This was not a central component of the media activism I have just chronicled, though it would move front and center—both as an issue for activism and as an invaluable tool for organizing—in the next decade, as I discuss in Chapter 4. If the activism and growing public concern about media had little influence upon the academic study of communication in the 1990s, the Internet did get the field's attention. By 1996, the *Journal of Communication* ran a special issue on the Internet—I wrote the article on policy—and I recall one of the other contributors telling me that "if the field doesn't embrace the Internet into the heart of its mission, it will be doomed." The Internet did enter into a good deal of research projects at this time, but the work was halting and of mixed value. It was very difficult to get a handle on what we were dealing with. That includes some of my own work.[28] We were in uncharted waters.

Or were we? What the Internet did do was open up space for discussions about fundamental questions of media institutional structures, about technology, about the relationship of media to politics, and about communication history in a way we hadn't seen for many decades. It was evident early on that broadband would eventually subsume all media, so that created space for critical inquiry. (The bias was for technocratic research that did not criticize the market, but the Internet challenged the existing commercial media model to such a large extent that even proponents of the status quo sometimes were scratching their heads.) Combined with the general crisis around journalistic decline and media consolidation, this provided a shot in the arm for critical research on media policy.

In particular the events of the mid- and late 1990s encouraged a new wave of research on critical junctures in the history of communication policymaking in the United States. Much work has been done on the rise of professional journalism and the first decades of the twentieth century. The traditional explanation for the emergence of professional journalism had relied upon technology—for example, the telegraph and Associated

Press making it necessary to have neutral content acceptable to a broad range of papers—or how it was in the economic interest of monopolistic publishers to publish nonpartisan journalism so as not to alienate part of the market. Although these were important factors, what tended to be missing was a crucial component: the public dissatisfaction with the sensationalistic and decidedly conservative journalism of the times.

New research, including extensive work by Ben Scott, highlighted just how significant a factor this public controversy was in pushing the emergence of professional journalism, as well as the occasionally intense struggle between newspaper publishers and journalists to define professional journalism and gain control over the newsroom.[29] This research makes it easier to understand the dilemmas and contradictions of professional journalism that have led to today's crisis.

The debates went far beyond newspapers and journalism. Inger Stole has chronicled the campaign led by the Consumers Union to strictly regulate advertising and limit commercialism in the 1930s. Here again was a chapter of American communication policy history almost entirely unknown heretofore.[30] Elizabeth Fones-Wolf and Victor Pickard unearthed a mother lode of material on the work that labor and other groups did to challenge the commercial media system in the mid- and late 1940s. In particular, labor led a valiant and relatively extensive effort to establish FM radio as a community and noncommercial medium, only to be crushed by the Red Scare.[31] Richard John's work on the post office made the case for the crucial role public policies and subsidies played in establishing the communication system in the United States.[32] With every new dissertation and new book, as we gain insight into the rich history of media policymaking in the United States, we also realize how much more there is to be done. In some respects, we have only scratched the surface. In particular, what has to be done is to link the American experience with the media policymaking histories of other nations. That work has barely begun.[33]

As a result of this new research, and stimulated by the critical juncture brought on by the Internet and the growing public concern about media, a handful of closely related "truths" about communication emerged by the beginning of the new century. These five closely related, at times overlapping, truths had been known before, but had not been given their due weight. Because of the successful dominance of the commercial media system, the system came to be taken for granted by scholars, and these truths drifted to footnote status. But when these truths are combined, their power increases exponentially, providing a powerful way to think about communication and changing the subfield of the political economy of communication.

The moribund field has been given a chance to get off the respirator. In fact, these five truths are of such importance that they demand that all media scholars reconsider the core presuppositions upon which their research and teaching have been based. And most important, they come to provide a way for communication scholars to share the significance of their work with a populace that has deep and pressing concerns about the role media play in their lives.

So what are they?

1. Media systems are created by policies and subsidies; they are not "natural" in any society.
2. The Founders of the Republic did not authorize a corporate-run, profit-motivated, commercially driven media system with the First Amendment.
3. The American media system may be profit-motivated, but it is not a free market system.

4. The policymaking process is of paramount importance in understanding how a media system is structured and how the subsidies are allocated.
5. The policymaking process in the United States has been dominated by powerful corporate interests with almost nonexistent public participation for generations; it must be addressed if the media system is to be reformed.

Let me go through each of these five points in more detail.

First, media systems are not *natural*; they are the result of explicit policies and subsidies. The types of media systems societies end up with are strongly influenced by the political economy of the nation, but it is not a mechanistic or vulgar relationship. That commercial media is not a "default" system is clear from liberal democratic political theory: Free people opt for the institution of private property because they regard it as the best way to advance their values. Likewise, a free people opt for commercial media because they determine it is the best way to promote the type of press system they deem desirable. And of course, in democratic theory, a free people may decide to have a noncapitalist economy, and likewise they may decide to have a noncommercial media system.

But, to be clear, the two matters are distinct in theory and in practice. Even in capitalist societies, it is not a given that the entirety of the media or communication system will be run for profit. Capitalist societies, including the United States, have had elements, sometimes significant, of their communication systems operating outside the marketplace during their history. When telegraphy came along, or radio broadcasting nearly a century later, the United States was certainly a capitalist nation, but there were debates about whether these emerging industries should be conducted by private, profit-maximizing concerns, even by people who favored capitalism otherwise. Even today, professional journalism, perhaps the defining characteristic of our free press in our media textbooks, is explicitly a public service that does not, at its best, follow the commercial logic of the companies that house it. A core principle of professional journalism is to provide a safe house for public service in the swamp of commercialism.

I understand that the practice of establishing viable nonprofit and noncommercial media has been getting a lot less practical, almost hypothetical, in advanced capitalist nations. One of the crowning achievements of the political economy of communication was to establish how much communication has become a core component of the market, how central it is to capitalism. Everywhere one looks one sees the spread of the market and commercialism into every nook and cranny of our lives. This analysis suggests that the degree of difficulty for establishing a viable nonprofit communication sector in the United States is astronomical, unless one also fundamentally changes or replaces capitalism. Although I think the empirical basis for this argument is strong, I do not think it leads to a strategy of abandoning all hope for reform in media and communication, and shifting all efforts to overturning the system as a whole, whatever that would look like. My point is that people should not concede media and communication to capital or to particular commercial interests. If the economic system cannot accommodate the legitimate democratic demands of the citizenry, then the system should be changed.

In short, media systems are created, even if the playing field is sloped at an ever greater angle toward dominant commercial interests. This is an argument made also by scholars who are far less critical of commercial media than I am. In 2004 two books were published that laid out this basic argument, Paul Starr's *The Creation of the Media* and my *The Problem of the Media*.[34] Starr relied upon secondary sources, but he did a masterful job nonetheless in marshaling the evidence and chronicling how the U.S. government had "created" the media with a series of policies and subsidies since the beginning of the Republic.

There was no natural "free market" default option. Starr contends that creating a viable free press is one of the nation's crowning achievements, and I agree. Nor is this a position that requires an antagonistic stance toward commercial media. Starr is far from critical of the way the media system has developed in the United States over time. Unlike me, Starr distinctly announces his support for the current corporate-controlled media system, which he regards as being largely a success, in need of only minor policy tinkering that can draw from the existing toolkit.[35] Mark Lloyd has done more research and made a compatible argument about the centrality of government policies to the formation of the communication system in his 2007 book, *Prologue to a Farce: Democracy and Communication in America*.[36] In fact, I know of no evidence that contradicts this position. Yet based upon my experience, it seems to be a minority view, even among communication scholars, compared to the notion that our media system is the natural result of free market competition.

The second truth is that the First Amendment is not a piece of protectionist legislation meant to grant special privileges to investors in the communication sector to be exempt from government regulation.[37] It does not lock us into the status quo and render all structural media reforms unconstitutional. The oft-stated "libertarian" or neoliberal position—the idea that the Constitution requires that capitalists be the natural rulers of all media to do as they please without government interference, regardless of the nature of the content they provide— is dubious, if not bogus. The "libertarian" position holds that almost any regulation of media is unconstitutional. Media companies have consistently argued that it violates the First Amendment to, among other things, limit how many broadcast stations or cable companies a corporation can buy. Their argument rests on the assumption that media companies are just like individuals and that a good democracy must treat them like individuals.

That is not the consensus opinion of the Supreme Court in

its handful of important cases on the meaning of freedom of the press. Yet the idea that freedom of the press means the government shall not interfere with media capitalists is commonly accepted. A good deal of the reason for this is that freedom of speech is often conflated with freedom of the press. Few people would condone government censorship of an individual's speech rights; by extension, how can we condone the government's regulation of an individual's free press rights?

C. Edwin Baker has done trailblazing research on the relationship of freedom of the press and freedom of speech. Baker concludes that court interpretations of the Constitution clearly see the press as a necessary institution distinct from people exercising free speech rights, and also as distinct from other commercial enterprises.[38] But in academic discourse the question is usually framed as: "Does the press get special privileges individuals do not have?"[39] It is not usually framed as: "Can the media be saddled with extra obligations that individuals do not have?" or "Can the people enact policies to create a press that meets its constitutionally understood functions better than the existing press is doing?" Baker's theory, although supported by the evidence, is outside the mainstream of constitutional law at present, and the implications have not been addressed by the Supreme Court, but it could become important in the years to come. Baker has argued persuasively that the First Amendment permits the government to play an active role in creating media and structuring the media system.[40]

I could never square the "libertarian" view of the Constitution as mandating commercial media with what I saw in the 1930s and my own analysis of history and of Supreme Court opinions. This point crystallized for me when I was doing my research on the 1930s broadcast reform movement. I was struck by the position of the American Civil Liberties Union at the time that commercial broadcasting, by its very nature, might violate the First Amendment. In essence, the ACLU argued that the profit motive in broadcasting was inconsistent with the First Amendment (which was Alexander Meiklejohn's position). The ACLU adjusted its position only after the commercial system became politically inviolate by the late 1930s, but its initial opposition to the emerging status quo was driven by a very different notion of the First Amendment than today's "libertarian" view.[41]

During my research I came across the work of Thomas Emerson, long considered a leading expert on the First Amendment in his stead at Yale Law School. Emerson made it clear that in the 1930s, nothing in the Constitution authorized commercial broadcasting or prevented the government from establishing a completely nonprofit radio and television system.[42] Indeed, all of the Supreme Court decisions on government regulation of broadcasting and cable to date, most famously the 1969 *Red Lion* decision discussed in Chapter 1, have made the First Amendment first and foremost a right of all Americans—rich or poor—not a private privilege for the handful of Americans who can afford to purchase successful commercial media.

A standard interpretation of freedom of the press acknowledged that broadcasting and cable were different from everything else, due to spectrum scarcity and government licensing. There the First Amendment belonged to the public, whose interests are represented by the government. But in this standard view, once spectrum scarcity ends and monopoly licensing ends, those areas will revert back to the unregulated media realm enjoyed by newspapers. Then freedom of the press will belong, as A.J. Liebling famously said, to those who own one.

But during the founding period, when freedom of the press was being discussed, often by Jefferson and Madison, there was no sense they regarded the press as an inherently market-driven institution, where the right to make profit was sacrosanct.[43] It is routinely thought that the term "marketplace of ideas" harkens back to Milton and the seventeenth century and was a guiding principle to Madison and Jefferson.[44] In fact, as

John Durham Peters demonstrates in his trailblazing research, the phrase was first used only in the 1930s and did not become a commonly used term until two decades later. Immediately thereafter it was assumed almost universally that the term had been the lodestar for freedom's thinkers for centuries. In fact, the Founders never framed the matter in such a manner.[45]

So how did they frame it? Madison and Jefferson have scores of quotations and passages in their writings and correspondence about the importance of the press. I even used one for the title of a book, *Tragedy & Farce*. (Madison in 1822: "A popular government without popular information or the means of acquiring it, is but a Prologue to a Farce or a Tragedy or perhaps both. Knowledge will forever govern ignorance, and a people who mean to be their own Governors, must arm themselves with the power knowledge gives.")[46]

Now consider Jefferson and his famous letter to Edward Carrington of January 16, 1787. A sentence from the middle of the letter has often been extracted: "Were it left to me to decide whether we should have a government without newspapers, or newspapers without a government, I should not hesitate a moment to prefer the latter."

But that doesn't capture Jefferson's far more important argument. I present a longer version here:

> The way to prevent these irregular interpositions of the people is to give them full information of their affairs thro' the channel of the public papers, and *to contrive that those papers should penetrate the whole mass of the people.* The basis of our governments being the opinion of the people, the very first object should be to keep that right; and were it left to me to decide whether we should have a government without newspapers, or newspapers without a government, I should not hesitate a moment to prefer the latter. *But I should mean that every man should receive those papers and be capable of reading them.* (emphasis mine)

In the same letter Jefferson praises Native American societies for being largely classless and happy, and criticizes European societies in no uncertain terms for being the opposite. Jefferson also stakes out the central role of the press in stark class terms when he describes the role of the press in preventing exploitation and domination by the rich over the poor:

> Among [European societies], under pretence of governing they have divided their nations into two classes, wolves and sheep. I do not exaggerate. This is a true picture of Europe. Cherish therefore the spirit of our people, and keep alive their attention. Do not be too severe upon their errors, but reclaim them by enlightening them. If once they become inattentive to the public affairs, you and I, and Congress, and Assemblies, judges and governors shall all become wolves. It seems to be the law of our general nature, in spite of individual exceptions; and experience declares that man is the only animal which devours his own kind, for I can apply no milder term to the governments of Europe, and to the general prey of the rich on the poor.[47]

Accordingly, Jefferson and Madison were obsessed with subsidizing the distribution of newspapers through the post office and supporting newspapers through printing subsidies as well.[48] An institution this important is not something you roll the dice of the commercial marketplace on and hope you get lucky. Their position became the consensus position among the Founders. By his fifth annual address, President Washington came out for free postage for newspapers through the mail, and even Treasury Secretary Alexander Hamilton, hardly a proponent of government deficit, conceded that the huge subsidy was necessary to spawn a viable press. (How significant was this subsidy? Newspapers accounted for 70 percent of the total weight handled by mail carriers, but only 3 percent of the total postal revenue.)[49] They understood the press in a precapitalist, if not noncapitalist, sense—and primarily as a political institution.[50] Nor did Madison or Jefferson have a romanticized notion of journalism. Jefferson's correspondence from his years as president is filled with screeds against the press of his day as an agent of destruction.[51] That pushed him not to censorship, but to policies to promote a better press.[52]

Moreover, when the Supreme Court has actually pondered what freedom of the press means under the First Amendment, it has not endorsed the neoliberal model of maximum profits equal maximum public service.[53] In some of the most important cases, the opinions suggest that freedom of the press is not an individual right to do as one pleases to make money. To the contrary, freedom of the press is in the Constitution to make self-government possible. Consider this from Hugo Black's magnificent majority opinion in the 1945 *Associated Press v. United States* case:

> It would be strange indeed however if the grave concern for freedom of the press which prompted adoption of the First Amendment should be read as a command that the government was without power to protect that freedom. The First Amendment, far from providing an argument against application of the Sherman Act, here provides powerful reasons to the contrary. *That Amendment rests on the assumption that the widest possible dissemination of information from diverse and antagonistic sources is essential to the welfare of the public, that a free press is a condition of a free society.* Surely a command that the government itself shall not impede the free flow of ideas does not afford non-governmental combinations a refuge if they impose restraints upon that constitutionally guaranteed freedom. Freedom to publish means freedom for all and not for some. Freedom to publish is guaranteed by the Constitution, but freedom to combine to keep others from publishing is not. Freedom of the press from governmental interference under the First Amendment does not sanction

repression of that freedom by private interests.[54] (emphasis mine)

Or consider what Black wrote twenty-six years later in the Pentagon Papers (*New York Times v. United States*) case:

In the First Amendment, the Founding Fathers gave the free press the protection it must have to fulfill its essential role in our democracy. The press was to serve the governed, not the governors. The Government's power to censor the press was abolished so that the press would remain forever free to censure the Government. The press was protected so that it could bare the secrets of government and inform the people. Only a free and unrestrained press can effectively expose deception in government. *And paramount among the responsibilities of a free press is the duty to prevent any part of the government from deceiving the people and sending them off to distant lands to die of foreign fevers and foreign shot and shell.*[55] (emphasis mine)

Or consider this brilliant passage from Justice Potter Stewart's opinion in the same case:

In the absence of the governmental checks and balances present in other areas of our national life, the only effective restraint upon executive policy and power in the areas of national defense and international affairs may lie in an enlightened citizenry—in an informed and critical public opinion which alone can here protect the values of democratic government. For this reason, it is perhaps here that a press that is alert, aware, and free most vitally serves the basic purpose of the *First Amendment*. For, without an informed and free press, there cannot be an enlightened people.[56]

These statements by Black and Stewart about the importance of the press for monitoring the government's proclivity for foreign wars are especially striking because this was a central concern of James Madison, who thought that unchecked militarism was probably the greatest threat to the Republic. Consider this from Madison:

> Of all the enemies of true liberty, war is, perhaps, the most to be dreaded, because it comprises and develops the germ of every other. War is the parent of armies; from these proceed debts and taxes; and armies, and debts, and taxes are the known instruments for bringing the many under the domination of the few. In war, too, the discretionary power of the Executive is extended; its influence in dealing out offices, honors and emoluments is multiplied; and all the means of seducing the minds, are added to those of subduing the force, of the people. The same malignant aspect in republicanism may be traced in the inequality of fortunes, and the opportunities of fraud, growing out of a state of war, and in the degeneracy of manner and of morals, engendered in both. *No nation can preserve its freedom in the midst of continual warfare.*[57] (emphasis mine)

In short, the spirit in several of these opinions is that the state has not only the right but the *duty* to see that a viable press system exists, for if such a media system does not exist the entire constitutional project will fail. If the existing press system is failing, it is imperative that the state create a system that will meet the constitutionally mandated requirements. At any rate, these opinions hardly suggest that the First Amendment is meant to provide a constitutional blank check to corporate media to do as they please, regardless of the implications for self-government. At the same time, this is nothing if not a complex matter. The problem of establishing a press system, providing direct and indirect subsidies, yet preventing censorship and state domination defies simple solution. And there may be no ideal solution, only a range of solutions where some are better than others.

So there remains debate on the First Amendment, and my position is one of many.[58] Those who disagree with my position tend to point to the *Miami Herald v. Tornillo* case, discussed in Chapter 2. This was where the Supreme Court ruled that the government could not regulate the press as it did broadcasting, and to some this is a clear indication of the Court's "media are innately capitalist" orientation. I agree this is supporting evidence for the view that spectrum scarcity is the primary justification for the different treatment of broadcasting from other media. But I hasten to point out, as Ed Baker says, that in that case the Supreme Court conflated the interests of editors and owners, making them identical. It made an eloquent argument for why the state could not censor editors, and at that level I quite agree with the Court's decision. But it did not really take up the issue of what happens if the interests of owners and editors are opposed. What does that mean in monopolistic or semimonopolistic markets where it is impossible for new owners to emerge to hire new editors? What happens to freedom of the press when the right to launch effective new media is nonexistent in the market or effectively limited to billionaires, and the investors have no more interest in journalism than they do in insurance or producing undergarments?

How precisely the Supreme Court will come to interpret freedom of the press and the First Amendment in the digital era is up in the air. I suspect that what happens with scholarship and, even more important, with citizen activism will go a long way toward influencing the outcome. If history is any guide, the Court's interpretation of the First Amendment will be flexible enough to accommodate what emerges from this critical juncture. For present purposes, my point is simply that there is nothing in the Constitution itself, or Supreme Court decisions to date, that mandates a neoliberal or libertarian course.

*   *   *

The third truth is that the American media system is not a free market. The media and communication systems in the United States have been the recipients of enormous direct and indirect subsidies, arguably as great as or greater than any other industry in our economy. When communication firms claim they work in free markets, it should provoke more howls than a Jerry Lewis film festival in France. All commercial enterprises benefit by government spending, and hence get indirect subsidies (roads, public health, public schools, etc.). But the subsidies provided to media and communication firms go far beyond that. One need only start with the value of the monopoly licenses that are given for free to commercial radio and TV stations or to spectrum for satellite television, or monopoly cable TV and telephone franchises. The best estimate of FCC staffers of the market value of the publicly owned spectrum today—which is given to commercial broadcasters at no charge—is around $500 billion.[59] When one considers all the wealth created on the backs of the free gift of spectrum to broadcasters since the 1920s, all the empires built upon it, the total transfer is certainly well into the hundreds of billions of dollars.

Although the spectrum granted to broadcasters is worth a large fortune, it is only a portion of the massive spectrum subsidy provided to private firms by the federal government at no charge. In addition to the "retail" spectrum used to provide services to the public, there is "industrial" spectrum used internally by television, cable, and telephone companies to transmit signals that eventually go to the public through wires or other sections of the spectrum or will be used for other purposes. Why did these companies get this spectrum? According to the leading expert on spectrum management, "The answer has less to do with any compelling public interest argument and more to do with the close relationship these industries have with the FCC."[60]

The "industrial" spectrum granted to the telephone and cable companies is the least of their subsidies. Lord knows the precise value of the indirect public subsidy created by AT&T's telephone monopoly over the years, or by the subsequent monopolies of the "Baby Bells." Or consider the massive empires people like John Malone and firms like Comcast built with the government-granted monopoly licenses for cable television systems they received. I suspect that the telephone and cable companies may well approach the broadcasters in generating private wealth from public subsidies and monopoly franchises, but no one to my knowledge has done the research yet.[61] It certainly is the last thing anyone in industry is pursuing. Economists of all stripes acknowledge that these companies earn "rent" (i.e., superprofits) from the government-created monopoly franchises, and much of the policymaking process is an effort by communities to get something in return for these rents, to get a piece of the action. Nor are these old media subsidies that need not concern us in the digital era. To the contrary, these firms are using their monopoly franchises and spectrum allocations to lock in their control over the Internet, as we will see in Chapter 4.

Although the public gifts to broadcasters, cable companies, and telephone companies are astronomical, they are not the only subsidies. Consider the following:

- The still considerable postal subsidies for magazines and periodicals, estimated by some in the many billions of dollars, though I know of no recent research.
- A broad range of federal, state, and local subsidies for film and television production, which Toby Miller, the leading scholar studying the matter, places on an annual basis somewhere "in the high hundreds of millions of dollars if you investigate all these areas."[62]
- The amount of money the federal, state, and local governments spend on advertising. Again, this totals in the billions of dollars annually. Granted this is not a subsidy per se, but it is a crucial market that supports media industries,

especially in the case of commercial broadcasters whose business model is based on government-granted monopoly access to the public airwaves. Policymakers could use this considerable government advertising spending to subsidize independent and alternative media.

- The indirect subsidy the government creates by allowing businesses to "write off" their advertising expenditures as a business expense on their taxes. It not only costs the government a great deal of money, but it encourages ever greater commercialism in our culture. S. Derek Turner of Free Press calculates that if we simply switched from an immediate write-off to a five-year write-off (80 percent first-year, balance spread over four years), it would generate as much as $40 billion in revenue over five years based on current patterns. During the critical juncture of the 1940s, there was a serious public debate over precisely this issue.[63]

- The billions spent on TV political advertising every election cycle. Policies effectively dictate that funds given to political campaigns end up in the pockets of those firms given monopoly licenses to the airwaves. This subsidy for commercial broadcasting has grown to where it accounts for more than 10 percent of the revenues of commercial TV stations and is now a major "profit center," with the ancillary outcome of making the broadcast industry the most powerful lobby against campaign finance reform.[64]

- Perhaps the largest subsidy of them all is copyright, a government-created and government-enforced monopoly right meant to eliminate the possibility of competitive markets. Accountants do not keep track of the value copyright creates for its holders, but lawsuits over the spoils suggest it is staggering.[65] And in crucial international policy deliberations, the U.S. government invariably represents the interests of copyright holders on the global stage.

- Along these lines, the federal government works as a powerful lobbying force for commercial media overseas, to see that foreign governments change regulations and divert subsidies to the benefit of U.S. communication firms.[66]

No one yet has done any of this math systematically,[67] but in combination these are subsidies of private firms to the tune of tens, perhaps even hundreds of billions of dollars annually. (This does not factor in more mundane government activities that boost the bottom lines of commercial media firms, such as government purchases of media products like books for schools and libraries.)

The term "government subsidies" is increasingly held in disrepute, so let me be clear about this. I think subsidies can be good, and I think that in principle they are necessary. Subsidies are costs that are supposed to have benefits. It is in our interest that the extent and role of subsidies in our media system be recognized and appreciated. Copyright, for example, is a necessary evil, a "tax on knowledge," as the Founders understood it in the Constitution. It is necessary to give authors an incentive to write books. The benefit of the massive printing and postal subsidies in the first few generations of the Republic, for example, was the establishment of an extraordinary press system and, with that, arguably the most advanced political democracy in the world. Our Founders regarded subsidies, in effect, as the price of civilization, or at least a viable republic. Many of our major communication revolutions, from the telegraph and radio to satellite communication and the Internet, were spawned as a result of massive government subsidies.

Even if one wanted a truly "free market" media system, without direct or indirect subsidies, it would be awfully difficult, if not impossible, to construct. And, ironically, to implement and maintain anything remotely close to a truly competitive market would require extensive government coordination, probably far beyond what currently exists.[68] It would never happen naturally. But the last thing the dominant commercial interests want is their subsidies removed; as far as I can tell, the "free market" think tanks are dedicated to promoting corporate domination in concentrated markets of the heavily subsidized communication system, rather than ending the heavily subsidized communication system. One need only look at how the self-proclaimed pro–free market editorial page of the *Wall Street Journal* carries water for AT&T and the big government-created telephone and cable powerhouses to see how the notion of free markets in the realm of media and telecommunication is mostly a rhetorical ploy to protect entrenched monopolistic power.[69]

This argument over subsidies leads directly to the fourth truth: the central importance of the policymaking process in structuring a media system. The question is not whether we will have subsidies and policies, but rather, what will the subsidies and policies be, what institutions will they support, and what values will they encourage and promote? When we talk about media, what most of us are concerned with, ultimately, is the content the media system produces and what effect that has upon our lives. But the content is shaped to a significant extent by the institutional structures of media systems, which is why political economists devote so much time to studying that issue. And the institutional structures are determined by policies and subsidies, which are in turn determined by the policymaking process. So that takes us to the nucleus of the media atom. This area has been overlooked for too long in communication studies.[70]

Allow me to refer to economics again for an analogy. As a student in the 1970s I had a professor who argued that in judging whether a nation was independent and advanced economically—whether it was "developed"—the key factor was not the level of GDP or the amount of consumer goods produced and consumed. He also said that the key was not the size of the capital goods sector, those industries like steel and glass and industrial machinery that provided the "plant and equipment" needed to produce consumer goods. In conventional reasoning, this was where the action was, and why nations like Japan and the Soviet Union were so gung-ho to establish powerful steel industries. No, he said, the key to evaluating an economy's vitality was the size and strength of its sector that *produced* capital goods, meaning, especially, the machine tools sector. If a nation was strong there, it could adapt to changing circumstances and it controlled its fate. This was why the U.S. economy could turn on a dime in 1941 and become the leading armaments manufacturer in the world; and it helps explain why the German and Japanese economies could rebound so successfully after the devastation of the war. This was striking to me and my fellow students, because while we knew about consumer goods and we knew all about the importance of plant and equipment, we had barely considered the seemingly minuscule industry of manufacturing the tools that made the plant and equipment. That, he said, was the key. So the rational conclusion for nations wishing to develop their economies was to use policies and subsidies to encourage the growth of this particular sector.

I do not know whether this theory is dismissed as hooey among economists today, but it provides a nice way to think about media. Consumer goods are the media content people consume. Capital goods are the policies, subsidies, and structures that determine the content. And the machine tool sector of media is the policymaking process that produces the policies and subsidies that create the media structures. That is where one must go to get to the root of the problem. If you understand that, it is a short path to understanding how the system will work and how it can be changed.

The detailed examination of the policymaking process has now, in my estimation, become the third core component of political economy of communication, joining the two aspects discussed in Chapter 2: evaluating how the media system fits into the broader economy and political culture; and exploring how market structures, profit motives, advertising support, policies, technologies, labor relations, and so forth affect the conduct, operations, and output of media firms and industries. When one examines the policymaking process, one can see what the real options were, and why a system later regarded as "natural" got put in place as it did. Policymaking is becoming a new area of intense research in communication history. For reasons already made clear, the research places particular emphasis upon critical junctures, as those are the moments in policymaking history when the range of debate is relatively broad and society can go in any number of directions with its media policies and subsidies. This is where communication revolutions truly take place.

These first four points lead directly to opening up new research areas for scholars; the *fifth and final truth* is the one that results inexorably from this research and fans the flames of citizen activism. This final truth is simply that the policymaking process in the United States has grown increasingly undemocratic as media and communication have become ever more lucrative industries. The policies and subsidies are made in the public's name but without the public's informed consent. In my talks and writings, I like to use the metaphor of the famous Havana patio scene in *The Godfather II*, where Michael Corleone and Hyman Roth and the American gangsters are dividing up Cuba between themselves during the dictator Batista's era. After divvying up the spoils, Hyman Roth states how great it is to be in Cuba, with a friendly government that "knows how to work with business."

That is pretty much how communication policymaking has been conducted in the United States. Monopoly broadcast licenses, copyright extensions, and tax subsidies are doled out all the time, but the public has no idea what is going on. Extremely powerful lobbyists battle it out with each other—like Michael Corleone and Hyman Roth—to get cushy deals from the FCC, whose members and top staffers almost inevitably move to private industry to cash in after their stint in "public service."

Above all else, the FCC has been dedicated to making the dominant firms bigger and more profitable. Congress too is under the thumb of big money. The one thing the big firms—just like Roth and Corleone—all agree upon is that it is their system and the public has no role to play in the policymaking process. And because the news media almost never cover this story in the general news, 99 percent of the public has no idea what is going on. If anything, they are fed a plateful of free market hokum, extolling an industry that "gives the people what they want."

This is actually a more complex point than the preceding two paragraphs suggest. In the sense that this is a capitalist society, what goes on in communication policymaking is not necessarily corrupt; it is what one would expect to be the outcome even if everyone plays by the rules. Once the decision has been made that communication shall be subject to the rules of the market and controlled by profit-maximizing corporations, a certain undemocratic outcome is all but guaranteed. Consider broadcasting: Once licenses are allocated to commercial concerns and rights to them are then resold on the market to the highest bidder, it limits the relevant pool of Americans who can afford to purchase a radio or television station to a tiny percentage of the population. (And when ownership caps are relaxed, the percentage plummets even further.) In a democracy, that is not a desirable outcome. But that's not corruption— that's capitalism.[71]

And while the decision to allow broadcasting to be developed by commercial interests was made secretively and dominated by money interests, no laws were broken (to my knowledge) during that political struggle in the 1930s. It was simply a playing field sharply sloped to the benefit of commercial interests. That's not corruption in the strict definition of the term; that's what happens when a few have a great many more resources to legally influence politicians than the vast majority. Ultimately, coming to terms with what may be termed "institutionalized" corruption means coming to terms with capitalism. That is why challenging antidemocratic communication policymaking is connected to other movements to strengthen the power of the many and weaken the privileges of the few in public life.

But while capitalism is a driving force in our society, it is not the only force. Ours is also a constitutional republic based upon the rule of law. As this book has chronicled, and as our Founders understood, there is often a tension between the needs of property and the needs of democracy. When the forces of property gain too much power, and democratic values get neglected, invariably the institutional corruption grows. So it was in the Gilded Age and so it is today. Certain powerful commercial interests unfairly dominate the policymaking system through a variety of mechanisms that while not technically illegal, are clearly unethical by nearly any conceivable standard of liberal democratic governance.

The empirical evidence is devastating: In the first six months of 2006 alone, communication and technology firms spent $172 million on lobbying in Washington, more than any other sector or group.[72] How serious is this lobbying army? Rep. Edward Markey of Massachusetts states that the largest communication firms each have a lobbyist assigned to *each* member of Congress on the relevant committees.[73] In January 2007, AT&T convened a meeting of its Capitol Hill lobbying army. A standing-room-only audience attended in a conference room described as "the size of a stadium."[74]

These firms also spend commanding amounts in candidate contributions and for public relations. When these firms do engage with the public on pressing policy matters, it is often in the form of phony "Astroturf" front groups—that is, the "fake grassroots."[75] Combine this with the extraordinarily high percentage of FCC members and top FCC officials (as well as members of Congress and congressional aides on the relevant committees) who leave the agency through the "golden revolving door" and go on to lucrative careers working for the firms and industries they were once theoretically regulating in the public interest.[76]

Even those who benefit from the policymaking system concede that it has been an insiders' game—with a bankroll in the hundreds of millions or billions the price of admission. In the past this situation was overlooked because, despite the corruption, the system seemed to be working. The policies seemed marginal in scope and technocratic, and therefore no big deal.[77] But now that the system is in crisis, it is becoming a very big deal. Policymaking is much like the man behind the curtain in *The Wizard of Oz*. The corporate media lobbies do not want you to look there because when people do, they see that the entire rationale for our media system rests upon a fairy tale about free markets.

The fairy tale of free markets protects the corporate media system from the public review it deserves. I recall an exchange I had with Jack Fuller, a top executive of the Tribune Company, at a 2002 University of Illinois conference on the future of family-owned newspapers. Fuller, the president of Tribune's publishing subsidiary, was presented as the thinking person's media boss because he has written some books. Fuller thundered to the audience about how offensive he found it that he even had to travel to Washington and countenance the right of the government to have any say whatsoever over the affairs of his company. He said he found that to be a dire attack on the First Amendment. I asked Mr. Fuller about the many extremely valuable monopoly radio and TV licenses the Tribune Company accepted from the government at no charge, and how that affected him as he was working up his anger over government meddling in the affairs of his company. Fuller paused and explained that the Tribune Company had no interest in broadcasting, but had been asked by the government to take the valuable monopoly licenses. We were left to assume nobody else wanted the opportunity to have a multimillion-dollar industry handed to them at no charge, and the Tribune Company was just being a good Samaritan, helping out a government in distress.

In fact, Fuller had it exactly wrong. Back in the 1920s, the Tribune Company sent its top lawyer, Louis Caldwell, to Washington to work for the government's newly created Federal Radio Commission, specifically to allocate the radio stations to commercial interests. At the time, Caldwell argued that the government needed to have draconian power over selecting who was allowed to have a monopoly radio broadcasting license and, conversely, who was not. Caldwell argued that determining the rulers of the airwaves was a government job of such magnitude that it could not be trusted to as democratic a body as Congress, which might be unduly influenced by people without sufficient expertise to make the right call. This expertise was to be found, apparently, exclusively in the hands of engineers and lawyers working for the commercial broadcasting industry. Coincidentally, as a result of Caldwell's labor, the Tribune Company's WGN was awarded at no charge one of the handful of clear channel signals, worth, even then, countless millions of dollars. Once the commercial system was in place and the lucrative monopoly licenses had been doled out in complete secrecy, Caldwell did a 180-degree turn and argued that any regulation of commercial broadcasting violated the First Amendment.[78] Jack Fuller was carrying on in Caldwell's tradition.

As the Fuller encounter demonstrates, the five truths undercut the positions of communication corporations and their advocates by shining a light on the two great and indefensible blind spots upon which their arguments for the status quo are based. The first blind spot was the "immaculate conception" notion of the American media system, the idea that corporations "naturally" assumed control because it was the American way. It requires the "immaculate conception" for industry and its defenders to shift seamlessly into a righteous lather about transgressions of the state. I recall being invited to appear on the Milt Rosenberg program on (Tribune-owned) WGN radio in 1999 to discuss my book *Rich Media, Poor Democracy*. To provide the home team perspective, Rosenberg also invited an editor from the *Chicago Tribune* to join us. Both the editor and Rosenberg conceded that some of my criticism of the media system was accurate, but waxed on about the evils of government censorship and how WGN had a First Amendment right to operate as it pleased. When I was asked to respond, I merely asked why WGN had been granted the monopoly license in the first place. Why not the Chicago Federation of Labor or some other commercial enterprise? Why did we assume that WGN was the rightful steward of that frequency? Initially flummoxed, both the editor and Rosenberg conceded the point and quickly moved to another topic.[79]

The second blind spot is the extent of public subsidies. Communication firms and their advocates love to wave the flag of free market economics; acknowledging the extent of their massive public subsidies blows up the free market argument. What was striking to me as I conducted research for this book was that the four main "free market" think tanks in Washington— the Cato Institute, Heritage Foundation, American Enterprise Institute, and Progress and Freedom Foundation—which often weigh in on behalf of communication corporations and against government "interference" with free markets, did no discernible research on the extent of subsidies.[80] When the state funnels tens of billions of dollars in subsidies to the firms that often bankroll these think tanks, it is not worth noting; if pressed, they confess it is troubling and move to another topic or they claim it's just a government appreciating the need to encourage "free enterprise." But when the government asks for anything in return for those subsidies, it is like the Sword of Damocles is being held over the very survival of freedom in our land.

Once the importance of the policymaking process is understood and the corruption of the process is grasped, our understanding of communication changes dramatically. Consider the term "deregulation," which is used frequently by journalists and scholars to describe it when big media firms look to see media ownership rules relaxed or eliminated. If we had a free market media system, this use of the term would be accurate, in the sense that market forces would play a larger role than the state in setting the terms of competition. But in telephony, broadcasting, cable, or satellite communication, the term is pure propaganda. It is meant to imply a competitive market outcome, when as often as not this "deregulation" leads to far less market competition.

So when radio ownership rules were "deregulated" in the 1996 Telecommunications Act, that did not mean that lots of new small firms could enter radio broadcasting and compete with the giants without having to get the FCC's permission. No. It meant, instead, that a small number of firms were permitted to gobble up ever more monopoly radio licenses from the government and establish vastly greater market power. The FCC was doing just as much regulation, only now it was simply regulating *on behalf* of the big guys. Deregulation in media policymaking means, in reality, *re-regulation* purely to serve powerful corporate interests with no concern for the general public whatsoever.

In sum, the government–corporation media nexus is tight. The public displays of antagonism by the Jack Fullers of the world toward Washington mask this truth, which leads to the great irony (and imposing challenge) that a free people must use the state to create viable media independent of the state and dominant business interests. This is more or less as Madison and Jefferson understood the situation.

* * *

By the early 2000s, signs of the beginning stages of a critical juncture were all around us. Of the three criteria that set the stage for a critical juncture, one was clearly in place, another looked to be in place, and the third factor loomed distinctly on the horizon.[81]

The first factor that leads to a critical juncture—a revolutionary communication technology that upsets the applecart—was the most certain. It was already clear that the Internet, cell phones, and digital technology were revolutionizing all forms of communication. Some media industries were already threatened with either extinction or complete overhaul, and within a decade or two all media industries would likely be radically transformed. New industries would be created and others would go the way of the horse and buggy. Whether society liked it or not, these new technologies were forcing a rethinking of communication in boardrooms and among policymakers across the nation. The future was absolutely unclear to anyone in 2001, as it pretty much remains in 2007, at the time of this writing.

A daunting question about the digital communication revolution was where it would fit in the broad sweep of human development. It was almost certainly the equal of the telegraph, or film, or television, in its impact as a social institution. But the real question is whether the digital revolution is much greater than that. Or, perhaps to put it better, whether it is a culmination of all the technological revolutions stretching from photography and telegraphy to broadcasting and computers, where the whole is exponentially greater than the sum of the parts? The question was whether the Internet, with its potential for instant communication by all people to each other and our collective knowledge at all times, would qualify as the fourth great communication "transformation" in human history. I use the term "transformation" to indicate a communication revolution of such stunning magnitude that it could alter the very way our species developed, creating consequences even our most brilliant science fiction writers would have difficulty imagining.

The first great transformative development in communication for humans was the emergence of speech and language. Although clearly there is a genetic instinct for language, it did not emerge overnight.[82] Some scholars place its development to roughly a mere 50,000 to 60,000 years ago. Some, perhaps many, anthropologists believe that it was this emergence of language that permitted a small band of hominids to avoid possible extinction and to move from one corner of Africa to dominate the planet in a geological nanosecond.[83] The acquisition of language helped human brains develop and made more advanced societies plausible. The eventual development of agriculture, which permitted the rise of surplus, and with that the beginning of civilization and history, would not have been possible without language.[84] So the first communication transformation was a big deal. In many ways it defined our species; it created us.

The second great communication transformation was writing, which came many thousands of years after agriculture, only around 5,000 years ago. Writing was not a "natural" development; many fairly advanced societies never had it, and there was never anything close to the diversity found in human languages.[85] Even today all the world's written languages come from three or four basic systems. Writing clearly was driven by the necessity of growing empires based upon surpluses generated by agriculture to record information, and those that did not have writing faced real limits to their expansion or survival. Indeed, empires with writing had a decided advantage over nonwriting societies, and tended to crush and absorb them. Writing also had enormous unanticipated consequences, with much of what we regard as our cultural heritage the direct and indirect result. Without writing, for example, it is impossible to imagine the human brain being capable of generating the scientific, philosophical, and artistic accomplishments that define us. Classical Athens is nothing if not a tribute to the written word.

The third great communication transformation was the printing press, and this is better understood among scholars as it has been the subject of considerable analysis and debate.[86] The printing press made possible the radical reconstruction of all major institutions, most notably religion. It is difficult to imagine political democracy, the scientific revolution, or much of an industrial economy without the printing press and mass literacy. By no means did the printing press generate democracy and an industrial economy on its own, but it was a precondition for either to exist.

Some of my friends and colleagues found the notion that the digital revolution could become a similar transformative development for our species preposterous. Perhaps. But if we broaden our notion of the digital revolution to include biotechnology and related scientific developments that are owed to some extent to notions of information, I think the case is more compelling. Nor should we assume that if the Internet and the digital communication revolution become the equal of these three communication transformations, it will automatically produce unambiguously progressive results. Language may have begat agriculture and civilization, but, as Jared Diamond has noted, for the great bulk of humanity the quality of life before agriculture was probably far superior to what followed.[87] As for the benefits of writing for humanity, Claude Levi-Strauss writes that "the immediate consequence of the emergence of writing was the enslavement of vast numbers of people."[88] And for all the wonders of the past five centuries, there is a long list of horror stories, from imperialism to slavery to genocide, much of it promulgated by societies with widespread if not near universal literacy and immersed in print culture.

Whether this current critical juncture develops into the fourth great communication transformation in the existence of our species is outside our control, and won't be understood as such until we are all long gone. Whether this is a democratic communication revolution is very much in our control. But unless one or both of the other factors that would promote a critical juncture materialize, we will almost certainly see this communication revolution directed from above, with results that may well be disastrous for the near-term prospects of our species. A corporate-directed critical juncture will end in a system that serves the profit needs of large communication firms and greases the wheels for marketing, because that is where the profits will be most readily found. They will find close allies in the upper echelons of the government. There will be no public participation in policymaking; it will remain behind closed doors, and the public will continue to get its regular serving of PR about the genius of the free market. In the minds of George Gilder and Newt Gingrich and Dick Cheney, this is heaven on earth. For many others, it will be a living hell. The revolutionary democratic potential of the digital revolution will be muted, if not extinguished.

So by the late 1990s, my attention was focused on whether the second or third factor generating a critical juncture would exist. The evidence was encouraging. I already discussed how there had been an upsurge of interest in media and media policy during the 1990s, and that interest only escalated in the new decade. For no small number of Americans, the dismal media coverage of economic "globalization," the 2000 presidential election, the environmental crisis exemplified by global warming, and the corporate crime wave typified by Enron were signs of a media culture that had lost its legitimacy. Millions of Americans, especially young people, were tuning out conventional journalism altogether. It was now fairly certain that the second factor for a critical juncture was coming into place: the lack of legitimacy and credibility of media content, especially journalism. And it was this concern about the deep flaws in the existing media environment—not abstract talk about new technologies—that was getting Americans off their couches and active. When John Nichols and I did the research for our first book, *It's the Media, Stupid*, in the late 1990s, we argued that Americans needed to take a page from all the media activism happening in other nations. When we did the research in 2002 for our second book, *Our Media, Not Theirs*, we were struck by how the tables had turned, and that there was more media criticism and burgeoning activism in the United States than just about anywhere else in the world.

The real measure of whether the second factor in a critical juncture was for real would be if significant political campaigns emerged to challenge the existing media system in the policy arena. Would concerns about lousy media content, and a desire to improve the situation, get people off their duffs? I imagine no one expected the first stirrings to come over the unlikely issue of low-power FM radio broadcasting.[89] This was a technology developed in the early 1990s that made it extremely easy and inexpensive to broadcast FM signals in the open sections of the FM spectrum, of which there were quite a lot. At night one of these low-power stations could cover an entire small or mid-sized city and up to half of a metropolitan area. Hundreds of so-called pirate broadcasters emerged in the 1990s to take advantage of the new technology, in a form of considerable civil disobedience. The FCC tried to stop this unlicensed broadcasting under pressure from the commercial broadcasters, but it was almost impossible to do. So FCC Chairman William Kennard decided to legalize LPFM and create a thousand new stations that would be turned over to nonprofit community groups to do noncommercial broadcasting. Kennard saw this as a way to get more minority voices in radio, as the massive wave of radio consolidation following the 1996 Telecommunications Act had decimated the ranks of minority broadcast station owners (of which there were never many to begin with). The FCC announced its plan in 2000.

The commercial broadcasters declared war on Kennard's LPFM plan.[90] The last thing they wanted was a number of additional stations in each community doing local programming without advertising. It might have forced them to pay more attention to the communities they were in and to ratchet down the advertising to keep their listeners. The commercial broadcasters claimed they were concerned that LPFM stations would create interference, but the engineering standards used in Kennard's plan had been developed by commercial broadcasting engineers and were used for a successful launch of several new commercial stations a decade earlier. But the National Association of Broadcasters got the House to radically overturn Kennard's plan and allow only a fraction of the LPFM stations that the FCC had authorized.

Then something remarkable happened. Scores of citizens from around the nation started visiting their senators' offices in their home states, or actually traveling to Washington. They explained how important LPFM was to them and their communities, and they demonstrated its nature with recordings. Enough members of the Senate, including, to his great credit, Republican Sen. John McCain of Arizona, paid attention—and the NAB could not get its plan to smash LPFM passed in the light of day. Instead, they added an anti-LPFM provision as a rider on the budget bill in the dead of night just before Christmas. They won, but the media lobby had not had to resort to such tactics against citizen activists since the great battle over commercial broadcasting in the 1930s.[91] At the time, the significance of this encounter was muted by the misery of yet another betrayal—but its importance would become clear in short order.

The third factor that contributes to having a critical juncture in media is whether there is a broader period of social upheaval and reform in the society as a whole. In an environment like this, it is easier for reform ideas that go against dominant commercial and political interests to gain traction and be successful. American history tends to have major reform periods every two or three generations. The most notable examples are the Jacksonian era, Reconstruction, the Progressive Era, the New Deal, and the Great Society. In my mind conditions were ripe—even overripe—for another such period of major reform. Inequality was growing, the U.S. economy was far too dependent upon militarism and debt, and political corruption at all levels was institutionalized and arguably approaching or surpassing the Gilded Age in sleaze.

But no uprising was on the horizon at the time, and it appeared unlikely in the foreseeable future. Increasingly, what fueled much media activism was the conviction that the dreadful media system was a serious factor in preventing peaceful and effective political reform. Media reform was seen as a means of getting social and political reform on the national agenda. Nicholas Johnson, one of the few former FCC members who did not parlay their valuable experience at the FCC into a big-ticket job working for the communication industry, put it this way: Whatever your first issue of concern is (the environment, civil rights, etc.), media reform has got to be your second. Because unless the media system is changed, it will be much harder, if not impossible, to win popular awareness and support for the first issue.

By 2002, I was aware of a growing popular momentum concerning media issues—but there was a real disconnect with these developments among communication scholars. Three events in particular crystallized this paradox.[92] In April, U.S. Rep. Bernie Sanders, the lone independent member of the House, invited Nichols and me to Vermont to do two "town meetings" on media policy on consecutive nights in Montpelier and Burlington. Sanders had been doing several of these town meetings every year—on issues like health care, education, economic inequality, women's rights, social security, the environment, and foreign policy—ever since he entered Congress in 1991. This was the first time he had devoted a town meeting to the problem of corporate control over media.[93] Both evenings the rooms were packed to the rafters, and the events ran well after the allotted time to allow people to speak. The questions and comments from the audience were passionate and informed, and sometimes striking and original. It led me to rethink some of the ways I have formulated my work. I wish every academic could have been there. People were energized to change the media system in the United States. Sanders told me that in all his years of conducting town meetings, maybe only one other time had there approached this level of intensity, enthusiasm, and participation.[94]

Fueled by that response, Sanders arranged a session on Capitol Hill to discuss the media crisis a couple of months later. Nichols and I joined Sanders, Democratic Rep. Sherrod Brown of Ohio, and Newspaper Guild head Linda Foley for a discussion of the media crisis and the implications for media policy.[95] We were especially concerned with media ownership. Although we were assigned a windowless room in the basement of a House office building on a boiling summer afternoon, the room was packed with people, including staffers from scores of offices on the Hill. We could have gone on for hours. Nichols and I had been coming to Washington to discuss media policy for a good three years by now. Usually the best we could do was to get a cup of coffee with one of our close allies like Sanders, Brown, Jesse Jackson Jr., or Paul Wellstone. But we never had any sense from any of them that there were any prospects of making this an issue on the Hill. The entrenched corporate money simply controlled the scene. This session in the basement of the House office building was a leap forward.

Sandwiched between these two episodes was a trip I made to London to give an address at the retirement celebration for Nicholas Garnham, the British political economist of communication whose work had been so central to my own development. Joining me from the United States were a good half-dozen communication scholars, most of whom worked in political economy and were, like me, in the prime of their careers. I was abuzz from the recent developments in the United States, and in my talk I discussed all the extraordinary changes taking place in the United States regarding popular interest in media as a political issue. In contrast, morale at the event was low. I felt like I was back in 1991. My talk, as far as I could tell, fell flat with much of the audience, though it was a hit with at least a couple of the grad students present. In fact, they were the ones who commented most strongly about how chilly the reception was to my talk.

For the next two days, I spent considerable time with my Yankee faculty colleagues—we were encamped in a dormitory on the distant outskirts of London—and there was little interest in discussing what was happening with media in our nation. When I raised the subject in conversation or discussed politics in general beyond aphorisms, the conversation faltered until the subject was switched. Instead all the talk was about consumer purchases, upcoming vacations, popular movies and TV shows, and, of course, academic politics: who got this job or that job, who got the big grant, and, after a few drinks, whose colleagues were the biggest schmucks. It was quite entertaining and the people were brilliant and charming, but that made it worse. Had this been some colleagues specializing in rhetoric or organizational communication, I would have been a tad dismayed but I would have understood. But these were mostly political economists, and all self-described critical scholars, people whose work was dedicated to democratizing media systems and creating a more just and humane society. They seemed almost afraid of addressing a world where their work was suddenly relevant; it looked to me like they had grown comfortable in their quiet and dimly lit corners of the academy, writing books and articles that few would read.

I returned from London in as deep a depression as I am

capable of about the state of academic communication studies in the United States. I actually thought about abandoning the field, and maybe setting up shop in a public policy program. The one thing I knew for certain was that my energy was best applied off-campus, because that was where the action was. Little did I know all hell was about to break loose.

4
Moment of Truth

It was sometime in the late fall of 2001 that I received a phone call out of the blue from someone identifying himself as Josh Silver. He said he was working at the Smithsonian in Washington, but in a previous life he had directed the successful campaign to establish publicly funded elections in Arizona. Silver said he was convinced that deplorable news was the main barrier to success in the issues he cared the most about, and he wanted to organize a campaign to change the media system. He was familiar with my writings on this subject and wanted to get together. Would I be willing to meet with him to map out a strategy? I had received many queries along these lines over the years, usually from well-intended but not especially practical souls, and I had little reason to think Silver was much different. But since John Nichols and I planned to be in Washington in January 2002, I agreed to meet with him and a couple of other people at his apartment to discuss the matter.[1] We had a nice chat that day but nothing came of it. I remember thinking at the time—this was just as Nichols and I did the town meetings in Vermont—that this might be the moment to get serious. After not hearing from Silver for a good eight months, I assumed he had dropped the matter.

Silver called again in the autumn of 2002, and explained he had been tying up some loose ends professionally and personally, and now was ready to act. He was moving from Washington to Northampton, Massachusetts, near where he had grown up. By this point, I was less concerned about whether Silver was a flake than I was about the state of our media system and the need to organize a serious movement to change it. So Nichols, Silver, and I formed Free Press after a series of phone conversations in November and December 2002. Josh was our only staffer, working out of Sut Jhally's Media Education Foundation in Northampton. We managed to find a couple of courageous funders—God knows how—willing to give us initial funds, so Josh could have a very modest income and we could eventually add a few more people by the middle of 2003.

The vision we had for Free Press was pretty simple. Our goal was to make media policymaking a political issue in the United States. We thought that the core problem was that the media system was based upon policies made in the public's name but without the public's informed consent. The more informed and engaged public involvement there was with regard to policymaking, the better the policies and the better the media system.

Nichols pointedly said we should use the environmental movement as our guide. Nichols spent a good deal of time interviewing and conversing with Gaylord Nelson, Wisconsin's former senator, who had been the first major environmentalist on Capitol Hill and was the guiding force behind the creation of Earth Day. Nelson agreed with us about the importance of media, and after much thought, concurred that it shared the same properties as the environmental movement in that it affected all people, cut across ideological lines, could be changed by public policies, and rightfully belonged in the heart of public debate. In the early 1960s, the environment was a nonissue in American political life; within fifteen years there was not a politician in the country who dared run for office without some sort of position on the matter. That was going to be one of our yardsticks for success.[2]

In our view, we needed to have one foot in Washington to be credible on the pressing matters of the day; and we needed another foot outside Washington organizing popular awareness and support for media reform policies. To get people engaged required that we not let the range of debate be determined by what was possible in Washington. That would not excite many people. Rather, we had to strike out boldly with visionary ideas to garner popular enthusiasm, and then parlay the momentum into political capital in D.C. In particular, we wanted to reach out to all those already organized groups—labor, feminists, civil rights groups, environmentalists, educators, journalists, artists, and so on—that had a stake in improving the media system but were, with only a couple of exceptions, missing in action. Looking back on our earliest discussions, we factored in almost no role for academics, including communication scholars, in our vision. I am not sure why; what is striking is that we didn't even pause to discuss the matter.

We knew we were onto something when Nichols and I appeared on the PBS program *NOW with Bill Moyers* in February 2003 to discuss our latest book, *Our Media, Not Theirs.* We did not discuss Free Press then—the group did not even have a website yet—but we laid out our basic critique of the failing U.S. media and the need to have citizens change the system and establish a truly free press. Moyers was so taken with the topic that he gave it his longest segment in the show's history, and then he said the program received as much immediate and positive feedback as any he had ever done. John and I received an avalanche of positive feedback. On the Amazon.com bestseller list, we watched after the show as *Our Media, Not Theirs* climbed from around 5,000 to end up in the top ten. It was exhilarating.

John, Josh, and I thought it would take years of hard organizing to get to the point where we could really have any appreciable effect on media policymaking. The system was so corrupt, the entrenched players were so powerful, and the news media coverage of media policy debates was so nonexistent, we thought it was going to require great patience to be successful. When the FCC announced it was going to review several of its core media ownership rules in the fall of 2002, Nichols and I thought it was almost certain the Republican-controlled FCC would relax or eliminate the ownership rules in a manner that would please the largest media conglomerates. In early 2003, with the Republicans taking control of the Senate, we put all our limited resources into fighting the rules changes while we were thinking about what Free Press would do *after* the FCC had handed the keys to the kingdom to GE, Clear Channel, Tribune Company, and Rupert Murdoch. To think otherwise seemed not only unrealistic, but absurd.

Then something wonderful and magical happened: The massive grassroots uprising against media consolidation that caught everyone, including me, by surprise. Some three million people from across the nation sent letters and e-mails, made telephone calls, or signed petitions protesting the relaxation of media ownership rules. Free Press became one of the groups doing the organizing work, but we were very much back-benchers. This was a moment in the sun for Consumers Union's Gene Kimmelman, Center for Digital Democracy's Jeff Chester, Media Access Project's Andy Schwartzman, and Consumer Federation of America's Mark Cooper. They used their skills and experience to drive the campaign, and they were clearly energized by the throngs of new activists and supporters coming to the issue. Outside Washington, existing and emerging media activist groups like Reclaim the Media, Media Alliance, Media-Tank, and the Prometheus Radio Project—which had been fighting for low-power FM—generated grassroots attention to the issue. And then the big guns, MoveOn.org, Common Cause, and even the National Rifle Association, joined the party. Media reform became arguably the second hottest issue in Washington in 2003 following only the war in Iraq, and it had no big corporate lobby behind it.

I will not chronicle the details of the media ownership fight here. That has been done elsewhere.[3] For present purposes, understand that while the FCC voted 3–2 to relax the ownership rules in June 2003, the Republican-controlled Congress, facing enormous popular pressure, voted to overturn some of the rules changes later that year. Then, in June 2004, the federal courts threw out the FCC's rules changes altogether—sending the FCC back to the drawing board. We were victorious, in a manner of speaking, at least for the time being. Nor will I attempt to provide a cursory history of Free Press or the broader media reform movement as it developed from 2002 to the present. That will be done down the road by many of the participants as the dust settles and as time permits. In time, I suspect it will receive systematic treatment by historians who were not participants. To do that properly requires the distance that comes with the passage of more time.

What the 2003 media ownership fight did accomplish, for Free Press in particular and the media reform movement in general, was to permit us to gain experiences in less than a year that would have taken a good five or ten years otherwise. We became battle-tested and seasoned, like raw recruits who had studied warfare at West Point and now were thrown into the heat of battle. We learned several crucial lessons over the course of 2003, most of which we wouldn't necessarily have anticipated. Perhaps the most immediate lesson: Our idea that this movement required a slow and gradual ramp-up to be viable was wrong. Media reform had a prehistory in the 1980s and 1990s, when energy and awareness were growing below the radar. But there are brief windows when social movements either build up momentum to take off like jet planes or run out of gas. The window of opportunity for this movement is presented by the critical juncture. It will not be here forever. This is not about building a permanent bureaucracy; this is a social movement. We grow quickly or we disappear.

The 2003 ownership fight provided at least six other definitional lessons for our critical juncture that merit discussion:

1. People actually cared enough about media issues to organize around them;
2. People were quite capable of sophisticated and thoughtful positions on media issues;
3. Media reform could be a "gateway" issue to draw people into public life and citizen activism;
4. The Internet and digital technologies dramatically changed the nature of political organizing, and made possible work that would have been impossibly expensive in years past;
5. Media reform was both a nonpartisan movement and a progressive movement;
6. Conservatism as it had evolved in American politics was incapable of addressing the concerns of the media reform movement, and was increasingly incapable of providing a coherent governing philosophy.

First, we had speculated that people would become active in media if they understood it as a political issue. But before 2003 this was largely a theoretical claim. We knew that many people cared a great deal about media; we did not know if this would translate into activism. In 2003 it went from theory to practice. The people who became active in the fight over media ownership were motivated by a variety of issues, including concerns about the lack of localism in media; unhappiness about the limited and unimaginative musical fare found on radio; dissatisfaction with news media coverage of a variety of issues, not the least of which was the U.S. invasion of Iraq; the paucity of quality programs; the representation of women and people of color in the media; the decline in minority and women media owners; the general decline of resources for journalism; the vulgarity and commercialism of commercial broadcasting; and the commercial marination of childhood, to mention the most striking. Not all of these areas would have necessarily been made appreciably worse by what the FCC proposed to do in 2003, though none would improve. But what was crucial in 2003 was that a light switch went on for millions of Americans. They did not have to accept all the problems with media as an "unalterable" given. The media system was not natural; it resulted from policies. The media ownership campaign exploded because once people realized that the failing system was the result of government policies, they found a place to vent their rage. Media ownership became a lightning rod for all media activism. People's long-standing bottled-up concerns about media found a target and became legitimate.

Second, much of the public already had thoughtful and substantive positions on media issues. A crucial development in 2003 was the organizing of a series of mostly unofficial town meetings and public hearings to discuss media ownership. There were around fourteen of these in 2003. I was a speaker at the first one at Columbia University in January 2003, and all five FCC members were present. (At only one other hearing in 2003, an FCC-sanctioned hearing in Richmond, Virginia, did the three Republican members reappear.) The panels at Columbia were split almost evenly between industry representatives and nonindustry folks: academics, artists and journalists, or public interest advocates. What was striking was the incessant bellyaching of the industry representatives about how "one-sided" the discussion was, and how it was "anti-industry." This was because it was the first time in memory that the noncorporate perspective had any noticeable presence at any proceeding connected to the FCC, and it was not a pleasurable experience for an industry used to having the floor to itself.

Throughout 2003 these hearings took place, almost always

with panels split between industry and nonindustry representatives. People from the audience could give their testimony and say whatever they wished. Sometimes the hearings lasted for hours and hours. Almost without exception, people opposed media consolidation, for the broad range of reasons mentioned above. These public forums were generally packed with people who were enthralled to be in the company of hundreds of people in the community who shared their concerns about media. It reminded me of why the "right to peaceably assemble" is one of the core protections in the First Amendment; there is nothing quite like the power that comes from physical proximity, even in the digital age.[4] These hearings proved so successful that Free Press has continued the practice, convening and organizing many more across the nation since 2004. Other groups around the nation have done the same. Even in the digital age, public hearings and town meetings are an indispensable form of democratic political organizing.

What we also learned from the public hearings is that people are much more complex and thoughtful about media than is generally acknowledged. Many media reformers and certainly most of the academics I knew, including those on the left, seemed to think that the entertainment content of the commercial media system (and possibly even the journalism) accurately reflected the tastes and desires of the audience. If people were given a "vote," the thinking went, they may well make the media system even worse than it already is. To some extent this was a reflection of the elitist and class bias of academics. What we discovered was that the media market choices people made did not reflect their values effectively, because the market did not provide a full range of options for people to choose from. People were citizens as well as consumers, and they understood that we needed a media system that did more than amuse, entertain, or hawk products. The media system was more than a conveyor belt to serve their particular immediate interests. This became clear in 2005, when Free Press conducted focus groups of working-class adults on their attitudes toward public broad-casting. We were astonished to see how many people wanted to make public and nonprofit broadcasting stronger—even if they did not watch the stations themselves—because they thought it important for children's programming and as a broader alternative to commercial stations.[5]

I think at least a few liberals and progressives had a suspicion of democracy, because they feared that people were basically morons, even if through no fault of their own. (This was the liberal paternalism that conservative populists feasted upon like a starving lion on its prey.) During 2003, it became clear that the more people become engaged with media policy-making, the more likely good things would happen. The success of the current system has been based to a large extent on the fact that people do not exercise their constitutional right to participate in policymaking. The big media corporations understand this and do everything in their power to minimize the public role. Our battle, in the end, remains just to make this a legitimate issue. If it is, we win.

Third, media reform is not only a legitimate basis for attracting popular political participation; it may indeed be a surprisingly effective means for drawing people into political activity. Before 2003 the operating assumption was that this was the last issue people would organize around, if only because it seemed so "wonky." This assumption was an article of faith among most activists and in the academic community. It has proven incorrect. And people who get interested in politics due to media issues sometimes begin to get interested in other issues. Media reform, rather than being the last issue people will turn to, may actually be a gateway issue for political engagement. What we learned was that media reform appealed to diverse constituencies, who could understand technical issues and terminology and who, in combination, could make for powerful coalitions. Moreover, since 2003 we have learned that there are numerous media reform issues that can draw people into the mix. Some groups might be active in one area and less inter-ested in another area. Free Press tries to get all these people working together on every issue. It is a strategy that has proven successful.

Along these lines, and something else we did not anticipate, media reform activism allows the possibility of discreet victo-ries on specific measures. Even in a corrupt political environ-ment, you can actually win. So we won the last round in the media ownership fight. We were able to stop the Bush adminis-tration from paying journalists like Armstrong Williams under the table and having its cronies at the Corporation for Public Broadcasting harass programs seen as insufficiently flattering toward President Bush. In 2006, our movement stopped a sweeping overhaul of our nation's telecommunications laws in Congress to protect the principle of Network Neutrality on the Internet. Contrast media reform activism with work on cam-paign finance reform, where unless you win the whole thing— publicly funded elections—you leave a crack in the edifice that will undermine whatever reforms you attempt to enact. Media reform offers short-term satisfaction as well as the possibility for grand victories down the road. It is a political winner.

Fourth, the Internet and the digital revolution have lowered the cost of doing political organizing and made it much easier to be effective with fewer resources. The campaign in 2003 was waged by a variety of groups that, added together, had dedicated budgets that were laughably small. Moreover, mainstream news media black out almost any coverage of me-dia policy debates, making the degree of difficulty that much higher.[6] In years past, that combination would have killed any organizing effort and guaranteed success to the Hyman Roths and Michael Corleones of the corporate media world. In 2003 we were able to use e-mail and the Internet to build up an army that could move quickly and decisively. MoveOn organizers, for example, found that media issues generated the largest response of any issue they worked on, and that has continued to be the case in subsequent years on other media issues, like protecting public broadcasting and Net Neutrality. But merely collecting names on an e-petition was hardly sufficient. The key was to build a list of activists, educate them on the issues, and mobilize them effectively. It is new territory for political organizing, and media reform has been at the cutting edge.

In 2003, for example, we initially just had people bombard Congress and the FCC with e-mails protesting media consolidation. The problem was that these were easily deleted and ignored. Our opponents claimed they were auto-generated and did not reflect any significant segment of public opinion. So one morning in the summer of 2003 we learned that the House would vote that afternoon on whether to overturn one portion of the FCC's relaxation of media ownership rules. The House leadership gave as little notice as possible, but as soon as we got word, we swung into action, e-mailing hundreds of thousands of people, organized by their congressional district. We had them telephone their member of Congress in Washington to express the importance of overturning what the FCC had done. As one of the organizers of the campaign told me, "We took advantage of a window there when taking in 100 calls per office in an afternoon was still relatively new. That impact has since faded and become more common, but at that time, it was like lightning."

No one knows how many people called that afternoon, but most estimates put it at around 40,000. We blew out the phone systems in many offices. Nor does anyone know how many votes were changed as a result, but it certainly got everyone's attention. When I came to the Hill to meet with aides to discuss media issues in October 2003, I suddenly had a bunch of members sign up to meet with me. "I want to meet the guy who closed down Congress this summer," an influential southern Democrat told me. "I have never seen anything like that in my career in this town." I had just a little to do with that operation, aside from cheerleading, but I accepted the compliment on behalf of the real organizers. Before the Internet, before e-mail, such organizing would have been impossible, or impossibly expensive.

We are still at the beginning of exploring the use of the Internet for political organizing, but we have proceeded light years from the phone campaigns and e-mail petitions of 2003. In the 2006–2007 SavetheInternet.com campaign—coordinated by Free Press to fight for Net Neutrality—thousands of bloggers, MySpace, and YouTube became important vehicles for generating awareness and involvement. Not too far down the road, I suspect there will be many more adaptations to the communication revolution, and the integration of digital activism with traditional political work will become seamless. I do not wish to romanticize this work or exaggerate its effect in shifting power to the previously powerless. As the Project for Excellence in Journalism stated in 2006, these technological developments "will probably also make it easier for power to move in the dark. And the open technology that allows citizens to speak will also help special interests, posing as something else, to influence or even sometimes overwhelm what the rest of us know."[7] For present purposes, it is sufficient to note that media reform activism has been among the pioneers in effectively using the new media for grassroots political organizing.

Fifth, media reform activism has unusual politics. It is both nonpartisan *and* progressive. It is nonpartisan because the reform proposals being proffered, with few exceptions, are viewpoint-neutral, and their aim is to expand the range and quality of viewpoints. One could argue that public broadcasting is more likely to lean left if well funded; likewise one could argue that increasing the number of small local owners could possibly put a more aggressive conservatism in control of the media. But neither is a certainty. The movement's abhorrence of censorship also is a popular position. At any rate, most of the issues covered by the movement have appeal across the political spectrum. This became evident in the media ownership fight of 2003.

Perhaps the most striking development in 2003 was the number of self-described conservatives who joined a movement that was led by people who were unabashed liberals or leftists. William Safire wrote numerous columns in the *New York Times* arguing that stopping media concentration was a conservative issue.[8] The National Rifle Association and Brent Bozell's Parents Television Council both came out in opposition to the FCC's rules relaxations, even though this put them in direct conflict with the Bush administration. This conservative support has not translated into as many votes in Congress as we would have thought. The Republican Party is very much under the thumb of corporate interests, and they tend to rule the party with iron discipline. But since we needed Republican votes to win, we were delighted to have conservative support.[9]

The conservative support in 2003 made for some difficult coalition politics. At one point, we had so many conservatives opposing media concentration on the Free Press website that a friend contacted me and asked me if I had pulled a "David Horowitz" and become a right-winger. One prospective funder withdrew her support for Free Press when she saw that Republican Sen. Trent Lott of Mississippi was also opposed to relaxing media ownership rules, and that we promoted this on our site. That just about every major civil rights group in the nation was working with Free Press or some other media reform group on this issue did not seem to register. In her mind, any cooperation with Lott was a de facto endorsement of white supremacy. She has had nothing to do with media reform ever since. Likewise, Free Press lost a board member in protest of our working with Parents Television Council; Bozell had been an antagonist of the progressive organization where she was employed. (Bozell also criticized Free Press and me in a manner that was far from flattering, once terming me a "socialist sob sister.")[10] We never sacrificed our principles in working with conservatives, we never endorsed their viewpoints on other issues or their critiques of media, nor did they endorse ours. We simply focused on our common ground.

The rank-and-file Republicans and self-described conservatives tended to be far more open-minded on media reform than right-wing politicians in Washington. I have had many conversations along the lines of one in 2006 with a right-wing radio station manager in Illinois, who said to me, "Keep up the great work, Bob, of battling the big liberal media conglomerates and their efforts to use the FCC to gobble up all the radio and TV stations in this country." We have discovered that many self-described conservatives like the idea of local media ownership and content, dislike TV political advertising, despise the commercialization of our culture, are suspicious of the power of the cable and telephone giants, and even welcome public broadcasting. It was Mr. Conservative, Barry Goldwater, after all, who in 1984 decried cutting any government funding to public broadcasting because that would force PBS stations to solicit corporate support. Goldwater argued that the rise of commercialism on public broadcasting "marks the end of the only decent source of broadcasting in this country."[11] We can hope rank-and-file conservatives will be more effective in the coming years, as the Republicans balance the need to get voters with the need to fill up their campaign coffers with corporate donations.

And we have discovered that the vast majority of people, once they realize how the system actually works, dislike the idea of important media policies being made corruptly behind closed doors. But inside the Beltway, top Republicans not only serve the corporate interests with impunity; often they view control over the media as essential to promoting their political agenda. Hence, rather than actually debate specific media policy issues and try to rally rank-and-file conservatives to a pro-industry position, Republican operatives dismiss the media reform movement as simply trying to introduce a liberal bias to the media, to counterbalance their success at moving journalism to the right.[12] So far this tack has generated little traction among rank-and-file conservatives.

Media policymaking does not necessarily fall along partisan lines. It is not an issue that contrasts liberals and conservatives, left and right, as much as it is a case of moneyed interests versus everyone else. When everyone else is silent, the game belongs to the moneyed interests. And when the Democrats have been in power, they have been very much in bed with the Roths and Corleones of the world. The 1996 Telecommunications Act is a classic case in point, as this gift to the corporate community was passed with overwhelming bipartisan support. That is another reason why this is a genuinely nonpartisan issue; it depends upon grassroots pressure to keep all politicians honest. No party should be accepted as the party of media reform, and no party should be let off the hook. What has gotten the Democrats' attention, and will get the Republicans' attention, is when we generate sufficient grassroots activism that politicians know they cannot serve corporate interests without paying a price on Election Day. That moment is on the horizon.

Being nonpartisan does not mean that media reform is value-free, even if most of the policy reforms we advocate are "viewpoint neutral." It is a bedrock progressive issue, because it is all about establishing the institutional basis for effective and accountable self-government. It is a natural issue for the disenfranchised in our society because they, more than others, require a viable free press to have the information necessary to govern their lives. This was exactly how Jefferson framed the matter in 1787. Those who own and control society will always have access to such information. The truth is that there are people in our society who, rhetoric notwithstanding, hold popular rule in contempt, and who believe private property should trump democracy at all turns. They have no interest in measures that reduce inequality or challenge their prerogatives. They will never embrace media reform, for they fear it could lessen the power of business in our society. In the end, combined with the explicit corporate lobbies, these are the forces that oppose us. They are, in the correct use of the term, political reactionaries: Their position is that corporate power should reign, with no role for the public in policymaking.

Finally, the dissension we saw among conservatives in 2003 was not an aberration. It continued on other media issues and then contributed to the Republican collapse in the 2006 elections. It signifies tensions in the conservative base and the growing contradictions in the conservative philosophy. As conservatism has been the dominant political ideology for what is approaching three decades, this is an important development. It is what we might expect if we are entering a sustained critical juncture.

Allow me to develop this and put it in a personal context. I was raised in a household devoted to conservative Republicanism in Cleveland, Ohio. My father's holy trinity was Robert Taft, Barry Goldwater, and Ronald Reagan. We talked about politics all the time; it is probably where much of my passion for the subject originates. I was so hardcore that in the 1964 presidential race I repeatedly wore a shirt jammed with countless Goldwater buttons to my sixth-grade class in my overwhelmingly Democratic school. The principal received so many complaints, she banned the wearing of political buttons except on Election Day, and then we were restricted to one measly button. (If only I had been born forty years later, Rush Limbaugh and Bill O'Reilly could have made me a cause celebre.)

I cut my teeth on a strict canon of conservatism: yes to small government; yes to honest and accountable government; yes to competitive markets; yes to a government that doesn't mess with people's private lives; yes to respecting tradition; yes to balanced budgets; yes to a strict enforcement of the rule of law; yes to a strong military response to the Cold War; yes to lower taxes and regulation on business; no to labor unions. Although our family attended church every Sunday, religion never factored into the equation. In fact, one of our ministers was active in the civil rights and antiwar movements, and hardly a political soulmate to my father. I abandoned conservatism as a teenager when I saw it as far too complacent toward racism, inequality, corruption, and militarism for my tastes—I came to regard it as an ideology for self-interested rich people—but I got an education in the area second to none.

If we look at the canon today, we can see the source of the problems with the current state of conservatism in American politics. Conservatism has pretty much abandoned its principles. Honest and accountable government? Small government? Balanced budgets? Respecting individual privacy? Competitive markets? Strict enforcement of the rule of law? Who is kidding whom? All that conservatism has devolved to is a blatant defense of the interests of corporations and entrenched wealth by any means necessary. Barry Goldwater's famous line from his 1964 acceptance speech at the Republican convention has been transformed to: extremism in the defense of wealth and privilege is no vice.[13] The flip side of the coin is an endless quest for increasingly transparent and cynical efforts to manipulate voting blocs using patriotism, racism, religion, chauvinism, and so-called wedge issues.[14]

In the realm of media policy, this contemporary conservatism is a nonstarter—it almost literally has no popular support, even among Republicans outside the Beltway—and this appears to increasingly be the case in other areas as well. It was only a matter of time until corruption, arrogance, devastating wars, economic mismanagement, and fatigue would undermine the power of conservatism as a coherent philosophy for governance. That time appears to be now. In 2006, principled conservatives of the Taft-Goldwater-Reagan variety began raising hell about the unprincipled nature of the current "conservative" government. In 2007, the legendary conservative movement activist Richard

Viguerie blasted the Bush administration precisely on several of the points mentioned herein, including Bush's corrupt support for "big business."[15] Where we will go as a result is very much up in the air.

Likewise, the bottom has come out of the cup for one of the cornerstones and rallying cries of the conservative movement: the alleged left-wing bias of the mainstream U.S. news media. The generous and largely uncritical treatment of President Bush in the years following September 11, grotesquely represented in the atrocious coverage of the U.S. invasion of Iraq, revealed this to be a canard. It is still thrown as red meat to the denizens of *Hannity and Colmes* on Fox News, but now it is increasingly understood as propaganda. For the right to concede that it has effectively dictated the news cycle in the United States would undermine its organizing principle that conservatives are populists organizing to take power from the liberal bloc that controls the government and the nation. After nearly three decades in power, that shtick only works with the true believers.

2003 was capped by the first National Conference for Media Reform, which Free Press hosted in Madison, Wisconsin. To give some sense of the explosion in the movement, when we were planning for the conference in the beginning of 2003, we anticipated that maybe 200 or 300 people would brave a Midwest winter and attend. Come November we had to suspend registration as we approached the 1,700 mark. The conference was a magical event, with members of the FCC and Congress, Bill Moyers, Jesse Jackson, Studs Terkel, numerous other prominent figures and activists, dozens of journalists, and the kickoff of the "Tell Us the Truth" music tour with Billy Bragg, Tom Morello, and others. One of my favorite memories is Congressman (now Senator) Sherrod Brown of Ohio, who came for the entire three-day conference with his then fiancée Connie

Schultz, a columnist for the *Cleveland Plain Dealer*. In near total anonymity, he attended numerous sessions, sometimes sitting on the floor in crowded rooms, and took notes.

What was striking by comparison was how few of the 1,700 were academics, who had been mostly missing-in-action that year. We had only one panel with academics on it; otherwise, as far as I could tell by going through the records, no more than a dozen attended of their own accord. In Madison itself there were a few dozen communication faculty just a few blocks from the conference; but at best only one or two of them ever dropped by for a quick visit during the three days. I mentioned the conference to a few academic friends who I knew would be interested and they gave me the stock response: "If you invite me to deliver a talk, I might be able to attend, at least on the day I present." That was exactly what we wanted to avoid: having conferences so academics could lecture people on their re-search, soak up acclaim, and pad their résumés while not pay-ing any attention to anyone else. (Admittedly, that probably was the same response I gave to activist groups when I was not intimately associated with a movement. It is built into the aca-demic culture.) If you get the sense I was fairly cynical about my colleagues in academia by now, you are correct. What may have been most revealing to me was that hardly anyone at the confer-ence seemed to notice their absence.

But two developments would dramatically alter the relation-ship of communication scholars to media policymaking. First, it became apparent how necessary and important research was to media policymaking, and that it was imperative that the media reform movement generate quality research. The crucial factor that had the courts throw out the FCC's rules changes in 2004 was superb research by Mark Cooper of the Consumer Federa-tion of America that demolished the FCC's justification for relax-ing ownership caps.[16] (The credit for organizing the victorious legal case goes to Andy Schwartzman, Harold Feld, and the Me-dia Access Project.) In fact, the entire media ownership fight drew increased attention to what an irresponsible, even fraudulent, system the FCC had for generating the very research it used to justify huge decisions affecting billion-dollar industries. In 2003, under the direction of Michael Powell, it was clear the FCC wanted to have just enough research to justify changing the rules, but it had little idea what that entailed. And it had no interest in research that undermined Powell's predetermined outcome. This appeared to be the standard operating procedure for the agency.

At this point all of us in the movement grasped how important it was to have first-rate credible media research. I was humbled with the recognition that the sort of research I specialized in, historical and critical, was useful for framing but really did not address some of the pressing issues and needs. The immediate need was for traditional quantitative communication scholars, for economists, and for legal scholars. And these scholars needed to work with us so they didn't get swallowed up by baseless presuppositions. I saw the splendid results that occurred when critical minds used quantitative research methods. It was pretty obvious by now that a handful of public interest researchers could not and should not be doing this work by themselves; it was imperative to have communication scholars step to the fore. (And, eventually, the FCC should have a sufficient research staff and budget—as well as a commitment from the top down—to produce quality research, even if it goes against the interests of the corporate sector. Or if the FCC is simply incapable of doing research without internal political pressures, it should collect data and turn them over to the Government Accountability Office and independent researchers to assess.) Significant resources were devoted to all strains of communication research on college campuses. Why was it almost impossible to locate when core decisions about the future of our media system hung in the balance?

The second development was the formation of deeper linkages between communication scholars and the actual sausage-making of media policy on Capitol Hill. In 2003, Ben Scott, then an Illinois graduate student, began doing a residency in the office of Rep. Bernie Sanders of Vermont to work exclusively on media policy. There were few congressional offices working on an aggressive popular agenda for media policy at the time, and Scott was able to learn quickly and work with some of the top staffers on the Hill. As fate had it, the first week Scott showed up to work was immediately after the FCC's June 2 vote to relax media ownership rules, and the firestorm was about to descend upon Congress. Suddenly, instead of opening the mail and doing coffee runs, Scott found himself in the middle of one of the hottest grassroots political battles on Capitol Hill in years. It was a win-win situation: Sanders got a very smart and talented staffer who had a rich understanding of communication. Scott got priceless firsthand experience in the policymaking process, an understanding that was virtually nonexistent in the field itself. Other members of Congress noticed, and asked me, "Can I get a grad student like Scott to do a residency in my office?"

Even more important, friends of mine in other Ph.D. programs in communication took notice. They were aware of Scott and what he had accomplished; they were following developments in Washington closely; and they wanted the same opportunities for their best students. This could make the research in the field stronger and more relevant. This could be a boon for the field and for the nation. Universities could provide a genuine public interest research component to balance and call into question the pro-corporate vending-machine research the FCC had looked to uncritically.

During the course of 2004, the heads of communication programs at the Universities of Pennsylvania, Southern California, Michigan, and Illinois began meeting every few months to discuss putting together what Larry Gross of USC dubbed the Consortium on Media Policy Studies (COMPASS). The four programs were at the center because their heads—Gross,

Michigan's Susan Douglas, Penn's Michael Delli Carpini, and Illinois's Bruce Williams[17]—were explicitly committed to the project and had the authority to dedicate resources if need be. Heads of prospective communication Ph.D. programs at the City University of New York and University of California-Riverside also participated in the talks. At various times, faculty from Washington and Southern Illinois were included. The idea behind COMPASS was that the field of communication needed to seriously engage with the broad range of media policy issues and bring the full weight of the field to bear on the matter. The plan was for leading Ph.D. programs to work together to create a critical mass of students working in policy research such that it would become a cornerstone of the field, with journals, conferences, and academic lines. The idea was not to be proprietary, but to expand outward to include all Ph.D. programs that wished to participate. If anything, we would be evangelical. The conviction is that in a discipline where there are only a few score Ph.D. programs, a small group of dedicated people could, to paraphrase Margaret Mead, change the course of the field.

The point of COMPASS also is to make communication research relevant outside the discipline and the academy. A central aim of COMPASS in the near term is to establish a residency program for Ph.D. students from the member schools in congressional and FCC offices to work on media policy matters. Initially the plan was to set up a summer program as a first step toward year-long residencies. Our students would come from a variety of schools and meet to discuss common issues and establish relationships that could last a lifetime. Informally, Illinois sent graduate students to D.C. to do residencies in congressional offices in the summers of 2005 and 2006. The core COMPASS schools are scheduled to launch their summer residency program in the summer of 2007. Dealing with Gross, Douglas, Williams, Delli Carpini, ICA president Sonia Livingstone, and a handful of other leaders in the field, I found my cynicism waning and I became more optimistic about the prospects for the field of communication.[18]

In my view, the battle for getting the field of communication to embrace the critical juncture went beyond researchers at Ph.D. programs; it had to be all-encompassing. From my experience, I knew that there were scores, even hundreds of scholars interested in media at non-Ph.D.-granting institutions or working in other disciplines. Every bit as important, I knew there were many more graduate students who wanted to get involved but did not know how to do so. Often they felt isolated in their departments and in their field. We needed to draw them together. We also had to make it clear that there was a place for communication scholars from the full range of methodologies and interest areas. The critical juncture needed to permeate all our works in some manner; it wasn't just about explicit research that could immediately address an issue before the FCC. Hence a few of us organized an "Academic Brain Trust" (the name was meant to be tongue-in-cheek) to meet the evening before the second National Conference for Media Reform, which was organized by Free Press and met in St. Louis in May 2005. By now it was clear we could not afford a repeat of the Madison conference, where only a handful of scholars were in attendance. This movement needed an infusion of communication scholars if it was going to grow and be successful.

The organizing for the Academic Brain Trust began around ten weeks before the conference, without a budget. I simply sent out e-mails announcing an afternoon get-together to the academics in my address book and asked them to send the notice along to other faculty and grad students they thought might be interested. The Ford Foundation graciously chipped in with some stipends to support a couple of dozen grad students and assistant professors who would not be able to attend otherwise. Even with such short notice, a solid 150 academics attended the St. Louis conference. Our Academic Brain Trust session was packed. After a handful of talks, we broke up into a half dozen smaller groups based upon research interests. Scores of schools were represented, from community colleges to Ivy League research universities and everything in between. Nearly every tradition in the field was present as well. When these scholars and grad students then attended the conference for the next three days, it could not help but get their attention. There were more than 2,300 people from 49 states and all walks of life desperately interested in the issues they were studying. The convention center was packed to the rafters; the feeling was electric.

There was one note of controversy at the Academic Brain Trust session in St. Louis. Mark Cooper of the Consumer Federation of America gave one of the short talks to the assembled academics. Cooper had done more research to thwart the big media and communication firms than any single person, and even that might be an understatement. In his talk, Cooper took the opportunity to explain the importance of research to winning victories for the public interest, and to make it clear to the assembled academics that when they ventured into the realm of media policymaking, they were not in Kansas anymore. He passionately invoked another classic scene from *The Godfather II*, where Hyman Roth explains to Michael Corleone why he understood that his buddy Moe Green had been murdered. It came with the territory if you were in the underworld. "This is the business we have chosen." Cooper's point was that in the business of battling the communication corporations, researchers had to come up with whatever research would help the public interest. Cooper was not saying to distort the research, but merely to emphasize that which helps the cause and downplay findings that undermine the cause. Think like a soldier in battle rather than a scholar. *This is the business we have chosen.*

No one said anything at the time, but Cooper's comment certainly touched a raw nerve. Weren't scholars supposed to tell the whole truth as they saw it, with unimpeachable honesty, and let the chips fall where they may? Or were they supposed to be, in effect, propagandists for a good cause, and shape their scholarship to best serve the political requirements of the cause? My argument had always been and will be the former: We think that the more people know, the more likely we will get healthy policies. We need to change the culture to expose the vending-machine research and demand a commitment to integrity. Cooper had spoken from years of experience, during which he and one or two other people were constantly doing battle with the massive piles of coin-operated research paid for by the communication corporations. He understandably wanted and needed explicit research that would directly debunk the mountains of lies and distortions he stared at every day. Cooper certainly didn't want anyone to lie, but he wanted people to understand this was a real battle we were in, with enormous consequences, not a tea party at the summer house of the Marquis of Queensbury. It is a tension that no doubt will recur throughout the critical juncture.

Plans to formalize the Academic Brain Trust as an independent entity following St. Louis collapsed when the prospective funding fell through. Some of the scholars kept in touch with each other and collaborated on projects, but too much of the energy dissipated. Fortunately, the Ford Foundation funded the Social Science Research Council in this area and they began to assume the leadership reins by 2006. During the course of the year, the SSRC began giving out grants to academics for media policy research projects.

Between 2003 and 2007 the media reform movement crystallized. Activism moved far beyond the issue of media ownership during those years. In 2004 and 2005 much attention went to the Bush administration's efforts to undermine freedom of the press through a series of illegal or unethical acts: producing fake news promoting Bush administration policies that was disseminated to television stations and aired as the real thing;[19]

paying ostensibly legitimate journalists under the table to promote Bush administration policies in their work;[20] placing a "ringer" in the White House press corps to lob softball questions at the president and the press secretary;[21] putting a crony in charge of the Corporation for Public Broadcasting to harass programming seen as critical of the Bush administration, and to encourage more pro-Bush shows.[22] When the Bush administration attempted to slash funding for public broadcasting in 2005, it produced more than a million letters and petitions in protest;[23] this was arguably a greater show of support than at any time in the history of U.S. public broadcasting. As all this was going on, the Bush administration set records for the volumes of government activities it made inaccessible to citizens or journalists.[24]

Along similar lines, the cozy and incestuous nature of the relationship between corporate media and the government became even more stark. In 2004, Sinclair Broadcasting attempted to broadcast *Stolen Honor*, a blatant and factually challenged attack on Democratic presidential candidate John Kerry, as a "news documentary" shortly before Election Day. Sinclair seemed intent on manipulating public opinion while sidestepping Federal Election Commission reporting requirements. But the company was forced to adjust its program after concerted action by media reformers.[25]

But the mainstream media didn't appear to learn a lasting lesson from Sinclair's retreat. Viacom's CBS hastily shelved a *60 Minutes* report on Bush administration deceptions on Iraq—in the wake of a report on Bush's military record that had used apparently forged documents.[26] Earlier, however, Viacom's Showtime had showed no qualms about airing a hagiographical salute to President Bush's actions surrounding the events of September 11, *DC 9/11: Time of Crisis*, which had a loose connection to the factual record and made President Bush look like a cross between Winston Churchill and Abraham Lincoln.[27] Then, in September 2006, Disney's ABC Network aired *The Path to 9/11*, a "docu-drama" on the history of the "War on Terror" that included fictionalized conversations of former President Clinton and top aides, which cast the Democrats as soft on Al Qaeda. Again, despite considerable protest, the slightly edited program aired.[28] At the same time, it was revealed that AT&T had participated in the Bush administration's illegal program of spying on U.S. citizens.[29]

Many viewed these episodes as highlighting how closely the large media firms are attached to the Bush administration and the Republicans. As Viacom CEO Sumner Redstone, a lifelong Democrat, put it shortly before the 2004 elections, "from a Viacom standpoint, we believe the election of a Republican administration is better for our company."[30] And while there may be a general convergence of political views among the corporate elite and the Republican Party, this conclusion is incomplete and misleading. It is closer to the truth to say that these episodes pointed to the corrupt nature of the "you scratch my back, I'll scratch yours" relationship between politicians and the big communication companies to whom they deliver monopoly licenses in a so-called deregulated environment.

One suspects that if a Democrat were in the White House and had the ability to deliver the goods to the corporate media sector, media coverage might skew in that direction. Famed right-winger Rupert Murdoch was notorious for getting in bed with Laborite Tony Blair in Britain when it was clear he would have a good shot at taking power, and is all but putting new sheets on the mattress for Hillary Clinton, should she get elected president in 2008.[31] The real problem here is the corruption of the system, which has made a mockery of the notion of the independent free press. And it was this corruption that became more apparent and drove hundreds of thousands, perhaps millions, of Americans to media policy activism.

Even more important, a number of substantive policy issues also moved to the fore, issues that were less tinged with partisan politics. A classic struggle has emerged in Washington and across the country about what the future of the Internet should look like. The Internet began as a testament to public sector investment and ingenuity. It developed as a Pentagon project, which then was shared with research universities. The architects built the network to operate on the same common carriage assumptions that had always made the phone system an open network, a policy that is written into the Communications Act of 1934. In many respects it was a policy that created the Internet, not a magical, unalterable technology. As the Internet became a source of spectacular revenues and potential profits, principles like common carriage interfered with commercial ambitions. The largest telephone and cable companies were attempting to use their immense political muscle to effectively privatize the Internet and make it their own.

The fight over the future of the Internet took place at two distinct levels beginning in 2005. First, communities were increasingly frustrated by the lousy and/or expensive Internet access the telephone and cable monopoly companies were providing to them. These industries had effective duopoly control over nearly the entire residential and business Internet market. Indeed, over 40 percent of the nation's zip codes are either monopoly markets or have no broadband Internet service at all.[32] As a result, communities began to explore setting up their own "Community Internet" systems, usually wireless. The telephone and cable giants reacted like Hyman Roth and Michael Corleone would have if they'd discovered that municipalities had entered the gambling and prostitution trade. They immediately went to state governments across the nation, trying to keep communities from getting in the broadband business to provide low-cost broadband to all its citizens. This led to a flurry of battles at the state level. In an extraordinary and arguably unprecedented burst of popular politics concerning telecommunication, the phone and cable giants lost in virtually every state where they attempted to rig the system.[33] By 2007 they were resigned to community Internet; they shifted to a scheme where they would attempt to win the licenses from communities for themselves.

The second crucial Internet policy fight concerned Network Neutrality—or Net Neutrality for short—the formal policy that prohibited Internet Service Providers from discriminating between websites on the Internet. Net Neutrality ensures that all content, applications, and services traveling on the Internet would be treated on just, reasonable, and nondiscriminatory terms by the owners of the interconnected networks that make up the Internet. This is the much-heralded principle of end-to-end networking, a neutral transmission system with the intelligence in the network collected at the edges.

Net Neutrality has become such a defining issue for this critical juncture, and for the media reform movement, that it merits a review of the relevant history. Congress did not formally establish Network Neutrality in the 1996 Telecommunications Act. In fact, the neutrality provisions actually date back to the 1934 Communications Act, which the 1996 Act amended. What Congress did in 1996 was to establish the Internet de facto as a telecommunication service (just like telephones), and therefore it was subject to the nondiscrimination provisions from the 1934 Act. It is subject to nondiscrimination because that is one of the many common carriage regulations that apply to all telecommunications networks. If Congress had *not* wanted the Internet to be neutral, they would have explicitly defined it differently. Otherwise, Congress decided to give the new network a very light regulatory touch. The law would simply guarantee equal treatment for every online speaker—from large corporations to small businesses to citizen websites. Conceptually, Net Neutrality is the First Amendment for the Internet.

The relationship of the telecommunication and cable giants to the development of the Internet is not in doubt: It is almost nonexistent. As Rep. Edward Markey, Democrat of Massachusetts and chair of the subcommittee that oversees the Internet and telecommunication matters, put it in a 2007 speech, "AT&T

was offered, in 1966, the opportunity to build the Internet. They were offered the contract to build it. But they turned it down. Now let me ask you this: what has AT&T done since then to develop the Internet? The answer is: nothing. What has Verizon done to help invent the World Wide Web? Nothing. What did they do in order to invent the browser? Nothing. These companies did virtually nothing to develop anything that has to do with what we now know as the Internet today."[34]

What the telephone and cable companies are singularly distinguished in is lobbying; their entire business models have been built on wooing politicians and regulators for monopoly licenses and sweetheart regulations much more than serving consumers. It is the basis of their existence.[35] They hope to parlay their world-class lobbying muscle into carving out a digital gold mine in this critical juncture by eliminating Net Neutrality.

In the late 1990s the cable companies began to roll out cable modem service, and they took dead aim at Network Neutrality as a barrier to their profits.[36] They appealed unsuccessfully to the Clinton FCC to allow them to exempt the Internet access they provide from the principles of neutrality. The industry also lost an effort in the courts in 2000, which ruled that cable firms needed to be held to the same standards as the telephone companies in Internet service provision. Then, stunningly, the Bush FCC under Michael Powell agreed to another appeal by the cable companies in 2002. Lacking the authority to undo the statute, the commission simply redefined cable modem service into a different regulatory category, an "information service." By doing so, they simply removed cable broadband from any of the requirements of the Telecom Act—including its explicit prohibitions on discrimination.

Consumers and competitors immediately sued to reverse this decision. Thereafter followed three years of litigation to determine whether the FCC had the authority to make such a radical change; and whether there was merit in the idea of removing neutrality principles from the Internet. In the summer of 2005 the Supreme Court ended the debate in the *Brand X* case. The Court ruled that the FCC did indeed have the authority to make this decision. Though some of the justices strongly disagreed with the substance of the FCC's decision, they ruled that the FCC was within its power to make a bad decision and that only Congress could overrule the agency.

Almost immediately after the Supreme Court ruling, the FCC then ruled that now that cable modem would not be subject to the neutrality rules of the Act, neither would the telephone companies' DSL broadband service. As of August 2005, when the DSL order went into effect, the free market guarantees set in place by the Act no longer applied to cable modem and DSL—technologies that control 98 percent of the broadband market. With almost no coverage in the media and no participation by Congress, the FCC had fundamentally altered the foundation of the Internet. To whitewash its abrogation of the neutrality principles in the Act for cable modem and DSL, the FCC put forward a policy statement on Network Neutrality and attached it to its August 2005 DSL deregulation for a period of two years. But Net Neutrality was off the books. It would take legislation passed in Congress to reinstate it.[37]

The huge cable and phone companies are champing at the bit to set up a "fast track" on the Internet for their favored sites or those sites that give them a cut of the action. Websites that refused to pay a premium would get the slow lane, and probably oblivion. The cable and telephone companies claim they need to have this monopoly power to generate sufficient profits to build out the broadband network, but the evidence for this claim is nonexistent. Jeff Chester states that "Cable and telephone subscribers have paid for a super-fast broadband network several times over. Network Neutrality will do absolutely nothing in terms of denting returns or slowing down deployment. Look, the reason that the cable and phone companies oppose Network Neutrality is they're desperate to extend their monopoly business model from multichannel video to the broadband world."[38]

One Missouri business columnist familiar with the telecommunication beat put it this way: "The cable and telecommunications industries have undergone wave after wave of deregulation—all in the name of providing better service, more and faster access, increased choice and cheaper rates to the customer. But instead we have gotten higher rates, lower customer service, less local programming and have fallen more behind in broadband access compared with other industrialized nations. That is because deregulation has never been about any of these issues. It has always been about increasing profits."[39] As an appalled Markey put it in 2007, "And now they say they have a right to put up the toll roads, showing up as though they should own it all."[40] Or as Columbia University law professor Tim Wu described what the phone and cable companies are trying to do: "You know, companies can do two things, they can either offer more value, or they can try and extract cash from companies because they're in a position to threaten them. The first helps the economy, the second is just extortion. It's the Tony Soprano system, you know, it's like a protection racket, and it's not an economically productive activity."[41]

The battle for Network Neutrality became the great rallying cry for the media reform movement in 2006 and 2007. Free Press formed the SavetheInternet.com coalition, which ultimately included more than 800 organizations from across the political spectrum—including MoveOn.org, the Christian Coalition, the ACLU, the National Religious Broadcasters, the American Library Association, and every major consumer group in the country. Much of the business community—including big Internet companies like Google and E-Bay, but also countless electronic retailers and small businesses—supported Net Neutrality, too. But the story was too often miscast in the press as a corporate clash of the titans—Google versus AT&T, or Yahoo! versus Verizon—when the real story was the unprecedented involvement in a media policy issue from the grassroots.[42] During that period, nearly two million Americans came together to demand that the government reinstate Network Neutrality into the law. The coalition was so powerful it was able to derail the telecommunication legislation that the industry was railroading through Congress in 2006. This was no small accomplishment, as industry was estimated to have spent more than $175 million on a lobbying/PR blitz to get its desired legislation passed.

The public clamor for Net Neutrality emboldened the Democratic members of the FCC to insist that Net Neutrality be a condition for any telecommunication company mergers. They got their chance when one of their GOP colleagues recused himself due to a conflict of interest from voting on the pending union of AT&T and BellSouth. That meant there was a 2–2 split on the commission. When the colossal merger of AT&T and Bell South was approved by the FCC in the final days of 2006, it included explicit protection of Net Neutrality for twenty-four months. The language of the agreement is worth quoting at length because it so clearly exposes the company's lie that Net Neutrality can't be defined. The final agreement hammered out by the two Democratic commissioners clearly states that the biggest opponent of the free and open Internet will:

> Maintain a *neutral* network and *neutral* routing in its wireline broadband Internet access service. This commitment shall be satisfied by AT&T/BellSouth's agreement not to provide or to sell to Internet content, application, or service providers, including those affiliated with AT&T/BellSouth, any service that privileges, degrades or prioritizes any packet transmitted over AT&T/BellSouth's wireline broadband Internet access service based on its source, ownership or destination.[43]

This was a shocking win for the public interest community. As one of the main lobbyists on this issue summarized the year in Washington, "It was like a high school football team playing the Chicago Bears in Soldier Field and playing to a 0–0 tie. And then in overtime (ATT merger), our guys sack Grossman in the endzone for a safety."[44]

In 2007 the battle returned to Congress to win permanent protection for the free and open Internet. Senators Byron Dorgan, a Democrat from North Dakota, and Olympia Snowe, a Republican of Maine, reintroduced their bipartisan legislation to formally make Network Neutrality the law of the land. In the House, Ed Markey—the chamber's strongest Net Neutrality proponent—took control of the key subcommittee shaping new telecom legislation. Already, grassroots pressure has commanded the attention of most Democrats in Congress—and every major Democratic presidential candidate came out for Net Neutrality at the start of the campaign. As one Democratic consultant put it in February 2007, "if you're not for Net Neutrality, then the blogs will kick your rear."[45] Only a few years ago it would have been laughable that grassroots organizations could take on the most powerful corporate lobbies in America on a once obscure technical-sounding issue and fight to a draw in a Republican-controlled Congress. We are entering uncharted waters.

Media ownership also returned to the fore in late 2006 and 2007, as the FCC was required to revisit the ownership rules that triggered the activist firestorm in 2003. Because of the scandalous manner in which the FCC had botched the ownership review in 2003, and the popular uprising, the FCC committed to holding six formal public hearings around the nation to gauge public opinion on the matter. As in the past, these hearings—the first two of which took place in late 2006 in Los Angeles and Nashville—produced massive turnouts of nearly

1,000 people each, nearly all of whom were opposed to media concentration. For both hearings, FCC Chairman Kevin Martin did everything in his power to reduce the turnout. He gave little advance notice of the hearings, did no advertising or advance publicity, and scheduled them for daytime slots on weekdays. But his efforts were insufficient to quiet the voices of people who are appalled by the concentration of media ownership, especially at the local level.

Martin's contempt for public participation was reduced to the absurd for the third formal public hearing on media ownership held in Harrisburg, Pennsylvania, on February 23, 2007. The FCC intensified the pattern set in Los Angeles and Nashville, announcing it very quietly on February 8, and then doing no publicity for the event, which was scheduled to start at 9:00 A.M. on a Friday morning. Only after four members of the Pennsylvania congressional delegation sent a letter of protest to the FCC because the location and time was still not announced a week before the event did the FCC finally post the information on its website. No efforts had been made to publicize the event, at least to the public. Despite this hostile approach, the event drew more than 300 people. The audience was spirited and expressed a wide range of concerns about media consolidation at the local level, and the only discernible support for loosening media ownership rules came from industry representatives and local broadcasters who were being paid to attend the event. Bottom line: Media consolidation is an issue the public cares about, and that scares the bejesus out of Kevin Martin and the pro-industry cabal at the FCC.

The FCC again commissioned research to provide hard data upon which any changes could be based. Precisely as the FCC launched its new rules review in the fall of 2006, it was revealed that the FCC under former chairman Michael Powell had suppressed (and ordered destroyed) two studies it had conducted in the previous three years which concluded that media concentration had been little short of disastrous for local journalism and music. These studies had been suppressed, as far as anyone could determine, because the conclusions contradicted the Bush administration's agenda of delivering lucrative rules changes to the big media companies.[46] Apparently no research supporting the Bush agenda was ever suppressed, though how much credible research fit that description in the first place is unclear.

It was difficult to escape the notion that the Republican-led FCC under Kevin Martin would do the bare minimum necessary to make the prospective rules changes pass constitutional muster with the courts, and would ignore whatever information was received from the public hearings and the research, unless some scraps could be located to support pro-industry goals. In particular, the big media conglomerates were leaning on the FCC to see two key rules eliminated. The first—and arguably their top priority—was the long-standing ban on newspaper/broadcast cross-ownership. This was the rule that prohibited one company from owning the major daily newspaper and a TV or radio station in the same town. The other rule in their sights was the limit on the number of broadcast stations one company could own in a single market. If both rules were gutted—as the Republican majority at the FCC had voted to do in 2003—then one company could potentially own three TV stations (eventually broadcasting multiple channels), the daily newspaper, eight radio stations, and the cable company in a single community. The vision of building media "company towns" was heaven to the media moguls because they could slash their costs to the bone with one newsroom serving all and face little competitive pressure. To just about everyone else, such local monopolies would be a living hell.

Martin appeared desperate to deliver the goods to his benefactors. The way the FCC commissioned new research did not inspire confidence, nor did its seeming indifference to examining how its earlier studies had been censored and ordered destroyed.[47] The Democratic victory in the 2006 congressional

elections suggested that Martin might be unable to get his media rules changes to stick, but this only seemed to make him
throw caution to the wind. Martin acted as if he planned to use
every administrative fiat at his disposal to advance the Bush administration agenda, regardless of the positions of the two
Democrats on the five-person FCC, Congress, non–vending machine researchers, or the vast majority of the American people.

It was this type of arrogance and corruption that ignited the
media reform movement in 2003; it only produced more of the
same in 2006 and 2007. In 2007, Eric Klinenberg's *Fighting for
Air: The Battle to Control America's Media* was published. It was
the first scholarly examination of this burgeoning movement
that grasped its historical significance.[48] It will not be the last.

During the course of all these campaigns, and others I have not
mentioned, the contours of the media reform movement itself
and its relationship to other types of activism and media work
have become clearer. As already mentioned, media reform
work developed as both nonpartisan and distinctly progressive, because of its commitment to effective self-governance
and political democracy. In this sense media reform work, in its
broadest strokes, is closely related to reform work on campaign
finance, voting rights, and electoral systems reform. In combination, these can be characterized as a "democracy movement,"
and I suspect that over the course of the next decade this will
become a more familiar construct. But nearly all of the organizing work to link these movements, and to coordinate research
on their areas, remains to be done.

The media reform movement, too, has evolved to have four
distinct segments. First, there is the media policy activism typified by Free Press and the numerous other groups that focus
upon core policies and subsidies at the various levels of government. Second, there is the burgeoning realm of producing
independent and alternative media, which has exploded with

the utilization of digital communication technologies. Third, there is the work of providing criticism of the media and educating people on how media work, done by groups like Media Matters for America, the Center for Media Education, and FAIR. Efforts to promote and develop media literacy in school curricula fit in here, too. Fourth, there is the organizing done by independent media owners, creative workers, journalists, and communication workers in general to protect their position in the media system, generally through trade union or trade association activity. The interests of communication workers, local owners, and the broader population tend to overlap in important ways. In each of these four areas the specific concerns of communities of color, of women, of labor, and of the dispossessed—what is often termed the media justice movement—play a necessary role.

These four areas cannot help but compete for resources and attention at one level, so principled leaders are working to build strong alliances between the four elements of the movement to emphasize their common interests. It does not require a genius to see that they are very much intertwined and dependent upon each other's success for their own. They are the Four Musketeers, so to speak.[49] One key development in the three National Conferences for Media Reform is that they have evolved from being exclusively about media policy activism to including sessions on the other components of the movement and how they link together. And there is a key role for research in each of the four areas.

The specific realm of media policy activism, the focus of this book, is heterogeneous as well. There is a broad range of issues covered and many groups that work on some issues, but not others. The experience of Free Press provides the most compelling evidence of the movement's growth. In the four years since its creation, Free Press has grown to some thirty staff members, and is approaching 400,000 members. (As the co-founder and because of my public visibility, I often receive credit for the work of the extraordinary Free Press staff; this credit is entirely misplaced.) Free Press emphasizes policies surrounding the Internet, media ownership, government and corporate propaganda, and viable noncommercial and nonprofit media, including public broadcasting. In every campaign Free Press undertakes, it works in broad coalitions. Free Press would not have been possible without the work done by our colleagues and allies for the past twenty years, continuing through the present. We have galvanized a strong, focused movement atop the foundation that they built, and we stand on that platform together with many allies that make our work possible.[50]

The dynamism of the media reform movement was apparent at the third National Conference for Media Reform, organized by Free Press and held in Memphis on January 12–14, 2007. As in Madison and St. Louis, registration had to be suspended because of the flush of demand to attend the conference. As it was, more than 3,500 people attended from all 50 states. Speakers included luminaries like Bill Moyers, Rev. Jesse Jackson, and Jane Fonda, and members of Congress and the FCC; and there were scores of sessions featuring the broad range of media activism in the United States.[51] Although the panels focused almost exclusively upon American media and politics, numerous international participants were struck by the degree of organization in the United States on this issue. Until quite recently, it was the United States bringing up the rear in any campaigns to democratize media policymaking; we were the nation most likely to assume that a corporate-dominated commercial media system was "natural." Now we are a leader in the global media reform movement. This points up the unique historical moment we are in.

Pause for a second and consider the nature and scope of this conference. Two decades ago a conference on media policy might have been fortunate to attract maybe 75 to 100 lawyers, insiders and diehards, if anyone would have even considered the prospect of having such a conference. Even at the height of the last critical juncture, in the early 1970s, four or five hundred people at a conference on media policy would have had people singing from the mountaintops about the impending revolution. Now we have thousands and thousands there physically, and hundreds of thousands, if not millions, active otherwise. It is arguably one of the most dynamic social movements in the nation.

Most striking was the dramatic increase in attendance and participation by communication scholars. It was like pulling teeth to get communication academics to take this movement seriously and attend the first National Conference for Media Reform in Madison in 2003; but by 2007 hundreds of scholars and grad students attended of their own volition, comprising about 10 percent of the attendees. The Social Science Research Council and Free Press organized a one-day pre-conference session for scholars on January 11, and 200 faculty and grad students convened to share research across a full range of policy issues. As in St. Louis, they came from the entire range of research traditions and academic institutions, including everyone from first-year graduate students to emeritus professors. There were eight distinct policy research areas that had their own sessions, as well as skills-oriented workshops.[52] Slowly but surely an appreciation for the importance of policy research, broadly construed, was arising in the field. The momentum and excitement among the scholars were palpable.

Between 2004 and 2007, a frank and overdue conversation began among academics and activists about how they could work together to each side's satisfaction. Activists pointed out that a fundamental reason academic research is typically useless to policymakers is that it presents evidence and arguments in jargon, or at least makes no effort to make the findings accessible. In addition, academic research often self-consciously avoids making a decisive conclusion. It offers evidence from all sides and makes a case for probability; then most conclusions in academic papers are filled with qualifications and calls for further study. This is the best way to doom a study to irrelevance in Washington. Policymakers, activists emphasized, need policy recommendations. This does not require lying, skewing the evidence, or omitting critical results. It simply requires stating your conclusions with conviction. And if scholars do not do so, they can be sure the industry players in the debate most certainly will.

Academics expressed their frustrations that research coming out of academia is difficult to plug into policy for institutional reasons. The peer-reviewed journal process is too time consuming. By the time new research is published, it's too late to matter. (It is not uncommon for for there to be a gap of two years between the time an article is submitted to a journal and the time it is published.) These professors understand that to be effective, research must be timely, targeted to specific policy debates that are ongoing, written in the language of those debates, and presented to the right decision makers at the right time and by the right people. Essentially, academic research must be injected into the political process, no matter how unwelcome that is to the existing culture of the academy. That culture is going to need to be modified. Notions of public service have to play a larger role in the evaluation of faculty performance.

What is necessary now is for these developments to translate into significant roles in the communication associations like AEJMC, ICA, and NCA, and in the leading journals. These tend to be conservative institutions that move at a snail-like pace, but we do not have the luxury of time. There are promising signs. One key development in addressing some of these problems was the creation by Larry Gross and Manuel Castells of a new online journal, the *International Journal of Communication*, which will be able to get articles peer-reviewed and formally published in a matter of weeks.[53] Even more important, ICA president Sonia Livingstone in 2007 made it a high priority to foster critical debate regarding the urgent research agenda for media policy and media reform under the auspices of ICA. It is a matter near and dear to her research heart, as well as a clear re-flection of a strong and growing train of thought within ICA.[54]

By 2007, too, it has become clearer what this all means for the content of the field of communication, though I hasten to add that this will no doubt change with more experience and greater academic involvement. The point of departure is a recognition by the entire field that we are in a critical juncture. This means that the classic Lazardsfeldian split between criti-cal and administrative research is becoming moot. There is no there there to administer. Some media industries are faltering, others are in crisis, and all are being fundamentally trans-formed. The assumption that existing commercial enterprises should be granted sway to operate as they have in the past is not a default position when the old system is crumbling.[55] It re-quires, at the least, a vigorous rethinking and reconceptualiza-tion even to re-create or maintain the supposed status quo. Propositions that would have seemed implausible or fanciful just a few years ago are increasingly looking realistic as we come to grips with the communication issues around us. We are all critical scholars now, whatever our politics may be.

This is beneficial for the field because the traditional splits between quantitative-oriented researchers and qualitative-oriented researchers no longer seem severe or important. Like-wise, the war between cultural studies and political economy seems fairly inconsequential nowadays. As scholars like Toby Miller are demonstrating, there is an important place for the cul-tural studies tradition in this process.[56] In St. Louis and Mem-phis, scholars from all these traditions met and discussed mutual concerns and how their research could enhance our understand-ing of the problem and our ability to craft wise solutions. The old aphorism about academics holds true: When the stakes are low, the differences among faculty seem much greater and the fight-ing is much more intense. When the field is moving forward dy-namically, the differences are seen in a broader perspective and seem less severe or consequential. In communication, more than any other field, dynamism is linked directly to political activity outside the academy, to the relationship between the work of scholars and the concerns of citizens. In a critical juncture we either move ahead dynamically like a flowing river, or we wash up irrelevantly on the banks. That is our choice.

This does not mean there will be no conflicts or crises if the field continues in the manner I propose. There are going to be obvious differences of opinion and research will come to conflicting conclusions. There are going to be tensions balancing the needs for independent research with the political aims of organized social movements, as the Mark Cooper speech to the Academic Brain Trust in St. Louis highlighted. This has its positive aspects and its drawbacks, as I can attest from personal experience. There is little doubt that my analysis has been sharpened considerably by my involvement in the media policymaking process; it has been a boon for my research. Giving talks to all sorts of audiences, answering questions from citizens from all walks of life, getting dirt under my fingernails in the political trenches has given me a perspective on my work, on what I could do better, that has been of tremendous value. I wish all of my colleagues could go through the same experience, because I think their work would improve too.

At the same time, the benefits of engaging with the politics of the day come at a cost. I have sacrificed some of my independence, not to a corporate benefactor, but to a movement in which I am a participant. I am a firm opponent of any television advertising to children, for example, and I am also opposed to candidate political advertising on television. In my writings from the 1990s I have come out foursquare for their respective abolition. I have deep concerns about global trade deals and about what has happened to copyright laws. Likewise, I support Dean Baker's plan to allow a $100 tax credit to every American to divert funds to the nonprofit medium of their choice.[57] Prior to 2003, I invariably mentioned the Baker idea in my talks and my writings. Since working with Free

Press, I am less likely to push these issues because they are so outside the realm of the possible in Washington, and I wish to emphasize those issues where there is some possibility of being effective in the visible future. So my policy interests today are first and foremost on devising ways to encourage multiple newsrooms in communities, to enhance nonprofit media, to create local media ownership, and to maintain the Internet as an open public resource and make broadband available to all at a reasonable price.

I have allowed what I emphasize to be determined by my desire to see the media reform movement grow, and that requires that it achieve political success in the next few years. But we still need people in the academy who are independent and who are willing to push the debate beyond what is politically realistic, even under the best of circumstances. That is why when I say the field must embrace the critical juncture, it does not mean people must toe any party line, or even get off-campus and rub shoulders with nonacademics. We still need independent scholars, willing to push the boundaries of debate and unconcerned about the immediate political ramifications for a controversial position. This is particularly true today, because in a critical juncture these positions may move into the mainstream of debate in short order. Let's hope so.

The most important barrier preventing the field from embracing the critical juncture is going to be the wealth and influence of the corporate sector. University administrators look to this sector to bankroll their communication programs to the greatest extent possible and will hardly be enthusiastic toward an approach that effectively lessens that possibility. Corporate interests are eager to encourage research that supports their agenda, and similarly can be expected to be alarmed if a visible body of research emerges that undermines their arguments before policymakers. There is no way around this conflict. The good news is that there are funders—including some in communication industries—who care deeply about the public interest, and if the field does work that commands attention, much more of that money will flow in our direction. But corporate money is like a big bird in the hand to administrators, and what I am talking about seems like a small bird in the bush. At any rate, when push comes to shove, the integrity of research cannot be determined by who pays for it. That is a principle we always have to keep front and center.

As I see it, in terms of research, the field of communication needs to approach the critical juncture at three distinct levels. The first level is what I call applied research. The second level is what I call basic research, and in many ways can be regarded as an outline for research areas for media policy studies, or a revamped political economy of communication. The third level addresses everything else in communication research, the preponderance of what exists in the United States.

"Applied" research is necessary to address immediate policy issues that are being determined in the near term and midterm. This includes research surrounding media ownership, use of spectrum, media content, public broadcasting, and Internet access, for example. The list is actually quite long, and academics have played too small a role heretofore. This is the work that concerns the researchers at Free Press, Consumer Federation of America, New America Foundation, Public Knowledge, and the Future of Music Coalition, and they need all the help they can get.[58] The Telecommunications Policy Research Conference has done a much better job of bringing nonindustry scholars into the mix, and under the auspices of the Benton Foundation, a group of scholars connected to the TPRC now meets to work on creating policies to promote universal access to the Internet. But the work from the academy largely remains tepid. Regrettably, public policy schools have all but neglected communication policy research; with the notable exception of Duke University, it is simply not taught at leading public policy programs, and very few faculty have any facility with the topic. This has to change; these programs have to be brought into the orbit of communication research, and communication programs have to promote this research as well. Every major Ph.D. program eventually should have faculty in this area. Much of this research tends to be quantitative or legal, and this is often what people think of when they think of doing research for media policymaking. But it is really only the tip of the iceberg.

I have alluded to the crisis in applied research throughout this book. The need for applied research is all the more pressing because the research component at the FCC (and, by extension, Congress, since Congress relies upon the FCC for expert analysis) has been inadequate.[59] A dire picture of the way research is produced and used at the FCC was provided in a candid talk by FCC commissioner Jonathan Adelstein to a group of communication scholars in 2007. His assessment of the corruption of the research process at the FCC left even grizzled public interest veterans shell-shocked. He said:

When it comes to issues like research, I like to think of myself as a proud member of the "reality-based community," as we call it, where we deal with the complexities of the facts. . . . We consider the public interest and not just what powerful, self-interested companies tell us, when it comes to competition, or localism, or diversity. And we develop reasoned regulatory options that are based on facts and principle, not pure ideology. Now too often, on the other hand, the Commission engages in what Marty Kaplan from USC has called "faith-based decision-making," where academic and empirical research is just ignored. . . . And the only view of reality convenient to the wishes of the most powerful companies happens to be the ones that get considered in policymaking. Too often, only those elements of competition that benefit their predetermined policy positions that they want to accomplish are worthy of discussion and consideration.

Adelstein continued, referencing the 2006 scandal involving suppressed FCC research, "So when an FCC radio industry study—our own study—finds out that the largest firm in each radio metro market has, on average, 46 percent of the market advertising revenue, well, the report vanishes. When an internal FCC study finds that local TV owners provide more local news, it vanishes, too." An FCC member since 2002, Adelstein provided this explanation:

> For those who seek to justify the positions that are in their corporate or their pecuniary interests, they have the means and the incentives to distort the truth, or try to make the facts fit the viewpoints that promote their own self-interests and their own goals. And as we all know, the fact of the matter is they have vast resources, and it gives them more access already than they should have, and a greater chance than regular Americans to affect the outcome. So they've got all that already, and then they've got all this power, and they are perfectly capable and willing of buying their own think-tanks, paying off their own researchers. And when their hired guns pump out their outcome-driven reports, they hire the finest PR machines to foist their views on the world. And of course, they own the very media that spreads the word while all too often ignoring the views of real experts that really are trying to get at the facts. The result is that the process, including academic research, has been politicized.

Adelstein continued at length, imploring the scholars to develop the applied research the FCC needs to act in the public interest:

> This is the kind of movement that we're up against. And indeed, over the last 20 years, government has been starved to the point where it's unable to make policy decisions based on quality, transparent public data. . . . I think as an expert

agency we should strive to make sure that we're doing all that we can to adequately grasp the complexities of the industries that we regulate and the policies that we enforce, and that we relay a range of thoughtful ideas about these dynamics to Congress. But we're not doing that job. We no longer gather and aggregate the relevant data; we generally have either nothing to contribute to the intellectual debate; or we have to make important policy decisions on all of these fields—not just media, but wireline and wireless and broadband—based on privately funded data, or, as I said, based on faith. We don't verify allegations made by the largest companies. But we accept everything that big companies say.[60]

The second level—where most of my own research has taken place—is research that goes deeper into the structures of media and policymaking and digs further into the past and looks further into the future. It is the "basic research," so to speak, that the more specific, near-term applied research must be based upon if it is to be effective. The applied researchers in Washington tell me they are desperate for this research, so as to ground and contextualize what they are doing.

A recent example of how basic research and applied research can work together is demonstrated in the debate over media ownership. Industry generated some research by economists knowing nothing about media or journalism "proving" that there was no concentration in local markets and we were in a golden age of competition. The problem with the research, as the public interest researchers like Mark Cooper pointed out, was that it equated a weekly shopper in the suburbs with a daily newspaper. When market share was taken into consideration, the alleged diversity crumbled. Subsequently, industry researchers have pointed to bloggers as solving the problem, since everyone under the sun can pontificate online. This is where the basic research came into the picture. Drawing from journalism history and political economy, applied researchers posited that the key to the health of journalism in a community was the number of paid working journalists and the number of autonomous competing newsrooms with paid working journalists. This idea never occurred to industry researchers, and was not necessarily the first thing public interest applied researchers considered either, but they grasped its import immediately when they discussed the matter with basic researchers, who were often historians. Viewed in this manner, the local media situation in the United States is mired in a deep crisis, as the number of working journalists in community after community has plummeted. (This was a point I discussed in the conclusion of Chapter 2.)[61] This approach is leading to powerful research about the actual state of local media in the United States, which should clarify what the real policy alternatives are to address the situation.

In a way, the relationship between applied and basic research is similar to the relationship between empirical research and social theory. In his 2005 ICA presidential address, Wolfgang Donsbach highlighted the importance of this relationship for the field of communication:

> Many scholars lack the knowledge of and/or interest in societal values that could guide research. This is a problem of socialization. My point here is that empirical research without normative goals can easily become arbitrary, random, and irrelevant. Of course, norms and values cannot be submitted to empirical tests, but they are easily available in statements of human rights and the constitutions of liberal social systems. A common denominator of all endeavors in communication research could be to strive for research that has the potential to serve such general human and democratic values and norms, that is, "research in the public interest."[62]

I can think of at least eight areas of "basic research" that require extensive research from communication scholars, and I dare say most of them are getting scant attention at present.[63] These eight areas all relate loosely to media policy studies, but they go far beyond that in scope. Likewise, they relate closely to the political economy of communication in spirit, but in practice this research agenda covers much more ground than political economy of communication was ever able to traverse. Each of these eight areas calls upon several traditions and methodologies within communication:

1. A study of the policymaking process, with an emphasis upon history;
2. A detailed examination of the relationship of communication and information to the evolving global system of capitalism;
3. A critique of the market, per se, and a critique of media markets specifically;
4. A critique and study of advertising and the relationship of communication to marketing;
5. An integration of media and communication into democratic theory, with a rigorous study of journalism in this light;
6. A political economy of the Internet—looking at a myriad of issues that will determine the control and structure of the digital communication system, in particular telecommunications, spectrum, copyright, and privacy;
7. A study of different institutional structures for media enterprises and policies that have promoted different types of structures;
8. A study of global communication that takes up all these issues in a comparative and transnational sense, and that examines issues unique to the global communication system.

First, we need a much richer understanding of the policy-making process. We need a detailed empirical and possibly ethnographic examination of the policymaking process today. We have to better understand contemporary practices. We need to develop theoretical understanding of policymaking, and we need hard empirical analysis of how people influence policy-making. We also need historical case studies; as Susan Douglas argues, we need to convey the truth about our history to under-mine the argument that what exists today is "inevitable." This has been my main area of research for two decades, yet I learn something new and striking almost every time I turn around. Just recently, for example, a new book by Elizabeth Fones-Wolf chronicled the public campaign for noncommercial FM radio, something I knew next to nothing about.[64] There are huge gaps in our understanding of the history and nature of the policy-making process in the United States and globally. As I noted in Chapter 3, this is now a core component of the work in the sub-field of the political economy of communication. This work, by its nature, also borders and overlaps with research on cam-paign finance, voting systems, and governance structures in general.

Second, it is often stated that capitalism is undergoing a dra-matic transformation—most significantly, "globalization"—and that these fundamental structural changes are due in large part to developments with communication and information technologies. Often there are elaborate claims about increasing competition and innovation, with considerable effects upon productivity and economic growth. But we get far more pieties than we do hard research on these claims, and we lack detailed examinations on how the "new economy" works compared to the old one, and what the precise role of communication may be. In view of the centrality of communication to the economy, it is a travesty that scholars and policymakers are working with an understanding of the global transformation of capitalism that is based more on clichés than research. What is happening to the economy, in the final analysis, may be at the epicenter of the critical juncture. Communication scholars have an important role to play, alongside economists, in generating this research.

Third, the application of the simplistic notion of the "free market" to media needs a rigorous examination, even by political economists of communication.[65] If the second point addressed capitalism as a "macro" system, here I turn to microeconomics, or market and firm structure. Too often the "free market" has been accepted uncritically as the ideal structure for media industries, with little evidence to support the assumption. We increasingly understand that the conventional model of free market economics has severe limitations in its applicability to any real-world economic situations. Some of the most important breakthroughs in economics in the past decade (e.g., the Nobel Prize–winning research of Joseph Stiglitz) have called into question the basic assumptions of the legitimacy of "free markets" as necessarily rational, efficient, and just regulators of human activity.[66] There is important work along these lines in the work termed the "new Keynesian economics," which has questioned the assumptions and claims of neoliberalism.[67]

That concern is doubly true for media markets, which tend to be much closer to nonrivalrous public goods, rather than traditional markets where the price tends to gravitate toward the marginal cost of the product. Some excellent economic analysis of media markets has been done, but nowhere near enough.[68] We also need a much harder examination of how media corporations actually operate, rather than assume that these complex bureaucracies follow the same pattern as the owner-operator small firm of the Adam Smith era. And we need a thorough examination of the notion that media firms, due to market pressures, "give the people what they want."[69] This canard has been left unchallenged all too long, even by critical scholars. It is ironic that intellectuals have accepted this premise while the "masses," in repeated public hearings over the past four years, have suggested that they do not feel the existing market accurately reflects their values or preferences.

Fourth, we need a systematic and comprehensive examination of the crucial role advertising plays, as it is the thread that connects communication to capitalism. Advertising is a fundamental aspect of commercial media markets, and has significant influence over media content, yet the amount of research examining it is paltry by almost any standard. All indications are that this commercial carpet bombing has a considerable effect upon our culture, and one is hard-pressed to locate much on the positive side of the ledger.[70] Inger Stole's new research indicates that advertising is evolving with the times, merging with public relations, and is even becoming a presence in the world of philanthropy, with dubious social implications.[71] Even if we go to a digital communication system, there is no reason to believe that advertising and marketing will go away. Quite the contrary. We need to conduct hard research on the role, nature, and effects of commercialism in the digital media world. If the communication revolution, in the final analysis, merely provides a way for Madison Avenue to get into the DNA of our social nervous system, we may rue the day the computer was invented.[72] In particular, the commercial indoctrination of children, as documented by Juliet Schor, is largely unexamined and, as far as I can see, indefensible. Jeff Chester, too, has done yeoman's work to uncover what marketers are up to online.[73]

Fifth, as I discussed in Chapter 1, there is an enormous disconnect between political theory and communication studies, particularly journalism. Both suffer as a result. We need to integrate the two and make strong arguments about the role of communication in a self-governing society, and the sorts of institutions and values that must guide them. This theoretical inquiry must be informed by history and empirical research. There are many good reasons for this avenue of research to be pursued, but let me provide you with the most pressing one: Invariably, what occurs in a critical juncture will be reviewed by the Supreme Court, and its constitutionality will be measured. What the First Amendment means for freedom of the press is likely to be determined in the coming generation, and scholars need to start preparing for it now. There has been tremendous pressure to make the First Amendment into a piece of protective legislation for media corporations and commercial values, although the courts have not gone all the way in that direction.

Specifically, Supreme Court rulings have defended the principle that the First Amendment belongs to the public, and not media owners, on the basis that spectrum scarcity permits the government to intervene on behalf of the citizenry. This is a very thin reed to hang such an important principle on, and it is unlikely to empirically survive the digital era. Our challenge is to answer this call, working with what has been left to us by Jefferson, Madison, Black, and Stewart to generate a democratic vision of freedom of the press as a necessity for all Americans and for self-governance—not just a privilege for investors and companies that happen to have holdings in the media sector. As cases work their way through the system in the coming generation, we need to have hard empirical research as well as thoughtful treatises on the relationship of a free press to self-governance and what this means for the First Amendment. It is still to be determined. The important point is that this is not a legalistic matter to be left to the lawyers; it is the most fundamental of policies that requires the active participation of communication scholars and engaged citizens. The simplistic interpretation of the First Amendment proffered by many communication scholars at present is insufficient to the task at hand.

The next two areas of "basic" research are somewhat more substantial and require greater explanation. Sixth, we have to think broadly about the Internet and what type of digital communication world we wish to build. What we need is a political economy of the Internet. So far the best work along these lines by far has been done by a handful of legal scholars.[74] Such a political economy entails a multitude of issues. On the one hand, it requires some big picture analysis of the relationship of the Internet to global capitalism and to democratic institutions. On the other hand, it includes a handful of specific areas that all boil down to crucial policy debates that loom on the horizon. This means that telecommunication research must be more closely integrated into media studies. Convergence is obliterating the distinction.[75]

Arguably, our goal should be to have ubiquitous broadband access as a civil right for all Americans, at a nominal direct fee, much like access to water. This is not simply for political and cultural reasons, but for economic reasons as well. Already the decline of broadband speeds and penetration in the United States compared to European and Asian rivals is a factor undermining economic innovation and growth. A 2007 article in *Information Week* put the U.S. situation in context: "The United States currently ranks 12th in broadband adoption rates, significantly down from its ranking of fourth in 2001, according to the Organization for Economic Co-operation and Development, a 30-member-nation group committed to the development of democratic governments and market economies. The International Telecommunications Union lists the U.S. as 21st worldwide for broadband penetration rate in 2005. Point Topic shows the United States is in 20th place by number of households with broadband access and in 19th by individual broadband access. Those ranks have been falling, not rising, in recent quarters."

Regrettably, though not surprisingly, *Information Week* finds that the FCC has done an inadequate job collecting and interpreting the data:

And even the good news isn't that good. Some of the more positive data that has been reported is questionable, such as

figures presented in a letter written by FCC Chairman
Kevin Martin in 2005 and published in *The Wall Street Journal*, showing what seems to be tremendous growth in U.S.
broadband access. The July 2005, FCC report that he was citing, which promoted and defended the state of broadband
access in the U.S., has received pointed criticism for defining
a "high-speed" line as one delivering service of at least 200
Kbps in at least one direction, and for defining a ZIP code as
"covered" by broadband access even if just a single broadband line is active in that region. It is true that 200 Kbps was,
even in 2005, a minimal definition of "broadband," but it's a
level that's largely inadequate for delivering much of what is
commonly accepted as "broadband-level service," such as
streaming video and swift downloads of large files. It seems
clear that measuring "broadband access" by even the relatively modest speeds of 1Mbps or higher would drastically
cut the estimate of U.S. broadband penetration.[76]

What policies and structures would get us closest to the goal
of ubiquitous high-speed Internet access? We need to examine
which policies and industrial structures can deliver that outcome most efficiently and effectively. In this vein, Community
Internet is an enlightened policy, and Net Neutrality is a necessary principle. Without Net Neutrality, there is no hope for
ubiquitous high-speed broadband, because the business model
of the ISPs is built on there being a very visible and decrepit
"slow lane" to scare websites and users into paying the cable
and telephone giants more to get the fastest possible service.
Indeed, the next great battleground for Net Neutrality is probably going to be cell phones and wireless communication. "We
are about to open a new front in the Net Neutrality wars: wireless," writes Michael Calabrese of the New America Foundation. "Cellular phone and data today is a nightmare image of
what the Internet would be like without Net Neutrality—and,
as the world goes wireless, it may be the way of the future,

unless we push back."[77] Tim Wu and Milton Mueller have launched research into this area, but much more needs to be done.[78]

And we must consider whether the current domination of the Internet by the handful of telecommunication and cable firms is conducive to the desired outcomes or a hindrance. We must not assume that the telephone and cable companies are the natural stewards of the digital era; they must win that role in an open competition, in which all the viable options are considered. Their power at present has less to do with their satisfying consumers or publicly determined needs than it does with their extraordinary lobbying power over politicians and regulators, and a kept press that barely pauses to cover these issues and bring them to the public's attention. Estimates of how much it would cost to establish ubiquitous super-fast broadband in every American home and appliance vary, but one of the highest estimates I have seen by far is a one-time investment of $300 billion, with an annual expense of $30 billion. That is roughly $1,000 annually per person in the United States. This is an area that requires a great deal more attention, and close examination of policies and practices in other nations.

One of the most important policy issues for a political economy of the Internet revolves around the management of the spectrum. Here, especially, the field of communication has produced little research or analysis of value. In fact, hardly anyone has. In Chapter 3, I discussed the enormous amount of spectrum turned over to private interests at no charge. That is just the beginning of the problem. Vast sections of the spectrum—over 60 percent—are currently controlled by the government and barely used at all.[79] The military gets nearly half of this government spectrum and operates in nearly complete secrecy. All of this government spectrum allocation is outside FCC control, administered by the Commerce Department. It is under the domain of the secretive Interdepartment Radio Advisory Committee.[80] Most of the information about the spectrum assigned to federal agencies by the IRAC is classified.[81] As J.H. Snider of the New America Foundation notes, "IRAC also has more impact on FCC rulemakings than is commonly appreciated. That is because unlike business and public interest groups, IRAC can lobby the FCC with complete secrecy."[82]

It is likely that a great deal of the public airwaves set aside by IRAC lie dormant most of the time. With new technologies that permit the smart use of spectrum without interference, this policy is growing outdated, even absurd. It is the equivalent of keeping two lanes on every interstate highway unused because once every month a government truck may need to use it. Yet scholars have done virtually no work on this aspect of the spectrum, and how it may be incorporated into policies for a superior communication system. It was striking that in 2005 a number of public interest advocates (led by Snider), after much wrangling, were able to get a meeting with officials of IRAC to discuss how the spectrum is allocated to government agencies. When the public interest advocates asked IRAC how it determined the allocation of spectrum to government agencies (including those that have nothing to do with national security), they were told that this was top secret. Dumbfounded, the public interest advocates asked why. The IRAC officials conferred among themselves and conceded they did not know why, exactly. The agencies themselves determined the level of secrecy for this information, and the practice had never been challenged before. Upon further review, they noted that this was apparently the first time in memory that anyone from the public had asked IRAC to explain how it functions.[83]

The point is simple: If we have enlightened and progressive policies for the disposition of spectrum, we can dramatically enhance the quality of our media system and significantly reduce the cost of having ubiquitous broadband. With sufficient spectrum, it would be easier to replace costly wire to the home and offices—the expensive "last mile"—with effective wireless connections. The spectrum is there. We need research that understands it and policies that provide it.

A number of other research and policy issues surround the Internet. Digital communication is radically overturning most media industries. Music is already on the chopping block; terrestrial broadcasting, daily newspapers, and film are in the on-deck circle.[84] All the other media industries are in line behind them, waiting their turn. We need to rethink copyright and intellectual property laws so that creative workers can receive just compensation for their labor without letting corporations put up barbed wire all over cyberspace, destroying the public domain and handcuffing creativity. Some new and pathbreaking communication research has developed the social and political implications of copyright.[85] In many respects, the commercial media system as it has developed is a very bad fit for digital technology. Copyright has become, to some extent, a policy to protect out-of-date industries from change that would benefit everyone else, rather than a progressive policy and subsidy to promote creativity and culture. Similarly, we need to conduct research on privacy, surveillance, and data mining. How can we best protect privacy from both governments and commercial interests? We need much more sustained research that leads to coherent policy proposals.

Seventh, even if we have a ubiquitous and affordable Internet, Net Neutrality, strict privacy protection, less restrictive copyright laws, and appropriate curbs on commercialism, all will not be settled in the digital media universe. Every bit as important, we have to use our intellects, imaginations, and research skills to develop alternative models for media organizations. Perhaps the most important lesson we have learned in the past decade has been that doing good media, even in the digital era, requires resources and institutional support. The Internet does many things, but it does not wave a magic wand over media bank accounts.

To do great media requires resources and compensated labor, and as a society we are going to have to generate policies, not unlike those created by the Founders, to spawn a vibrant media in the digital era. This is true across the board, but the crisis is most striking in the case of journalism, where the Internet not only doesn't fatten the bankroll, it doesn't offer protection when powerful government or business figures come after you. And good journalism will invariably antagonize someone in power. We need research that examines the institutional structures most conducive to vibrant journalism, as well as research that clarifies what factors produce the most negative effects. If one thing is clear, simply mixing the profit motive with digital technologies does not solve the problem.

I recall a conversation I had with a prominent retired television journalist in February 2004. He told me with great enthusiasm that with the Internet all of his journalistic needs were met: He could find all the reporting he needed from around the world on his computer. He went on and on about how he now read the great newspapers of the world online every morning. He compared his blissful situation with the Dark Ages B.I. (Before Internet), when access to such a range of news media would have been pretty much impossible, even for world leaders and corporate CEOs. I asked this retired journalist what the Internet informed him on doings in Schenectady, New York. He looked at me quizzically, thinking I must be from Schenectady and probably feeling some measure of sympathy for me. But, as I explained, my point was that the Internet made existing journalism available, but it was not creating lots of new journalism, and by that I mean research and reporting, not just commenting on someone else's research and reporting. And, I told him, it was not clear how existing journalism would segue to the Internet and maintain its revenue base while commercial pressures were lowering the resources going to journalism overall. In community after community, like Schenectady, there was precious little journalism, and *Le Monde* was assigning no correspondents to cover the Schenectady School Board meeting. He conceded the point.

Allow me to put the crisis in journalism in somewhat different terms, to highlight how the conventional thinking of scholars has been so inadequate to address the current situation. As I discussed at the end of Chapter 2, over the past two decades corporate media have dramatically reduced the resources and commitment to journalism. Local journalism barely exists in many communities, while the number of foreign correspondents has dropped sharply right alongside all the ballyhoo about globalization.[86] Now imagine if the federal government had issued an edict demanding that there be a sharp reduction in international journalism, or that local newsrooms be closed or their staffs and budgets slashed. Imagine if the president had issued an order that news media concentrate upon celebrities and trivia, rather than rigorously investigate and pursue scandals and lawbreaking in the White House. Had that occurred, there would have been an outcry that would have made Watergate look like a day at the beach. It would have been second only to the Civil War as a threat to the Republic. Professors of journalism and communication would have gone on hunger strikes; hell, entire universities would have shut down in protest. Yet, when quasi-monopolistic commercial interests effectively do pretty much the same thing, and leave our society as impoverished culturally as if it had been the result of a government fiat, it passes with only minor protest in most journalism and communication programs. That response is no longer satisfactory. It has contributed to the crisis that has been foundational to the critical juncture.

In short, it is imperative that we conduct research on alternative policies and structures that can generate journalism and quality media content. Already, on the margins of the academy, people like Orville Schell, dean of the University of California-Berkeley School of Journalism, and Geneva Overholser, former editor of the *Des Moines Register* and now professor at the

University of Missouri School of Journalism, are putting their minds to this project.[87] This research is slowly entering the field of communication, as the recent book by Lance Bennett, Regina Lawrence, and Steven Livingston suggests.[88] We need to turn the trickle into a torrent. We need to consider policies to encourage local ownership, employee ownership, and/or community ownership of daily newspapers, and understand that newspapers may well be largely digital within a generation. We need to look to history and look abroad for relevant case studies and practices. What was once considered "radical" is now fair game for some of the more established members of the journalistic profession.[89] We know we are in a critical juncture when the heir to the Chandler newspaper fortune acknowledges the failure of the system that made him fabulously wealthy and calls for community ownership of newspapers in 2006.[90]

The hard truth is that the existing commercial system has lost interest in journalism, or has lost much incentive to produce it; and what it does produce tends to have serious problems, owing to commercial pressures. We need creative plans to create institutions that will produce journalism and provide resources for reporting. This research will also need to see how the Internet can transform journalism as an institution, and do so for the better.

This logic applies not only to journalism, but to the full range of cultural production. Along these lines, we can now see that the obituary for public broadcasting was premature. In the 1990s it was widely assumed that the plethora of digital channels rendered publicly subsidized media moot, because there would be an array of commercial options for every conceivable need. Now it is clear that not only is that not the case, but we have the tools to rethink public media in a revolutionary manner. It can be a pluralistic and heterogeneous sector with a variety of structures and missions. Noncommercial and nonprofit public media remain strikingly popular in those nations where the institutions have been well established, and even in the

United States, where public broadcasting has been at most a marginal institution, it has shown surprising resiliency. (Britain spends more than fifty times more per capita in public funds on the BBC than the United States does on NPR and PBS.) It is true that the *broadcasting* in "public broadcasting" may soon be obsolete, but the *public* will not. We are now in a period when we have to re-imagine the forms and structures of nonprofit and noncommercial media, developing a palette of policy options to study, debate, and consider. This is a job that must be done by communication scholars. And the vision must be broad, going far beyond what has been done in the past—and beyond journalism to broader cultural production as well. Moreover, if this work is not done and done successfully, there is every reason to believe that U.S. public broadcasting, specifically public television, will continue to decline, if not disintegrate.[91]

Finally, we need to expand all of the above research to a global basis and internationalize our research. If the premises for U.S. communication are disintegrating in a critical juncture, so must the assumptions of American scholars as we look at the world. We must work sympathetically with scholars and citizens in other lands facing situations similar to our own; they probably have more to teach us than we have to teach them.[92] This means doing hard comparative analysis of communication policies and systems in other nations. And we need to be more critical, in the intellectual sense of the term, toward the U.S. government and commercial activities abroad; if we learn nothing else from the disastrous invasion and occupation of Iraq, it is that the assumption that the United States is a benevolent force for good in the world needs to be established with evidence. A good starting point would be to regard the intentions and motives of the U.S. government and corporations with the same skepticism—that is, demand the same evidence for claims—we use in assessing the motives of other governments, especially those not on friendly terms with the U.S.

government. The double standard has never been defensible, but in a critical juncture it becomes pure propaganda.

Most important, while crucial policy decisions guiding the communication revolution are significantly national, and that is what I have emphasized herein, the global arena is growing in importance—and in an increasing number of cases, it will override national policymaking. Moreover, these issues are closely tied to how the global political economy will develop, and how nations might improve the conditions for the mass of impoverished peoples. Already the question of whether media policies should be connected to global trade agreements has emerged; if they are so subsumed, that would override national policies.[93] Currently, there are major debates globally over intellectual property and control and regulation of the Internet.[94] There are serious questions concerning advertising and the disposition of the spectrum. There are also important questions about global economic development using the new communication technologies. American communication scholars need to elevate these issues to the center of their curricula and see that they receive ample attention, with a rich context. At present, the opposite is the case—what research is being done is outside the field and tends to be largely obscure, technocratic, and bereft of much understanding of what the discipline of communication has to offer.

The third level beyond "applied" and "basic" research at which the field of communication needs to engage with policymaking and the critical juncture extends to all the other research and teaching it conducts; in other words, to the vast majority of its work. In my view, all of our work and teaching are affected by the critical juncture, because it changes the presuppositions upon which our research and teaching are based, and the context for how we think about our work and our times. Consider cultural studies, which now has an opportunity to infuse its work with a sense of political immediacy that has been absent for years. Or consider all the research conducted on media effects, or political communication, or health communication, or children and media, or even interpersonal and organizational communication; or even, ironically enough, much of the research on aspects of the Internet and new communication technologies. All of it is based on a certain notion of the existing media environment being there as a known and fixed entity. What if that media environment is radically changing so that the assumption no longer holds? More important, what if the changes can be shaped by society in a positive direction? Would that affect the research in these areas? To the extent the answer is yes, the case for embracing the critical juncture *in toto* is now complete.[95]

I am not naïve. I have already chronicled the numerous barriers that prevent the field from moving in the direction I propose. In the months before writing these words, I have had conversations with a couple of leaders in our field, people who have some interest in policy, and it is clear they still think we are living in a bygone era, and that the U.S. communication system and the field of communication in U.S. universities are doing just fine, thank you. They are oblivious to the developments of the past five years, or are straining to fit them into a 1983 or 1992 worldview. Others I speak to acknowledge the deep crisis we are in, but they persist in trying to promote worn-out solutions like enhanced professional education and corporate self-regulation. They are desperate to avoid the political implications of a critical juncture, for society and for our field. I understand; it is unnerving, even to one whose work has been expressly committed to social change. There is a side of me that would like nothing more than a quiet life of teaching, digging through the archives, hanging out with friends and family, talking about politics like it was a spectator sport, and watching basketball games on television. But that is not an option.

In my view the evidence points clearly in another direction:

The present course for the field of communication studies is a road to nowhere, or, at best, to remaining a largely irrelevant and ignored back-bencher in U.S. academic and social life. What I propose entails risk but it also opens the possibility of the field moving forward dramatically, as it did during its founding critical juncture in the 1930s and 1940s. Communication can assume a leadership position on campuses and in society, and inspire not just its own ranks, but those in the other social sciences as well. If we take advantage of this juncture, we can advance the field for generations, not merely in status but, more important, in terms of its intellectual work.

Communication may not be a wealthy and powerful field, but it is not without influence. In addition to explicit research, it can marshal its resources to help guide public awareness, understanding, and informed participation on the crucial media policy issues before us. It has the power to greatly enhance the visibility of media policy not only in the academy, but in everyday life. It can make a difference. Consider that Columbia University held a much-publicized forum on "Media Reform and Journalism" in February 2007. This was not a partisan affair; Columbia went to great lengths to see that the industry position was as well represented as that of critics. But by holding such a conference, Columbia was saying to the campus, to journalists, to the city that this is an important issue which deserves your attention. Ohio University held a similar public event in May 2007.

Imagine if every communication department and journalism school followed this lead and held similar public events in their communities, where their faculty could interact with politicians and everyday people in the community. Imagine if every communication department built these concerns into its curricula where appropriate. Imagine if journalism schools held seminars for journalists on these issues. Imagine if lecture series on campuses brought speakers to campus to discuss and debate these issues. Imagine if the radio and television stations associated with colleges and universities ran programs on media reform. Imagine if media reform was a debate topic in high schools and universities across the nation.[96] Would it make a difference? Based on our experiences over the past three years with hearings and media coverage, I can tell you it might make all the difference in the world.

I confess to ulterior motives. I am not solely interested in the field of communication per se. I think that whether this critical juncture has a progressive solution is very much in doubt and depends significantly upon the quality and quantity of public participation in core communication policy issues over the coming period. If these policies remain the province of large corporate lobbyists, the regulators and politicians they bankroll, and their PR flaks, then the digital communication universe will be a shadow of what it might be otherwise and possibly do as much damage as good. It will be their system, not ours. The chances of effective popular participation taking place will be enhanced measurably if the field of communication embraces and participates in the democratization of media policymaking. This does not mean that popular efforts to engage with media policymaking cannot be successful if academia continues its present course, only that the degree of difficulty will be much higher.

Moreover, my interest is not in media and communication systems per se. It is in participatory democracy, which I believe is the best system for generating social justice and human happiness and providing the basis for a humane and sustainable society. This is pure undistilled Jefferson. Viable media are indispensable to and unconditional for a self-governing society, as Hugo Black put it so famously in 1945. I believe that unless we have informed popular participation in media policymaking, we will be less likely to generate the media system that will best encourage participatory democracy. And, in view of the importance of media to our politics and lives, I believe that if we are unsuccessful in the realm of media, it will be a pronounced setback for progressive and humane politics in this country. In my darkest moments, I believe this could be catastrophic. The fates of media reform and social justice are closely intertwined. They will rise and fall together.

This means that for media reform to be successful, in the final analysis, it will take more than the participation of academics. It will require a broad "politicization" of society and a massive increase in popular politics, as happened in the 1960s, the 1930s, and other reform eras in American history. I don't believe this is impossible. As Bill Moyers writes, it is not about "changing people" as much as it is about "reaching people." It is not about having people reject their nation and its history; it entails understanding our actual history and the tension in our nation's history between competing values.[97] The grounds to encourage such a process—deepening corruption, growing inequality, reckless militarism, personal insecurity and unhappiness—are in place. The extent to which we see such an upsurge in the coming decade or two is the great unanswered question. A lot is riding on it.

I can certainly understand why many communication scholars and even some nonacademics who have gotten this far might be reluctant to change course. The conventional signals we all get tend to encourage us to play it safe, take care of number one, and don't make waves. What I am proposing may be rational, even tantalizing, but it isn't safe. Shortly before his death, the sociologist Pierre Bourdieu considered this dilemma and argued that what we need today is to rekindle reasoned utopianism—the notion that it is the right of the world's people to use their imaginations to construct the media, the economy, and the world to suit their democratically determined needs. In this enterprise, there is a necessary role for intellectuals and scholars. (Bourdieu noted in the same address that the necessary starting point for citizen activism was with regard to media reform, and creating vibrant, noncommercial institutions.)[98]

In a critical juncture, what Bourdieu proposes is less utopian and more plausible because conventional wisdom doesn't hold. We have more control over our destiny now than we usually do, and there is a crying need for what we communication scholars have to offer our fellow citizens. In the final analysis, each scholar, just like every citizen, has to take a long, hard look in the mirror and consider the following: If we act as if social change for the better is impossible, we guarantee it will be impossible. That is the long-standing human dilemma, except that in critical junctures our powers increase and the odds can swing dramatically in democracy's favor. We hold immense power in our hands. Let's not blow this opportunity. Let's have a real communication revolution.

Notes

Introduction

1. In addition to my work on the history and political economy of the media, I have written several essays over the past fifteen years criticizing communication research, and at least seven or eight of them have been published in journals. See, for example, Robert W. McChesney, "Critical Communication Research at the Crossroads." In *Journal of Communication*, special double issue, "The Future of the Field," Vol. 43, No. 4 (Autumn 1993): pp. 98–104; Robert W. McChesney, "Radical Scholarship in the Academy: The View from Communications," *Monthly Review*, Vol. 45, No. 8 (January 1994): pp. 27–35; Robert W. McChesney, "Is There Any Hope for Cultural Studies?" *Monthly Review*, Vol. 47, No. 10 (March 1996): Review of the Month, pp. 1–18; Robert W. McChesney, "Communication for the Hell of It: The Triviality of U.S. Broadcasting History," *Journal of Broadcasting and Electronic Media*, Vol. 40, No. 4 (Fall 1996): pp. 540–52; Robert W. McChesney, "Whither Communication?" *Journal of Broadcasting and Electronic Media*, Vol. 41 (1997): pp. 566–72; Robert W. McChesney, "The Political Economy of Communication and the Future of the Field," *Media, Culture & Society*, Vol. 22 (2000): pp. 109–16; Robert W. McChesney, "Radio and the Responsibility of Radio Scholars," *Journal of Radio Studies*, Vol. 8, No. 2 (Winter 2001): pp. v–viii; Robert W. McChesney, "AE-JMC and the Quality of Communication Research," *QS News*

(Spring 1994): pp. 6, 8. See also: Jean Folkerts, "JQ Editor Responds to McChesney Criticism," *QS News* (Summer 1994): pp. 1–2.

This criticism has been a subplot in several of my other articles. It seems fair to say that this has been a minor preoccupation of mine. The tenor of some of the pieces has had, to my regret, a trace of arrogance. An unsympathetic interpretation of my basic argument could be summed up like this: "A lot of you guys are doing crap and you should be doing great work like me and my friends." I was never especially happy with some of those essays, though I imagine they have historical value, because they were more about chest-pounding and my expressions of frustration than they were about providing the basis for constructive change. This current argument is fundamentally different. It is not about which tradition, which approach, which methodology is best, because there is a necessary role for all of us in a critical juncture. It is not an argument about which political philosophy is superior or more important, because all political viewpoints need an effective hearing if a critical juncture is to reach the best possible outcome. The old fights now look irrelevant. This is truly an opportunity that can unite the study of communication in a manner that was unthinkable only a few years ago. It is an opportunity we cannot let pass.

2. For the sake of students, primarily, I will provide detailed notes of core readings for some of the authors and topics I discuss in the text, especially in Chapters 2 and 3. (I am putting this in a footnote rather than the preface itself because my publisher says that only academics read footnotes, and I don't want to scare away any readers from the general public.)

3. Let me be clear: This book is in no way a history of the field in the United States and it is anything but comprehensive. There are numerous important scholars and schools of thought I will not mention—indeed, the overwhelming preponderance of the field—because they do not fit into the train of my specific argument, not because they are unimportant or inconsequential.

4. Some friends suggested I call the book "Bob's Book of Lists." You will see why soon enough.

1: Crisis in Communication, Crisis for Society

1. I will use the terms "communication" and "media studies" interchangeably in this book to refer to the study of media and

communication at colleges and universities, both in the United States and worldwide. Such research is conducted under other departmental names as well. I understand that the term "communication" has many uses in this book, and I endeavor to be clear in its usage. At times I will use the term "communication studies" to make clear that I refer to the academic study of communication.

2. Nicholas Garnham, "Toward a Theory of Cultural Materialism," *Journal Of Communication*, Vol. 33, No. 3 (Summer 1983): p. 314.

3. Dave Berkman, "Living a Professional Lie," *Shepherd Express Metro*, April 6, 2000. Available at http:#www.shepherd-express.com/shepherd/21/15/cover_story.html.

4. The article approvingly cites the seminal article by Philip Wander and Steven Jenkins, "Rhetoric, Society, and the Critical Response," *Quarterly Journal of Speech*, Vol. 58 (December 1972): pp. 441–50.

5. Raymie E. McKerrow, "Scholarship, Influence, and the Intellectual Community," *Spectra*, April 2000, p. 4.

6. Wolfgang Donsbach, "The Identity of Communication Research," *Journal of Communication*, Vol. 56 (2006): pp. 437–48.

7. The political right has used and understood media as a political weapon more astutely than liberals or the left. See, for example, Richard A. Viguerie and David Franke, *America's Right Turn: How Conservatives Used New and Alternative Media to Take Power* (Chicago: Bonus Books, 2004).

8. See Ruth Berins Collier and David Collier, *Shaping the Political Arena: Critical Junctures, the Labor Movement, and Regime Dynamics in Latin America* (South Bend, IN: Notre Dame University Press, 2002; first published by Princeton University Press in 1991).

9. This was an obsession of James Madison, and likewise explains his obsession with having a viable independent press that would keep the government from becoming an empire. I return to this point in Chapter 3. One scholar who has drawn the connection between U.S. empire and domestic crisis that resonates well with a critical juncture analysis is Chalmers Johnson. See Chalmers Johnson, *Nemesis: The Last Days of the American Republic* (New York: Metropolitan Books, 2007).

10. http://www.thebulletin.org/.

11. Michel Crozier, Samuel P. Huntington, and Joji Watanuki, *The Crisis of Democracy: Report on the Governability of Democracies to the Trilateral Commission* (New York: New York University Press, 1975); an excellent discussion of this point can be found in Noam

Chomsky, *Necessary Illusions: Thought Control in Democratic Societies* (Boston: South End Press, 1989), pp. 2–5.

12. Friedman was a political theorist as much as an economist. His work is mandatory reading. See, in particular, Milton Friedman, *Capitalism and Freedom* (Chicago: University of Chicago Press, 1962). Chapters 1 and 2 lay out the premises of neoliberalism and its implications for notions of democracy as well as anything I have read.

13. Herbert J. Gans, *Democracy and the News* (New York: Oxford University Press, 2004); Herbert J. Gans, *Deciding What's News: A Study of* CBS Evening News, NBC Nightly News, Newsweek *and* Time (London: Constable and Company, 1980); Herbert J. Gans, *The Uses of Television and Their Educational Implications: Preliminary Findings from a Survey of Adult and Adolescent New York Television Viewers* (New York: Center for Urban Education, 1968); William A. Gamson, *What's News: A Game Simulation of TV News: A Coordinator's Manual* (London: Collier Macmillan, 1984); David Croteau and William Hoynes, *Media/Society: Industries, Images, and Audiences* (Thousand Oaks, CA: Pine Forge Press, 1999); David Croteau and William Hoynes, *The Business of Media: Corporate Media and the Public Interest* (2nd ed.) (Thousand Oaks, CA: Pine Forge Press, 2005); David Croteau and William Hoynes, *By Invitation Only: How the Media Limit Political Debate* (Monroe, ME: Common Courage Press, 1994); William Hoynes, *Are You on the* Nightline *Guest List? An Analysis of 40 Months of* Nightline *Programming* (New York: Fairness and Accuracy in Reporting, 1989).

14. Robert Darnton, annual address of the president of the American Historical Association, delivered in Chicago, January 5, 2000. From the *American Historical Review*, Vol. 105, No. 1, http://www.historians.org/info/AHA_History/rdarnton.htm. See also: Robert Darnton, "An Early Information Society: News and the Media in Eighteenth-Century Paris," *American Historical Review*, Vol. 105, No. 1 (February 2000): pp. 1–35.

15. See, for example, Robert A. Dahl, *On Political Equality* (New Haven, CT: Yale University Press, 2006); Ronald Dworkin, *Is Democracy Possible Here?* (Princeton, NJ: Princeton University Press, 2006); Amy Guttmann and Dennis Thompson, *Democracy and Disagreement* (Cambridge, MA: Belknap Press, 1996); Iris Marion Young, *Inclusion and Democracy* (New York: Oxford University Press, 2000); Ronald Dworkin, *Freedom's Law* (Cambridge, MA: Harvard University Press, 1996); Ronald Dworkin, *Sovereign Virtue*

(Cambridge, MA: Harvard University Press, 2000); John Rawls, *The Law of Peoples* (Cambridge, MA: Harvard University Press, 1999); Arthur Lupia and Mathew D. McCubbins, *The Democratic Dilemma: Can Citizens Learn What They Need to Know?* (Cambridge, England: Cambridge University Press, 1998). One of the very few works in political philosophy that considers what the best manner to structure the media system would be for a democracy is Michael W. Howard, *Self-Management and the Crisis of Socialism* (Lanham, MD: Rowman & Littlefield, 2000).

16. See, for example, Robert D. Putnam, *Bowling Alone: The Collapse and Revival of American Community* (New York: Simon & Schuster, 2000); Derek Bok, *The Trouble with Government* (Cambridge, MA: Harvard University Press, 2001).

17. See, for some recent examples, C. John Sommerville, *How the News Makes Us Dumb: The Death of Wisdom in an Information Society* (Downers Grove, IL: InterVarsity Press, 1999); Carla Brooks Johnston, *Screened Out: How the Media Control Us and What We Can Do About It* (Armonk, NY: M.E. Sharpe, 2000); Andrei Cherny, *The Next Deal: The Future of Public Life in the Information Age* (New York: Basic Books, 2000); Morris Berman, *The Twilight of American Culture* (New York: Norton, 2000); Ed Shane, *Disconnected America: The Consequences of Mass Media in a Narcissistic World* (Armonk, NY: M.E. Sharpe, 2001); Jeffrey Scheuer, *The Sound Bite Society: Television and the American Mind* (New York: Four Walls, Eight Windows, 1999).

18. When I first arrived in Madison in 1988, I recall having dinner at the home of a senior colleague from the School of Journalism and Mass Communication. Also invited was a professor in the distinguished Department of Sociology and her husband. During the course of the evening my colleague and the sociology professor got into an argument over a matter concerning media. I cannot even remember the substance of the dispute. What I do recall, very clearly, is what happened the next day when I ran into the husband of the sociology professor. "Can you believe the nerve of your colleague?" he said to me. "He thinks someone from journalism knows more than a professor in sociology? Incredible." I learned the husband had a reputation for shooting from the hip, but I sensed he merely said out loud what was possibly beneath the surface.

19. Wolfgang Donsbach, "The Identity of Communication Research," *Journal of Communication*, Vol. 56 (2006): pp. 437–48.

20. Discussed splendidly in James Carey, "A Plea for the University Tradition," *Journalism Quarterly*, Vol. 55 (1978): pp. 846–55.

21. John Michael, *Anxious Intellects: Academic Professionals, Public Intellectuals, and Enlightenment Values* (Durham, NC: Duke University Press, 2000).

22. Cited in: Greg Philo and David Miller, eds., *Market Killing: What the Free Market Does and What Social Scientists Can Do About It* (Harlow, England: Longman, 2001), p. xiv.

23. Carol Posgrove, *Divided Minds: Intellectuals and the Civil Rights Movement* (New York: Norton, 2001).

24. See, for example: Jennifer Washburn, *University, Inc.: The Corruption of Higher Education* (New York: Basic Books, 2005); Derek Bok, *Universities in the Marketplace: The Commercialization of Higher Education* (Princeton, NJ: Princeton University Press, 2003).

25. Christopher Lasch, *Revolt of the Elites* (New York: Norton, 1995).

26. Quoted in Neil Tudiver, *Universities for Sale* (Toronto: James Lorimar, 1999), p. 155.

27. For a good discussion of this point, see Dan Schiller, *How to Think About Information* (Urbana: University of Illinois Press, 2007). For a provocative book on information theory, see Charles Seife, *Decoding the Universe* (New York: Viking, 2006).

28. Jeff Chester, *Digital Destiny: New Media and the Future of Democracy* (New York: The New Press, 2007), p. 84.

29. I make no attempt to present a comprehensive or even quasi-comprehensive history of the field. Two books I recommend to get a general sense of the field's origins and history are: Everett M. Rogers, *A History of Communication Study: A Biographical Approach* (New York: Free Press, 1994); John Durham Peters and Peter Simonson, eds., *Mass Communication and American Social Thought: Key Texts, 1919–1968* (Lanham, MD: Rowman & Littlefield, 2004).

30. See, for example, Edward Bellamy, *Looking Backward: 2000–1887* (New York: Signet Classic, 2000).

31. See Robert W. McChesney and Ben Scott, eds., *Our Unfree Press: 100 Years of Radical Media Criticism* (New York: The New Press, 2004); see also: Elliott Shore, *Talkin' Socialism: J.A. Wayland and the Radical Press* (Lawrence: University Press of Kansas, 1988).

32. Duane C.S. Stoltzfus, *Freedom from Advertising: E.W. Scripps's Chicago Experiment* (Urbana: University of Illinois Press, 2007); Pulitzer reference in Ben H. Badgikian, *The Media Monopoly* (Boston: Beacon Press, 1983), p. 46.

33. Upton Sinclair, *The Brass Check: A Study of American Journalism* (Pasadena, CA, self-published by the author, 1920). A new

edition was issued by the University of Illinois Press in 2002, with an introduction by Robert W. McChesney and Ben Scott.

34. Robert M. La Follette, *The Political Philosophy of Robert M. La Follette*, compiled by Ellen Torelle (Madison, WI: Robert M. La Follete Co., 1920).

35. Inger L. Stole, *Advertising on Trial: The Consumer Movement and Corporate Public Relations in the 1930s* (Urbana: University of Illinois Press, 2006).

36. See Robert W. McChesney, *Telecommunications, Mass Media, and Democracy: The Battle for the Control of U.S. Broadcasting, 1928–1935* (New York: Oxford University Press, 1993).

37. William Allen White, "Don't Indulge in Name-Calling with Press Critics," *Editor & Publisher*, April 22, 1939, p. 14.

38. John Dewey, *The Public and Its Problems* (New York: H. Holt and Company, 1927); Walter Lippmann, *Public Opinion* (New York: Macmillan, 1922).

39. Dan Schiller, *Theorizing Communication: A History* (New York: Oxford University Press, 1996), ch. 2; for a sense of the intellectual tenor of the times, see Robert S. Lynd, *Knowledge for What? The Place of Social Science in American Culture* (Princeton, NJ: Princeton University Press, 1939).

40. Harold D. Lasswell, *Propaganda, Encyclopedia of the Social Sciences*, Vol. 12 (1934): pp. 521–27; Harold D. Lasswell, *Propaganda Technique in World War I* (Cambridge, MA: MIT Press, 1971).

41. Paul F. Lazarsfeld, "Administrative and Critical Communications Research." In Paul F. Lazarsfeld, ed., *Qualitative Analysis. Historical and Critical Essays* (Boston: Allyn and Bacon, 1972), pp. 155–67.

42. See Steven H. Chaffee, "George Gallup and Ralph Nafziger: Pioneers of Audience Research," *Mass Communication & Society*, Vol. 3, Nos. 2 and 3 (Spring and Summer 2000): pp. 317–27.

43. Robert Leigh, ed., *A Free and Responsible Press* (Chicago: University of Chicago Press, 1947); William Ernest Hocking, *Freedom of the Press: A Framework of Principle* (Chicago: University of Chicago Press, 1947).

44. See Christopher Simpson, *The Science of Coercion* (New York: Oxford University Press, 1994); Timothy Glander, *Origins of Mass Communications Research During the American Cold War* (Mahwah, NJ: Lawrence Erlbaum Associates, 2000).

45. See Robert W. McChesney, "Springtime for Goebbels," *Z Magazine*, December 1997, pp. 16–18.

46. This is the point Christopher Simpson makes in his book. Simpson, *The Science of Coercion*.

47. Considerable historical research has recast the 1940s as a pivotal decade in recent U.S. history, where progressive political forces were far stronger than much of the conventional thinking had presumed. See, for example, George Lipsitz, *Rainbow at Midnight* (Urbana: University of Illinois Press, 1994).

48. C. Wright Mills, *The Sociological Imagination* (New York: Oxford University Press, 1959).

49. See, for example: Michael E. Kinsley, *Outer Space and Inner Sanctums: Government, Business, and Satellite Communication* (New York: John Wiley & Sons, 1976); Dallas Smythe, *Counterclockwise: Perspectives on Communication*, edited by Thomas Guback (Boulder, CO: Westview, 1994), ch. 10; Charles Tate, ed., *Cable Television in the Cities* (Washington, DC: The Urban Institute, 1971); Ralph Lee Smith, *The Wired Nation: Cable TV: The Electronic Communications Highway* (New York: Harper & Row, 1972); Nancy Jeruale, with Richard M. Neustadt and Nicholas P. Miller, eds., *CTIC Cablebooks, Volume 2: A Guide for Local Policy* (Arlington, VA: The Cable Television Information Center, 1982); Brenda Maddox, *Beyond Babel: New Direction in Communications* (Boston: Beacon Press, 1972).

50. See, for example: David Armstrong, *A Trumpet to Arms: Alternative Media in America* (Los Angeles: J.P. Tarcher; Boston: distributed by Houghton Mifflin, 1981); Abe Peck, *Uncovering the Sixties: The Life and Times of the Underground Press.* (New York: Pantheon, 1985); Robert J. Glessing, *The Underground Press in America* (Bloomington: Indiana University Press, 1970); Laura Kessler, *The Dissident Press: Alternative Journalism in American History* (Beverly Hills, CA: Sage Publications, 1984); Margaret Blanchard, *Revolutionary Sparks: Freedom of Expression in Modern America* (New York: Oxford University Press, 1992), pp. 351–54; Bob Ostertag, *People's Movements, People's Press: The Journalism of Social Justice Movements* (Boston: Beacon Press, 2006); Robert J. Glessing, *The Underground Press in America* (Bloomington: Indiana University Press, 1970).

51. In National Advisory Commission on Civil Disorders, *Report of the National Advisory Commission on Civil Disorders* (Kerner report) (Washington, DC, 1968), http://historymatters.gmu.edu/d/6553.

52. It is also known as the New World Information and Communication Order (NWICO).

53. See, for example: Michael P. McCauley, *NPR: The Trials and Triumphs of National Public Radio* (New York: Columbia University

Press, 2005); Jack W. Mitchell, *Listener Supported: The Culture and the History of Public Radio* (Westport, CT: Praeger, 2005); Glenda R. Balas, *Recovering a Public Vision for Public Television* (Lanham, MD: Rowman & Littlefield, 2003); Michael P. McCauley, Eric E. Peterson, B. Lee Artz, and Dee Dee Halleck, eds., *Public Broadcasting and the Public Interest* (Armonk, NY: M.E. Sharpe, 2002); John Witherspoon and Roselle Kovitz, *A History of Public Broadcasting* (Washington, DC: Current, 2000); Tom McCourt, *Conflicting Communication Interests in America: The Case of National Public Radio* (Westport, CT: Praeger, 1999); Ralph Engelman, *Public Radio and Television in America: A Political History* (Thousand Oaks, CA: Sage Publications, 1996); James Day, *The Vanishing Vision: The Inside Story of Public Television* (Berkeley: University of California Press, 1995); Jim Robertson, *Televisionaries: In Their Own Words, Public Television's Founders Tell How It All Began* (Charlotte Harbor, FL: Tabby House Books, 1993); Michael Tracey, *The Decline and Fall of Public Service Broadcasting* (Oxford: Oxford University Press, 1998); John Macy Jr., *To Irrigate a Wasteland: The Struggle to Shape a Public Television System in the United States* (Berkeley: University of California Press, 1974).

54. Opinion located on line at http://www.epic.org/free_speech/red_lion.html. The opinion also includes a reference to a related opinion from 1964: "Speech concerning public affairs is more than self-expression; it is the essence of self-government." *Garrison v. Louisiana*, 379 U.S. 64, 74–75 (1964).

2: The Rise and Fall of the Political Economy of Communication

1. See Christian Appy, *Working-Class War: American Combat Soldiers and Vietnam* (Chapel Hill: University of North Carolina Press, 1993).

2. See, for example: Robert L. Allen, *Black Awakening in Capitalist America: An Analytic History* (Garden City, NY: Doubleday & Co., 1969); Floyd B. Barbour, ed., *The Black Power Revolt: A Collection of Essays* (Boston: P. Sargent, 1968); Stokely Carmichael and Charles V. Hamilton, *Black Power: The Politics of Liberation in America* (New York: Vintage Books, 1992); Peniel E. Joseph, *Waiting 'Til the Midnight Hour: A Narrative History of Black Power in America* (New York: Henry Holt and Co., 2006); Judson Jeffries, ed., *Black Power in the Belly of the Beast* (Urbana: University of Illinois, 2006);

Jeffrey Ogbar and Ogbonna Green, *Black Power: Radical Politics and African American Identity* (Baltimore, MD: Johns Hopkins University Press, 2004); James Edward Smethurst, *The Black Arts Movement: Literary Nationalism in the 1960s and 1970s* (Chapel Hill: University of North Carolina Press, 2005).

3. For an influential book from that period, see Juliet Mitchell, *Woman's Estate* (London: Penguin Books, 1971); for a recent assessment, see Ruth Rosen, *The World Split Open: How the Modern Women's Movement Changed America* (New York: Viking, 2000). A superb collection of texts from the 1970s is: Roslyn Baxandall and Linda Gordon, eds., *Dear Sisters: Dispatches from the Women's Liberation Movement* (New York: Basic Books, 2000).

4. A book I wish every American would read that deals with the implications of the U.S. policies in Latin America is John Dinges, *The Condor Years: How Pinochet and His Allies Brought Terrorism to Three Continents* (New York: The New Press, 2004); a powerful book on the Allende experience I had difficulty reading without being reduced to tears is Marc Cooper, *Pinochet and Me: A Chilean Anti-Memoir* (London: Verso, 2001).

5. A valuable analysis of the critical communication tradition in the United States can be found in: Hanno Hardt, *Critical Communication Studies: Communication, History and Theory in America* (London: Routledge, 1992). For a look at the development of the field from a mainstream perspective, see Wilbur Schramm, *The Beginnings of Communication Study in America*, edited by Steven H. Chafee and Everett M. Rogers (Thousand Oaks, CA: Sage Publications, 1997).

6. Karl Marx, "Letter to Arnold Ruge, September 1843." In Robert Tucker, ed., *The Marx Engels Reader* (2nd ed.) (New York: Norton, 1978), p. 13.

7. Edward S. Herman and Robert W. McChesney, *The Global Media: The New Missionaries of Global Capitalism* (London: Cassell, 1997).

8. An eye-opening book in this regard is former *New York Times* reporter Stephen Kinzer's *Overthrow: America's Century of Regime Change from Hawaii to Iraq* (New York: Times Books, 2006). In the interview with Kinzer for my radio program, he went on at some length about what happened when Che Guevara met Fidel Castro while Castro was in exile in Mexico in the 1950s. This was shortly after Guevara had left Guatemala, where the United States had just overthrown the democratic Arbenz government in 1954, again leading to a bloody regime. Che convinced Castro that it would be

impossible for the Cuban revolution to survive U.S. efforts to destroy a government not under the U.S. thumb and serving U.S. capitalist interests, if post-revolutionary Cuba was an open society.

9. Antonio Gramsci, *Selections from the Prison Notebooks of Antonio Gramsci*, edited and translated by Quintin Hoare and Geoffrey Nowell Smith (New York: International Publishers, 1971); Louis Althusser and Étienne Balibar, *Reading Capital*, translated from the French by Ben Brewster (New York: Pantheon Books,1970); Louis Althusser, *Lenin and Philosophy, and Other Essays*, translated from the French by Ben Brewster (London: New Left Books,1971); Louis Althusser, *For Marx*, translated from the French by Ben Brewster (London: Allen Lane, 1969).

10. Here are some of the main works: Theodor Adorno, *Negative Dialectics*, translated by E.B. Ashton (New York: Seabury Press, 1973); Theodor Adorno, *Aesthetic Theory* (London: Routledge and Kegan Paul, 1984); Theodor Adorno, *The Culture Industry: Selected Essays on Mass Culture*, edited with an introduction by J.M. Bernstein (London: Routledge, 1991); Max Horkheimer and Theodor W. Adorno, *Dialectic of Enlightenment*, translated by John Cumming (New York: Herder and Herder, 1972); Herbert Marcuse, *Reason and Revolution: Hegel and the Rise of Social Theory* (New York: Oxford University Press, 1941); Herbert Marcuse, *Eros and Civilization: A Philosophical Inquiry into Freud* (Boston: Beacon Press, 1955); Herbert Marcuse, *Soviet Marxism: A Critical Analysis* (New York: Columbia University Press, 1958); Herbert Marcuse, *One Dimensional Man: Studies in the Ideology of Advanced Industrial Society* (Boston: Beacon Press, 1964); Herbert Marcuse, *Negations: Essays in Critical Theory*, with translations from the German by Jeremy J. Shapiro (London: Allen Lane, 1968); Herbert Marcuse, *An Essay on Liberation* (Boston, Beacon Press, 1969); Herbert Marcuse, *Counterrevolution and Revolt* (Boston: Beacon Press, 1972); Herbert Marcuse, *Studies in Critical Philosophy*, translated by Joris De Bres (Boston: Beacon Press, 1973); Herbert Marcuse, *The Aesthetic Dimension: Toward a Critique of Marxist Aesthetics* (Boston: Beacon Press, 1978).

11. Arguably Williams's three most influential works for critical communication scholars were: Raymond Williams, *Culture and Society, 1780–1950* (London: Chatto & Windus, 1958); Raymond Williams, *The Long Revolution* (New York: Columbia University Press, 1961); Raymond Williams, *Marxism and Literature* (Oxford: Oxford University Press, 1977). As for the Mattelart influence, see: Armand Mattelart, *Communication and Class Struggle: An Anthology*

in 2 Volumes, edited by Armand Mattelart and Seth Siegelaub (New York: International General, 1979); Ariel Dorfman and Armand Mattelart, *How to Read Donald Duck: Imperialist Ideology in the Disney Comic*, translation and introduction by David Kunzle (New York: International General, 1975); Armand Mattelart, *Transnationals and the Third World: The Struggle for Culture* (S. Hadley, MA: Bergin & Garvey, 1983); Armand Mattelart, *Mass Media, Ideologies, and the Revolutionary Movement*, translated by Malcolm Coad (Atlantic Highlands, NJ: Humanities, 1980).

12. For a splendid discussion of the significance of Marxism for critical communication, see James Curran, "The New Revisionism in Mass Communication Research: A Reappraisal," *European Journal of Communication*, Vol. 5 (1990): pp. 135–64, especially pp. 136–37.

13. For a stronger position than I would take on the matter, but one to which I am sympathetic, see Gabriel Kolko, *After Socialism: Reconstructing Critical Social Thought* (New York: Routledge, 2006).

14. Edward S. Herman, "The Reopening of Marx's System," *New Politics*, Vol. VI, No. 4 (New Series) (Winter 1998): pp. 131–35.

15. The classic letter is Engels to J. Bloch, September 21, 1890; that and other correspondence can be found in K. Marx, F. Engels, and V. Lenin, *On Historical Materialism* (Moscow: Progress Publishers, 1972), pp. 290–308.

16. As a middle-class kid from the suburbs, my first serious questioning of the nature of capitalism was based on environmental concerns. After getting my driver's license in 1969, I recall driving all over Cleveland and the surrounding countryside in my parents' car. I saw the combination of the rapid conversion of lovely countryside and farmland into new suburbs alongside the continued deterioration of once magnificent residential neighborhoods in the city itself. I thought that this was a process that made little sense, and any economy that made this a rational outcome had fundamental problems.

17. John Bellamy Foster, *Marx's Ecology: Materialism and Nature* (New York: Monthly Review Press, 2000); Foster has also written a series of essays on this subject: see John Bellamy Foster, *Ecology Against Capitalism* (New York: Monthly Review Press, 2002).

18. Cited in Anatol Lieven, "The End of the West as We Know It?" *International Herald Tribune*, December 28, 2006, http://www.iht.com/articles/2006/12/28/opinion/edlieven.php?page=1. See also: Elisabeth Rosenthal and Andrew C. Revkin, "Science Panel

Says Global Warming Is 'Unequivocal,'" *New York Times*, February 3, 2007, pp. A1, A5.

19. For a multifaceted take on exactly this issue, see Leo Panitch and Colin Leys, eds., *Coming to Terms with Nature: Socialist Register 2007* (New York: Monthly Review Press, 2007).

20. http://www.democracy.ru/english/quotes.php.

21. See Yves de la Haye, ed., *Marx and Engels on the Means of Communication* (New York: International General, 1979).

22. Cited in Harold J. Laski, *The Communist Manifesto of Marx and Engels, with the Original Texts and Prefaces* (New York: Continuum, 1967), p. 161.

23. This point is made strongly in C. Wright Mills, *The Sociological Imagination* (New York: Oxford University Press, 1959), ch. 8.

24. I return to this point in my discussion of the First Amendment in Chapter 3.

25. Robert Heilbroner, *The Nature and Logic of Capitalism* (New York: Norton, 1985).

26. Laski, pp. 135, 136.

27. I took this description almost verbatim from John Bellamy Foster, "Introductory Notes to Chapter Four." In Ernst Fischer, *How to Read Karl Marx* (New York: Monthly Review Press, 1996), p. 67.

28. Karl Marx and Friedrich Engels, "The German Ideology." In *On Historical Materialism*, pp. 14–76.

29. Charles Blitzer, "Introduction." In Henry M. Christman, ed., *The American Journalism of Marx & Engels* (New York: New American Library, 1966), p. xxvii.

30. Ibid.

31. For a discussion of the influence of Marx on Stone, see Robert C. Cottrell, *Izzy: A Biography of I.F. Stone* (New Brunswick, NJ: Rutgers University Press, 1992).

32. See, for example, Saul K. Padover, "Introduction." In Saul K. Padover, ed. and trans., Karl Marx, *On Freedom of the Press and Censorship* (New York: McGraw-Hill, 1974), p. xiv.

33. Marx, *Freedom of the Press*, pp. 40–41.

34. Ibid., pp. 33–34.

35. For a sympathetic critique of Marx and the limitations in his understanding of communication, see John Durham Peters, *Speaking into the Air: A History of the Idea of Communication* (Chicago: University of Chicago Press, 1999), pp. 119–27. This is an excellent book and Peters raises good points, although I wonder if a rigorous reading of Marx's own work might lead to a revision of the

analysis. As far as I know, no one has read Marx systematically to tease out the notion of communication in its varied manifestations. When John Bellamy Foster did this to understand Marx's conception of ecology, he discovered what we had thought about Marx and nature was both incomplete and inaccurate. Foster's research proved to be a bountiful discovery of considerable importance. It is possible, only possible, that such might be the case with Marx and communication.

36. My reading of Marx from the 1970s stayed with me, though I don't know if I have ever cited Marx in anything I have written. I did use a quote from Marx as the title of a book I co-edited. See William S. Solomon and Robert W. McChesney, *Ruthless Criticism: New Perspectives on U.S. Communication History* (Minneapolis: University of Minnesota Press, 1993).

37. Stuart Hall, "Culture, the Media and the 'Ideological Effect'." In James Curran, Michael Gurevitch, and Janet Woollacott, eds., *Mass Communication and Society* (London: Edward Arnold, 1977), pp. 315–48.

38. Stuart Hall, "The Rediscovery of 'Ideology': Return of the Repressed in Media Studies." In Michael Gurevitch, Tony Bennett, James Curran, and Janet Woollacott, eds., *Culture, Society and the Media* (London: Metheun, 1982), p. 88. As James Curran points out, although published in 1982, most of the essays in this book are from the mid-1970s.

39. James Curran, "The New Revisionism in Mass Communication Research: A Reappraisal," *European Journal of Communication*, Vol. 5 (1990): p. 139.

40. Stuart Hall, "Media Power and Class Power." In James Curran, Jake Ecclestone, Giles Oakley, and Alan Richardson, eds., *Bending Reality: The State of the Media* (London: Pluto, 1986), p. 11.

41. For perhaps the best treatment of this split in U.S. academic and left intellectual circles, see Vivek Chibber, "On the Decline of Class in South Asian Studies," *Critical Asian Studies*, Vol. 38, No. 4 (2006): pp. 357–87.

42. See James Curran, Michael Gurevitch, and Janet Woollacott, eds., *Mass Communication and Society* (London: Edward Arnold, 1977); Michael Gurevitch et al., *Culture, Society and the Media*; James Curran et al., *Bending Reality: The State of the Media*. The 1982 volume was actually written around 1976, according to James Curran.

43. See, for example: James Curran et al., *Mass Media and Society*; Paddy Scannell, Philip Scheslinger, and Colin Sparks, eds.,

Culture and Power: A Media, Culture & Society Reader (London: Sage Publications, 1992).

44. See Lawrence Grossberg, Cary Nelson, and Paula Treichler, eds., *Cultural Studies* (New York: Routledge, 1992). It is worth noting, too, that the first Illinois cultural studies conference in 1983 led to a book with "Marxism" in the title: Cary Nelson and Lawrence Grossberg, eds., *Marxism and the Interpretation of Culture* (paperback ed.) (Urbana: University of Illinois Press, 1988).

45. As postmodernists and Marxists fractured over core issues during the late 1980s and early 1990s a number of important works restated the foundations of radical social theory and were invaluable to my understanding of what was at stake. See, for example: Ellen Meiksins Wood, *The Retreat from Class: A New "True" Socialism* (London: Verso, 1986); Roy Bhaskar, *Reclaiming Reality: A Critical Introduction to Contemporary Philosophy* (London: Verso, 1989); Aijaz Ahmad, *In Theory: Classes, Nation, Literatures* (London: Verso, 1992); Norman Geras, *Discourses of Extremity* (London: Verso, 1990).

46. See, for example, Lawrence Grossberg, "Cultural Studies vs. Political Economy: Is Anyone Else Bored with this Debate?" *Critical Studies in Mass Communication*, Vol. 12, No. 1 (March 1995); Nicholas Garnham, "Political Economy and Cultural Studies: Reconciliation of Divorce?" *Critical Studies in Mass Communication*, Vol.12, No. 1 (March 1995): pp. 62–71; James W. Carey, "Abolishing the Old Spirit World," *Critical Studies in Mass Communication*, Vol.12, No. 1 (March 1995): pp. 82–88; Graham Murdock, "Across the Great Divide: Cultural Analysis and the Condition of Democracy," *Critical Studies in Mass Communication*, Vol.12, No. 1 (March 1995): pp. 89–95; Nicholas Garnham, "Reply to Grossberg and Carey" *Critical Studies in Mass Communication*, Vol.12, No. 1 (March 1995): pp. 95–100. There were also impassioned debates involving Garnham and Grossberg at several conferences, including ICA in 1990 and 1993 in Dublin and Washington, DC, respectively.

47. For a superb recent example of this melding, see Janice Peck, *The Age of Oprah: Media Mind Cure in the Neoliberal Era* (Boulder, CO: Paradigm Publishers, 2007). Another recent book that draws from both traditions is James H. Wittebols, *The Soap Opera Paradigm: Television Programming and Corporate Priorities* (Lanham, MD: Rowman & Littlefield, 2004). I cite work by Miller, Grossberg, Meehan, Wasko, and Mosco elsewhere in the book.

48. Nicholas Garnham and Joan Bakewell, *The Structures of Television* (British Film Institute, 1972; rev. ed., 1978); Nicholas

Garnham, Richard Collins, and G. Locksley, *The Economics of Television* (London: Sage Publications, 1988); Nicholas Garnham, "Contribution to a Political Economy of Mass-Communication," *Media, Culture and Society*, Vol. 1, No. 2 (April 1979): pp. 123–46; Nicholas Garnham, "Telecommunications Policy in the United Kingdom," *Media, Culture and Society*, Vol. 7, No. 1 (January 1985): pp. 7–29; Nicholas Garnham, "Toward a Theory of Cultural Materialism," *Journal of Communication*, Vol. 33, No. 3 (Summer 1983): pp. 314–29.

49. James Curran, Anthony Smith, and Paula Wingate, eds., *Impacts and Influences: Essays on Media Power in the Twentieth Century* (London: Methuen, 1987); James Curran, "Capitalism and Control of the Press, 1800–1975." In James Curran et al., *Mass Communication and Society*; James Curran, "Advertising and the Press." In James Curran, ed., *The British Press: A Manifesto* (London: Macmillan, 1978); James Curran, "Advertising as a Patronage System." In Harry Christian, ed., *The Sociology of Journalism and the Press* (Keele, Staffordshire: Keele University Press, 1980); James Curran, "The Impact of Advertising on the British Mass Media," *Media, Culture and Society*, Vol. 3, No. 1 (1981): pp. 43–69; James Curran, "The Different Approaches to Media Reform." In James Curran et al., *Bending Reality: The State of the Media.*

50. Peter Golding, *The Mass Media* (London: Longman, 1974); Peter Golding, "Media Role in National Development: Critique of a Theoretical Orthodoxy," *Journal of Communication*, Vol. 24, No. 3 (Summer 1974): pp. 39–53; Peter Golding and Philip Elliott, eds., *Making the News* (New York: Longman, 1979); Peter Golding and Graham Murdock, "Theories of Communication and Theories of Society," *Communication Research*, Vol. 5, No. 3 (July 1978): pp. 339–56; Peter Golding, Graham Murdock, and Philip Schlesinger, eds., *Communicating Politics: Mass Communications and the Political Process* (New York: Holmes & Meier, 1986); Peter Golding and Sue Middleton, *Images of Welfare: Press and Public Attitudes to Poverty* (Oxford: M. Robertson, 1982); Andrew Sills, Gillian Taylor, and Peter Golding, *The Politics of the Urban Crisis* (London: Hutchinson, 1988).

51. Graham Murdock and Noreeene Janus, eds., *Mass Communications and the Advertising Industry* (Paris: UNESCO, 1984); Graham Murdock and Peter Golding, "Information Poverty and Political Inequality: Citizenship in the Age of Privatized Communications," *Journal of Communication*, Vol. 39, No. 3 (Summer 1989): pp. 180–95; James D. Halloran, Philip Elliott, and Graham

Murdock, *Demonstrations and Communication: A Case Study* (Harmondsworth: Penguin, 1970); Graham Murdock and Guy Phelps, *Mass Media and the Secondary School* (London: Macmillan, 1973); Philip Schlesinger, Graham Murdock, and Philip Elliott. *Televising "Terrorism": Political Violence in Popular Culture* (London: Comedia Pub., 1983); Graham Murdock, "Blindspots About Western Marxism: A Reply to Dallas Smythe," *Canadian Journal of Political and Social Theory*, Vol. 2, No. 2 (1978): pp. 109–19; Graham Murdock, "Cultural Studies: Missing Links," *Critical Studies in Mass Communication*, Vol. 6, No. 4 (1989): pp. 436–40; Graham Murdock, "Critical Inquiry and Audience Activity." In Brenda Dervin, Lawrence Grossberg, Barbara O' Keefe, and Ellen Wartella, eds., *Rethinking Communication. Vol. II: Paradigm Exemplars* (Newbury Park, CA: Sage Publications, 1989), pp. 226–49.

52. Graham Murdock and Peter Golding, "For a Political Economy of Mass Communications." In Ralph Miliband and John Saville, eds., *The Socialist Register 1973* (London: Merlin Press, 1974), pp. 205–34.

53. Some of the work from the political economy tradition that caught my attention (and not mentioned elsewhere in this book) in the 1980s included: Dan Schiller, *Telematics and Government* (Norwood, NJ: Ablex, 1982); Stuart Ewen, *Captains of Consciousness: Advertising and the Social Roots of the Consumer Culture* (paperback ed.) (New York: McGraw-Hill, 1977); Oscar H. Gandy, *Beyond Agenda Setting: Information Subsidies and Public Policy.* (Norwood, NJ: Ablex, 1982); Sut Jhally, *The Codes of Advertising: Fetishism and the Political Economy of Meaning in the Consumer Society* (London: Routledge, 1990); William Leiss, Stephen Kline, and Sut Jhally, *Social Communication in Advertising: Persons, Products, & Images of Well-Being* (Toronto: Methuen, 1986); Vincent Mosco, *The Pay-Per Society: Computers and Communication in the Information Age: Essays in Critical Theory and Public Policy* (Norwood, NJ: Ablex, 1989); Joseph Turow, *Media Industries: The Production of News and Entertainment* (New York: Longman, 1984); Joseph Turow, *Playing Doctor: Television, Storytelling, and Medical Power* (New York: Oxford University Press, 1989); Janet Wasko, *Movies and Money: Financing the American Film Industry* (Norwood, NJ: Ablex, 1982); Vincent Mosco, *Broadcasting in the United States: Innovative Challenge and Organizational Control* (Norwood, NJ: Ablex, 1979).

54. Vincent Mosco and Janet Wasko, eds., *The Political Economy of Information* (Madison: University of Wisconsin Press, 1988).

55. *Journal of Communication*, Vol. 33, No. 3 (Summer 1983).

56. Profiles of Smythe and Schiller can be found in John A. Lent, ed., *A Different Road Taken: Profiles in Critical Communication* (Boulder, CO: Westview, 1995).

57. Richard Meyer, "The 'Blue Book,'" *Journal of Broadcasting*, Vol. 6 (1962): pp. 197–98; Richard Meyer, "Reaction to the 'Blue Book,'" *Journal of Broadcasting*, Vol. 7 (1962): pp. 295–312; Victor Pickard, "Holding the Line in Dark Times: Radio Activism from Above and Below, 1945–1949" (National Communications Association. San Antonio, November 16–19, 2006); Michael Socolow, "Questioning Advertising's Influence over American Radio: The Blue Book Controversy of 1945–1947," *Journal of Radio Studies*, Vol. 9 (2002): pp. 292–302.

58. Dallas Smythe, *Counterclockwise: Perspectives on Communication*, edited by Thomas Guback (Boulder, CO: Westview Press, 1994). This includes much of his most important work.

59. Dallas Smythe, *The Structure and Policy of Electronic Communication* (Urbana: University of Illinois Press, 1957).

60. Political economy of communication was anything but a monolithic enterprise in this period. Smythe's arguments provoked considerable and spirited debate. See, for example: Graham Murdock, "Blindspots About Western Marxism: A Reply to Dallas Smythe," *Canadian Journal of Political and Social Theory*, Vol. 2, No. 2 (1978): pp. 109–19.

61. For an excellent overview of Schiller's intellectual history, see Richard Maxwell, *Herbert Schiller* (Lanham, MD: Rowman & Littlefield, 2003).

62. Herbert I. Schiller, *Mass Communications and American Empire* (1969). After initial success, Beacon Press bought the rights to the book, and a second edition was published in 1992 by Westview.

63. Herbert I. Schiller, *Culture, Inc.* (New York: Oxford University Press, 1989). Schiller's final book was a fine restatement of his core positions and showed that he was keenly aware of global developments. See Herbert I. Schiller, *Information Inequality: The Deepening Social Crisis in America* (New York: Routledge, 1996).

64. The classic piece in this regard is: Dallas W. Smythe, "Communications: Blindspot of Western Marxism," *Canadian Journal of Political and Society Theory*, Vol. 1, No. 3 (1977): pp. 1–28.

65. I want to thank Dan Schiller specifically for much of the material in this paragraph.

66. Edward S. Herman, "The Externalities Effects of Commercial and Public Broadcasting." In Kaarle Nordenstreng and Herbert I. Schiller, eds., *Beyond National Sovereighty: International Communication in the 1990s* (Norwood, NJ: Ablex, 1993), pp. 85–115.

67. Edward S. Herman and Noam Chomsky, *Manufacturing Consent: The Political Economy of the News Media* (New York: Pantheon, 1988).

68. Edward S. Herman, "The Propaganda Model Revisited." In Robert W. McChesney, Ellen Meiksins Wood, and John Bellamy Foster, eds., *Capitalism and the Information Age* (New York: Monthly Review Press, 1998), pp. 191–206.

69. Robert A. Brady, *The Spirit and Structure of German Fascism* (New York: Viking, 1937); Robert A. Brady, *Business as a System of Power* (New York: Columbia University Press, 1943).

70. Dan Schiller, "The Legacy of Robert Brady," *Journal of Media Economics*, Vol. 12, No. 3 (1999): pp. 89–102.

71. Noam Chomsky, *Necessary Illusions: Thought Control in Democratic Societies* (Boston: South End Press, 1989).

72. Vincent Mosco, *The Political Economy of Communication* (Thousand Oaks, CA: Sage Publications, 1996).

73. Sweezy also wrote arguably the finest introduction to Marxist political economy in the English language. See Paul M. Sweezy, *The Theory of Capitalist Development: Principles of Marxian Political Economy* (New York: Monthly Review Press, 1970; first published in 1942).

74. I had the privilege of co-editing *Monthly Review* with John Bellamy Foster, Harry Magdoff, and Paul Sweezy from 2000 to 2004. I left *MR* when my work with Free Press took off, although I continue on its Board of Directors.

75. See, for example, Josef Steindl, *Maturity and Stagnation in American Capitalism* (New York: Monthly Review Press, 1976; first published in 1952).

76. Paul A. Baran and Paul M. Sweezy, *Monopoly Capital* (New York: Monthly Review Press, 1966).

77. Raymond Williams, *Problems in Materialism and Culture* (London: Verso, 1980), pp. 170–95.

78. The literature is not empty, merely lean. I have found these books instructive in developing my understanding of advertising and public relations: Daniel Pope, *The Making of Modern Advertising* (New York: Basic Books, 1983); Stuart Ewen, *PR! : A Social History of Spin* (New York: Basic Books, 1996); Stuart Ewen and

Elizabeth Ewen, *Channels of Desire: Mass Images and the Shaping of American Consciousness* (New York: McGraw-Hill, 1982); Sut Jhally, *The Codes of Advertising: Fetishism and the Political Economy of Meaning in the Consumer Society* (London: Routledge, 1990); Sut Jhally, *The Spectacle of Accumulation: Essays in Culture, Media, & Politics* (New York: P. Lang, 2006); Richard Wightman Fox and T.J. Jackson Lears, eds., *The Culture of Consumption: Critical Essays in American History, 1880–1980* (New York: Pantheon Books, 1983); Jackson Lears, *Fables of Abundance: A Cultural History of Advertising in America* (New York: Basic Books,1994); Michael Schudson, *Advertising, The Uneasy Persuasion: Its Dubious Impact on American Society* (New York: Basic Books, 1984).

79. Vincent P. Norris, "Advertising History—According to the Textbooks." In Roxanne Hovland, Joyce Wolburg, and Eric Haley, eds., *Readings in Advertising, Society and Consumer Culture* (Armonk, NY: M.E. Sharpe, 2007).

80. For a superb recent overview of Mills, see Stanley Aronowitz, "A Mills Revival?" *Logos*, Vol. 2, No. 3 (Summer 2003): pp. 67–93.

81. C. Wright Mills, *The Power Elite* (New York: Oxford University Press, 1956).

82. Jurgen Habermas, *The Structural Transformation of the Public Sphere: An Inquiry into a Category of Bourgeois Society* (Boston: MIT Press, 1991).

83. Colin Sparks, "Media and Democratic Society: A Survey of Post-Communist Experience." In Margaret Blunden and Patrick Burke, eds., *Democratic Reconstruction in the Balkans* (London: Centre for the Study of Democracy, 2001), pp. 147–64; Colin Sparks (with Anna Reading), *Communism, Capitalism and the Mass Media* (London: Sage Publications, 1997); Yuezhi Zhao, *Media, Market, and Democracy in China: Between the Party Line and the Bottom Line* (Champaign: University of Illinois Press, 1998).

84. The classic statement of this position ironically located four theories, but really came down to us versus them. See Fred Siebert, Theodore Peterson, and Wilbur Schramm, *Four Theories of the Press: The Authoritarian, Libertarian, Social Responsibility, and Soviet Communist Concepts of What the Press Should Be and Do* (Urbana: University of Illinois Press, 1953).

85. Several people whom I respect followed the technological path to Jacques Ellul. That was never my trajectory, but for those interested, see: Jacques Ellul, *Propaganda: The Formation of Men's*

Attitudes, translated by Konrad Kellen and Jean Lerner (New York: Knopf, 1965); Jacques Ellul, *The Technological System*, translated by Joachim Neugroschel (New York: Continuum, 1980); Jacques Ellul, *The Technological Bluff*, translated by Geoffrey W. Bromiley (Grand Rapids, MI: Eerdmans, 1990).

86. Harold Innis, *Political Economy in the Modern State* (Toronto: The Ryerson Press, 1946); Harold Innis, *Empire and Communications* (Oxford: Clarendon Press, 1950); Harold Innis, *The Bias of Communication* (Toronto: University of Toronto Press, 1951).

87. For a terrific interview with James Carey where he discusses his intellectual antecedents, see Jeremy Packer and Craig Robertson, eds., *Thinking with James Carey* (New York: Peter Lang, 2006).

88. See Eric McLuhan and Frank Zingrone, eds., *Essential McLuhan* (New York: Basic Books, 1995); Marshall McLuhan, *Understanding Media: The Extensions of Man*, Introduction by Lewis H. Lapham (Cambridge, MA: MIT Press, 1999; first published in 1964); Marshall McLuhan and Quentin Fiore, *The Medium Is the Message: An Inventory of Effects* (New York: Bantam Books, 1967); Marshall McLuhan, *The Gutenberg Galaxy: The Making of Typographic Man* (1st ed.) (Toronto: University of Toronto Press, 1962).

89. The classic text is: Neil Postman, *Amusing Ourselves to Death: Public Discourse in the Age of Show Business* (New York: Penguin Books, 1986). See also: Neil Postman, *Building a Bridge to the 18th Century: How the Past Can Improve Our Future* (New York: Vintage, 2000); Neil Postman, *The End of Education: Redefining the Value of School* (New York: Vintage, 1996); Neil Postman, *Technopoly: The Surrender of Culture to Technology* (New York: Vintage, 1993); Neil Postman and Steve Powers, *How to Watch TV News* (New York: Penguin Books, 1992); Neil Postman, *Conscientious Objections: Stirring Up Trouble About Language, Technology and Education* (New York: Vintage, 1992); Neil Postman, *The Disappearance of Childhood* (New York: Vintage, 1994); Neil Postman and Charles Weingartner, *Teaching as a Subversive Activity* (New York: Delacorte Press, 1969); Neil Postman, *Crazy Talk, Stupid Talk: How We Defeat Ourselves by the Way We Talk and What to Do About It* (New York: Delacorte Press, 1976); Neil Postman, *The Soft Revolution* (New York: Delacorte Press, 1971).

90. I am not closed-minded on this issue. See David Williamson Shaffer, *How Computer Games Help Children Learn* (New York: Palgrave, 2006); for a provocative discussion about how our romanticization of the benefits of a print-dominated culture may obscure

our ability to understand the benefits of the coming digital communications era, see Mitchell Stephens, *The Rise of the Image, The Fall of the Word* (New York: Oxford University Press, 1998).

91. Alexander Meiklejohn, *Political Freedom* (New York: Harper, 1960), pp. 19–20.

92. Ibid., 73–75.

93. See Jerome Barron, *Freedom of the Press for Whom? The Right of Access to Mass Media* (Bloomington: Indiana University Press, 1973).

94. Most important of his works for my development was C.B. Macpherson, *The Political Theory of Possessive Individualism* (Oxford: Clarendon Press, 1962).

95. See Jules Townsend, *C.B. Macpherson and the Problem of Liberal Democracy* (Edinburgh: Edinburgh University Press, 2000).

96. C.B. Macpherson, *The Life and Times of Liberal Democracy* (New York: Oxford University Press, 1977).

97. See Robert Babe, *Canadian Communication Thought: Ten Foundational Writers* (Toronto: University of Toronto Press, 2000), ch. 6.

98. This is a point worth pursuing a bit further. In my view, too much intellectual energy among self-described radicals and liberals is devoted to policing the border between them. Each side hunts down and elevates the alleged weaknesses of the other. Those on the left castigate liberals for their impurity and their willingness to capitulate to capital. To the liberal border police, the left is a dangerous place that liberals must quarantine and castigate to establish their credentials to people in power as being capable of ruling the nation. There are important political and intellectual disputes between the two sides, but it's more productive to find the common ground between them—and in the study of communication it was not difficult to locate—and to regard each side with respect when there are differences. This approach was cemented by my dealings with nonacademics, who usually found the radical-liberal border debates a turnoff, if not incomprehensible or even childish.

99. Robert W. McChesney, "Sport and Newspapers in the 1920s: A Political Economic Interpretation of the Symbiotic Relationship." Special Research Session on Economic History, Association for Education in Journalism and Mass Communication National Convention, Norman, OK, August 1986.

100. See Oscar H. Gandy Jr., "The Political Economy Approach:

A Critical Challenge." *Journal of Media Economics* (Summer 1992): pp. 23–42.

101. Joseph A. Schumpeter, *Capitalism, Socialism and Democracy* (New York: Harper and Brothers, 1942).

102. See Robert Heilbroner and William Milberg, *The Crisis of Vision in Modern Economic Thought* (New York: Cambridge University Press, 1995).

103. See, for example: Ronald Coase, "The Federal Communications Commission," *Journal of Law and Economics*, Vol. 2 (1959): pp. 1–40; Ronald Coase, "The Problem of Social Cost," *Journal of Law and Economics*, Vol. 3 (1960): pp. 1–44; Ronald Coase, "Why Not Use the Pricing System in the Broadcasting Industry?" *The Freeman* (July 1961): pp. 52–57; Ronald Coase, "The Interdepartment Radio Advisory Committee," *Journal of Law and Economics*, Vol. 5 (1962): pp. 17–47; Ronald Coase, "Evaluation of Public Policy Relating to Radio and Television Broadcasting: Social and Economic Issues," *Land Economics*, Vol. 41 (1965): pp. 161–67.

104. Bruce M. Owen, "A Novel Conference: The Origins of the TPRC." In Jeffrey K. MacKie-Mason and David Waterman, eds., *Telephony, the Internet, and the Media: Selected Papers from the 1997 Telecommunications Policy Research Conference* (Mahwah, NJ: LEA Books, 1998), http://www.erlbaum.com/ME2/dirmod.asp?sid= 28807ECF50FE49F0837125BE640E681F&nm=Books&type=e Commerce&mod=CommerceProductCatalog &mid=CD22EA0F118949C09A932248C040F650&tier=3&id=54995 F0ED050430488AEFFD83BA1F212&itemid=0-8058-3152-5.

105. Ithiel de Sola Pool, *Technologies Without Boundaries: On Telecommunications in a Global Age*, edited by Eli Noam (Cambridge, MA: Harvard University Press, 1990); Lloyd S. Etheridge, ed., *Politics in Wired Nations: Selected Writings of Ithiel de Sola Pool* (New Brunswick, NJ: Transaction Publishers, 1998); Ithiel de Sola Pool, *Technologies of Freedom* (Cambridge, MA: Harvard University Press, 1983).

106. Benjamin M. Compaine, ed., *Issues in New Information Technology* (Norwood, NJ: Ablex, 1988); Benjamin M. Compaine and Douglas Gomery, *Who Owns the Media? Competition and Concentration in the Mass Media Industry* (3rd ed.) (Mahwah, NJ: Lawrence Erlbaum Associates, 2000).

107. See, for example: Oscar H. Gandy, Paul Espinosa, and Janusz A. Ordover, *Proceedings from the Tenth Annual Telecommunications*

Policy Research Conference (Norwood, NJ: Ablex, 1983); Vincent Mosco, *Policy Research in Telecommunications: Proceedings from the Eleventh Annual Telecommunications Policy Research Conference* (Norwood, NJ: Ablex, 1984).

108. Charles E. Lindblom, *The Market System* (New Haven, CT: Yale University Press, 2001), pp. 2, 3.

109. http://www.democracy.ru/english/quotes.php.

110. Accordingly, much of my own thinking about critical scholarship came from a graduate seminar at the University of Washington in 1986 where we spent much of a term closely examining Kaplan's classic text. See Abraham Kaplan, *The Conduct of Inquiry*, with a new introduction by Charles Wolf Jr. (New Brunswick, NJ: Transaction Publishers, 1998).

111. While writing, I have tried to imagine how someone who did not share my political views would respond to my research. I was quite fortunate to have a colleague in Madison, a Republican, who graciously read my early work in draft form and who often raised objections I would have never imagined.

112. Gyula Hegyi, "Learn from Our Failures and Create a Socialist Democracy," *The Guardian*, December 22, 2006.

113. Comment of Angela McRobbie. Cited in Lawrence Grossburg, "Cultural Studies vs. Political Economy: Is Anyone Else Bored with This Debate?" *Critical Studies in Mass Communication*, Vol. 12, No. 1 (March 1995), p. 81.

114. Stuart Hall, "Culture, the Media and the 'Ideological Effect.'" In James Curran et al., *Mass Communication and Society*, p. 324.

115. It was the emergence of Fiske to preeminence by the early 1990s that signaled the full divorce of cultural studies from political economy, as the two positions were irreconcilable. The journal *Media, Culture & Society*, which had been a leading sponsor of critical communication studies, saw this and came out firmly against the "Fiske turn." See William R. Seaman, "Active Audience Theory: Pointless Populism," *Media, Culture & Society*, Vol. 14, No. 2 (1992): pp. 301–11.

116. See John Fiske and John Hartley, *Reading Television* (London: Methuen, 1978), p. 102.

117. Comments of Susan Douglas at the "Back to the Future: Explorations in Communication and History" conference, University of Pennsylvania, Philadelphia, Pennsylvania, December 1, 2006. I happened to be in Madison during the late 1980s and early 1990s

when Fiske was also on the faculty, though in a different department. He was a charming man and a splendid teacher, which no doubt was part of his considerable appeal.

118. One way to interpret the politics of Fiske was to see it as a rejection of the defeat to neoliberalism by proclaiming that the traditional notions of politics no longer applied. It reminded me of the critics of the Vietnam War in the 1960s who argued the United States should simply withdraw all the troops and declare victory. Fiske seemed to survey the demoralized and ravaged landscape of the neoliberal era and see the masses in some sort of triumph. What would constitute a victory in this new world of politics was never established and remained unclear. As Bruce Cumings put it in 1992, after reviewing Fiske's arguments about all the power the audience has, and how this is working to the advantage of progressive politics: "I would like to think that Fiske is right, but I would also like to know where he finds 'a multitude of resistance' to mass television." See Bruce Cumings, *War and Television* (London: Verso, 1992), pp. 274–75.

119. Fiske wrote many books in the 1980s and 1990s along these lines. Perhaps his best statement was John Fiske, *Television Culture* (London: Routledge, 1988). See also: John Fiske, *Power Play, Power Works* (London: Verso, 1993). Many consider his last book his finest statement of his project: John Fiske, *Media Matters* (Minneapolis: University of Minnesota Press, 1994).

120. For a recent discussion of Fiske by one of his acolytes that disputes my interpretation of Fiske and defends Fiske's legacy vigorously, see Henry Jenkins, "Why Fiske Still Matters," *Flow*, Vol. 2, No. 6 (2005), http://jot.communication.utexas.edu/flow/?jot=view&id=801.

121. According to Eagleton, postmodernism (and the cultural studies it largely defined) emerged as "the theory of those too young to recall a mass radical politics, but who had a good deal of glum experience of drearily oppressive majorities. . . . Protest would still be possible; but because the system would instantly recongeal around the irritant like a jellyfish, the radical sensibility would be accordingly divided—between a brittle pessimism on the one hand, and an exhilarated vision of ceaseless difference, mobility, disruption on the other. The distance between all that, and the drearily determinate world of social and economic life, would no doubt bulk embarrassingly large; but the gap might be narrowed if one were to attend those few surviving enclaves

where these things could still find a home, where a pleasure and playfulness not wholly under the heel of power might still be relished. Primary candidates for this role might be language and sexuality." See Terry Eagleton, *The Illusions of Postmodernism* (Oxford: Blackwell, 1996), pp. 1–3.

122. As James Curran points out, much of the cultural studies tradition had moved toward a more liberal pluralist view, terminology and self-image notwithstanding, which made the work less threatening to mainstream scholars. See James Curran, "The New Revisionism in Mass Communication Research: A Reappraisal," *European Journal of Communication*, Vol. 5 (1990): pp. 135–64. Herbert Schiller similarly observed around the same time that the cultural studies approach tended to adopt a "limited effects" approach much like the dominant paradigm as well. In this model actual control and structure of the media tends to assume less importance. See Schiller, *Culture, Inc.*

It is also true that important victories from the 1960s and 1970s—specifically around rights for women and people of color—were not rolled back entirely. Officially, these victories were incorporated into the dominant culture, albeit in a truncated manner that failed to address structural inequality. Cultural studies was able to maintain a strong link to issues of race and gender around issues of identity and representation, which provided it with what political backbone and moral authority it had. Political economy, which was never oriented toward identity issues, but rather toward structural issues, was hard-pressed to address the immediate concerns of women and people of color during this nadir. This was part of the crisis it faced that led to its stagnation and demise.

123. When I left Wisconsin in 1998, although I had taught some of the most popular courses in the department for more than a decade and supervised several Ph.D.'s, there was no thought of hiring someone who did political economy to replace me. That tradition was terminated.

124. For a good discussion of one aspect of this issue, see Justin Lewis, *Constructing Public Opinion* (New York: Columbia University Press, 2001). For a critique of quantitative work, see Bent Flyvbjerg, *Making Social Science Matter*, translated by Steven Sampson (New York: Cambridge University Press, 2001).

125. *Journal of Communication*, special double issue, "The Future of the Field," Vol. 43, No. 4 (Autumn 1993).

126. Armand Mattelart, *The Information Society: An Introduction*, translated by Susan G. Taponier and James A. Cohen (Thousand Oaks, CA: Sage Publications, 2003); Armand Mattelart, *Mapping World Communication: War, Progress, Culture*, translated by Susan Emanuel and James A. Cohen (Minneapolis: University of Minnesota Press, 1994); Armand Mattelart, *Networking the World, 1794–2000*, translated by Liz Carey-Libbrecht and James A. Cohen (Minneapolis: University of Minnesota Press, 2000); Armand Mattelart and Michèle Mattelart, *Rethinking Media Theory: Signposts and New Directions*, translated by James A. Cohen and Marina Urquidi (Minneapolis: University of Minnesota Press, 1992); Armand Mattelart and Michèle Mattelart, *Theories of Communication: A Short Introduction*, translated by Susan Gruenheck Taponier and James A. Cohen (Thousand Oaks, CA: Sage Publications, 1998).

127. Nicholas Garnham, *Capitalism and Communication: Global Culture and the Economics of Information* (London: Sage Publications, 1990); Nicholas Garnham, *Emancipation, the Media, and Modernity: Arguments About the Media and Social Theory* (Oxford: Oxford University Press, 2000.)

128. James Curran, *Culture Wars: The Media and the British Left* (with Ivor Gaber and Julian Petley) (Edinburgh: Edinburgh University Press, 2005); James Curran, *Mass Media and Society* (edited with Michael Gurevitch) (4th ed.) (London: Arnold, 2005); James Curran, *Media and Cultural Theory* (edited with David Morley) (London: Routledge, 2005); James Curran, *Power Without Responsibility* (with Jean Seaton) (6th ed.) (London: Routledge, 2003); James Curran, *Contesting Media Power: Alternative Media in a Networked World* (edited with Nick Couldry) (Lanham, MD: Rowman & Littlefield, 2003); James Curran, *Media and Power* (London: Routledge, 2002); James Curran, *Bending Reality: The State of the Media* (Dover, NH: Pluto, 1986); James Curran, ed., *Media Organizations in Society* (London: Arnold, 2000); James Curran, *Media and Power* (London: Routledge, 2003); James Curran and Michael Gurevitch, eds., *Mass Media and Society* (3rd ed.) (London: Arnold, 2000); James Curran, *Policy for the Press* (London: Institute for Public Policy Research, 1995).

129. Ib Bondebjerg and Peter Golding, eds., *European Culture and the Media, Changing Media* (London: Intellect Books, 2004); Dennis McQuail, Peter Golding, and Els de Bens, eds., *Communication Theory and Research* (London: Sage Publications, 2005); David Deacon and Peter Golding, *Taxation and Representation: The*

Media, Political Communication and the Poll Tax (London: John Libbey, 1994); Peter Golding and Phil Harris, eds., *Beyond Cultural Imperialism: Globalisation, Communication and the New International Order* (London: Sage Publications, 1997); Peter Golding and Graham Murdock, eds., *The Political Economy of the Media* (Cheltenham, Glos, England: Edward Elgar, 1997); Marjorie Ferguson and Peter Golding, eds., *Cultural Studies in Question* (London: Sage Publications, 1997).

130. Jan Wieten, Graham Murdock, and Peter Dahlgren, eds., *Television Across Europe* (London: Sage Publications, 2000).

131. This is some of the more impressive research generated by the political economy of communication tradition since the 1990s through to today, that is not mentioned elsewhere in this book: Oscar H. Gandy, *Communication and Race: A Structural Perspective* (London: Arnold, 1998); Oscar H. Gandy, *The Panoptic Sort: A Political Economy of Personal Information* (Boulder, CO: Westview, 1993); Sut Jhally and Justin Lewis, *"Enlightened" Racism: The Cosby Show, Audiences, and the Myth of the American Dream* (Boulder, CO: Westview Press, 1992); Slavko Splichal and Janet Wasko, *Communication and Democracy* (Norwood, NJ: Ablex, 1993); Gerald Sussman, *Transnational Communications: Wiring the Third World* (Newbury Park, CA: Sage Publications, 1991); Joseph Turow, *Media Systems in Society: Understanding Industries, Strategies, and Power* (New York: Longman, 1992); Janet Wasko, *Democratic Communications in the Information Age* (Toronto: Ablex Publishing, 1992); Janet Wasko, *Hollywood in the Information Age: Beyond the Silver Screen* (Cambridge: Polity Press, 1994); Ingunn Hagen and Janet Wasko, eds., *Consuming Audiences? Production and Reception in Media Research* (Cresskill, NJ: Hampton Press, 2000); Janet Wasko, *Understanding Disney: The Manufacture of Fantasy* (Cambridge: Polity Press, 2001); Gerald Sussman, *Global Electioneering: Campaign Consulting, Communications, and Corporate Financing* (Lanham, MD: Rowman & Littlefield, 2005); Vincent Mosco, *The Digital Sublime: Myth, Power, and Cyberspace* (Cambridge, MA: MIT Press, 2004); Manjunath Pendakur, *Indian Popular Cinema: Industry, Ideology, and Consciousness* (Cresskill, NJ: Hampton Press, 2003); Stephen D. Reese, Oscar H. Gandy, and August E. Grant. *Framing Public Life: Perspectives on Media and Our Understanding of the Social World* (Mahwah, NJ: Lawrence Erlbaum Associates, 2001); Gerald Sussman and John A. Lent, *Global Productions: Labor in the Making of the "Information Society"* (Cresskill, NJ: Hampton

Press, 1998); Gerald Sussman, *Communication, Technology, and Politics in the Information Age* (Thousand Oaks, CA: Sage Publications, 1997); Joseph Turow and Andrea L. Kavanaugh, *The Wired Homestead: An MIT Press Sourcebook on the Internet and the Family* (Cambridge, MA: MIT Press, 2003); Joseph Turow, *Breaking Up America: Advertisers and the New Media World* (Chicago: University of Chicago Press, 1997); Janet Wasko, Mark Phillips, and Eileen R. Meehan, *Dazzled by Disney?: The Global Disney Audiences Project* (London: Leicester University Press, 2001); Janet Wasko, *A Companion to Television* (Malden, MA: Blackwell Pub., 2005); Janet Wasko, *How Hollywood Works* (Thousand Oaks, CA: Sage Publications, 2003).

132. Paul A. Baran, "The Commitment of the Intellectual." In Paul A. Baran, *The Longer View: Essays Toward a Critique of Political Economy* (New York: Monthly Review Press, 1970), pp. 3–15.

133. Although two of the books were published in 1980, they were all written in the 1970s. Herbert Gans, *Deciding What's News: A Study of CBS Evening News, NBC Nightly News, Newsweek and Time* (New York: Random House, 1979); Mark Fishman, *Manufacturing the News* (Austin: University of Texas Press, 1980); Gaye Tuchman, *Making News: A Study in the Construction of Reality* (New York: Free Press, 1978); Todd Gitlin, *The Whole World Is Watching: Mass Media in the Making and Unmaking of the Left* (Berkeley: University of California Press, 1980). One other excellent book on journalism produced in the 1970s was journalist Edward Jay Epstein's *News from Nowhere: Television and the News* (New York: Vintage Books, 1973). Another sociologist who wrote an influential book on journalism in this period was Michael Schudson, *Discovering the News: A Social History of American Newspapers* (New York: Basic Books, 1978).

134. The critical work in Britain in the 1970s produced a good deal of work on journalism; some of it was influential on this side of the Atlantic. But it never provided the basis for a critique that would generate fruitful studies of American journalism that would have significant staying power in the United States. A couple of the classic works that I read in graduate school and found eye-opening include: Glasgow University Media Group, *Bad News* (London: Routledge and Kegan Paul, 1976). There were several other volumes of this research group. See also: Stuart Hall, Chas Critcher, Tony Jefferson, and Brian Roberts, *Policing the Crisis* (London: Macmillan, 1978).

135. Chomsky and Herman had clear differences from Bagdikian in tone and emphasis, and much was made of their being radicals while Bagdikian was a liberal. Bagdikian was certainly accorded more respect by working journalists. There are important differences between them and they are worth pursuing, but they are in my opinion much less important than the common ground the three authors share. I have read their works closely and have had the privilege of getting to know all three of them quite well. The more I studied them and spoke with them, the more I found their critiques of journalism to be highly complementary.

136. One notable exception was my colleague Chuck Salmon, who wrote a thoughtful review of *Manufacturing Consent*, in *Journalism Quarterly*. Chuck is now at Michigan State University. See Charles T. Salmon, *Journalism Quarterly*, Vol. 66, No. 2 (Summer 1989): pp. 494–95.

137. Chomsky is getting more attention in the heart of communication studies in recent years, as his legacy and influence grow. For a recent cultural studies critique of Chomsky, see Gabriel Noah Brahm Jr., "Understanding Noam Chomsky: A Reconsideration," *Critical Studies in Media Communication*, Vol. 23, No. 5 (December 2006): pp. 453–61; for a perspective on Chomsky in the same issue I find more accurate, see Robert F. Barsky, "Anarchism, the Chomsky Effect and the Descent from the Ivory Tower," *Critical Studies in Media Communication*, Vol. 23, No. 5 (December 2006): pp. 446–52.

138. See, for example, Michael Schudson, *The Power of News* (Cambridge, MA: Harvard University Press, 1995), pp. 4–6; Daniel C. Hallin, *We Keep America on Top of the World: Television Journalism and the Public Sphere* (New York: Routledge, 1994), pp. 12–13; Nicholas Lemann, review of *Manufacturing Consent*, in *The New Republic*, January 9, 1989.

139. More recently, two prominent scholars engaged in a detailed exchange with Herman and Chomsky concerning the propaganda model in an academic journal. It would have been nice to see this 15 years earlier. See Kurt Lang and Gladys Engel Lang, "Noam Chomsky and the Manufacture of Consent for American Foreign Policy," *Political Communication*, Vol. 21, No. 1 (2004): pp. 93–101; Kurt Lang and Gladys Engel Lang, "Response to Herman and Chomsky," *Political Communication*, Vol. 21, No. 1 (2004): 109–11; Kurt Lang and Gladys Engel Lang, "Afterword," *Political*

Communication, Vol. 21, No. 1 (2004): p. 117; Edward S. Herman and Noam Chomsky, "Reply to Kurt and Gladys Engel Lang," *Political Communication*, Vol. 21, No. 1 (2004): pp. 103–7; Edward S. Herman and Noam Chomsky, "Further Reply to the Langs," *Political Communication*, Vol. 21, No. 1 (2004): pp. 113–16.

140. Leonard Downie Jr. and Robert G. Kaiser, *The News About the News: American Journalism in Peril* (New York: Alfred A. Knopf, 2002). See also: Eugene Roberts, Thomas Kinkel, and Charles Layton, eds., *Leaving Readers Behind: The Age of Corporate Newspapering* (Fayetteville: University of Arkansas Press, 2001).

141. The report details the hard decline in the number of reporters actually covering communities over the past two decades as well as the domination of commercial values of the public interest in the determination of news. See Project for Excellence in Journalism, "State of the Media 2006: An Annual Report on American Journalism," at: http://www.stateofthenewsmedia.org/2006/index.asp.

142. Paula Constable, "Demise of the Foreign Correspondent," *Washington Post*, February 18, 2007, p. B1, http://www.washingtonpost.com/wp-dyn/content/article/2007/02/16/AR2007021601713_pf.html.

143. Go to http://www.savejournalism.org/.

144. Michael Schudson, "Owning Up: A New Book Stops Short of Deepening the Discourse on Media Concentration," *Columbia Journalism Review*, January–February 2007, p. 58. See also Michael Schudson, *The Sociology of News* (New York: Norton, 2003), pp. 38, 40.

145. Several authors have assessed the news coverage of the Iraq invasion and occupation. My analysis can be found in John Nichols and Robert W. McChesney, *Tragedy and Farce: How American Media Sell Wars, Spin Elections and Destroy Democracy* (New York: The New Press, 2005). See also: Jeff Cohen, *Cable News Confidential: My Misadventures in Corporate Media* (Sausalito, CA: PoliPoint Press, 2006); Robin Andersen, *A Century of Media, a Century of War* (New York: Peter Lang, 2006); Norman Solomon, *War Made Easy* (Hoboken, NJ: John Wiley & Sons, 2005); Frank Rich, *The Greatest Story Ever Sold: The Decline and Fall of Truth from 9/11 to Katrina* (New York: Penguin Press, 2006); Sheldon Rampton and John Stauber, *The Best War Ever: Lies, Damned Lies, and the Mess in Iraq* (New York: Penguin Books, 2006); Michael Isikoff and David Corn, *Hubris: The Inside Story of Spin, Scandal, and the Selling of the*

Iraq War (New York: Crown Publishing Group, 2006); Bill Katovsky and Timothy Carlson, *Embedded: The Media at War in Iraq* (Guilford, CT: Lyons Press, 2003); Norman Solomon et al., *Target Iraq: What the News Media Didn't Tell You* (New York: Context Books, 2003); Philip M. Seib, *Beyond the Front Lines: How the News Media Cover a World Shaped by War* (New York: Palgrave MacMillan, 2004); Ralph D. Berenger, ed., *Global Media Go to War: Role of News and Entertainment Media During the 2003 Iraq War* (Spokane, WA: Marquette Books, 2004); Ralph D. Berrenger, ed., *Cybermedia Go to War: Role of Converging Media During and After the 2003 Iraq War* (Spokane, WA: Marquette Books, 2006); Michael Massing, *Now They Tell Us: The American Press and Iraq* (New York: New York Review Books, 2004); Howard Tumber, *Media at War: The Iraq Crisis* (London: Sage Publications, 2004); Alexander G. Nikolaev and Ernest A. Hakanen, *Leading to the 2003 Iraq War: The Global Media Debate* (New York: Palgrave MacMillan, 2006); David Miller, *Tell Me Lies: Propaganda and Media Distortion in the Attack on Iraq* (London: Pluto Press, 2004); David Dadge, *The War in Iraq and Why the Media Failed Us* (Westport, CT: Praeger, 2006); Danny Schechter, *When News Lies: Media Complicity and the Iraq War* (New York: Select Books, 2006).

146. Gilbert Cranberg, "Cranberg wants a serious probe of why the press failed in its pre-war reporting," *Nieman Watchdog*, February 7, 2007, http://www.niemanwatchdog.org/index.cfm?fuseaction=ask_this.view&askthisid=00261.

3: The Historical Turn, Critical Junctures, and "Five Truths"

1. Dan Schiller, *Objectivity and the News: The Public and the Rise of Commercial Journalism* (Philadelphia: University of Pennsylvania Press, 1981).

2. Robert W. McChesney, "The Battle for America's Ears and Minds: The Debate Over the Control and Structure of American Radio Broadcasting, 1930–1935" (Ph.D. dissertation, University of Washington, 1989); Robert W. McChesney, *Telecommunications, Mass Media, and Democracy: The Battle for the Control of U.S. Broadcasting, 1928–1935* (New York: Oxford University Press, 1993).

3. See Erik Barnouw, *A Tower in Babel: A History of Broadcasting in the United States to 1933* (New York: Oxford University Press, 1966); Erik Barnouw, *The Golden Web: A History of Broadcasting in the United States 1933–1953* (New York: Oxford University Press,

1968); Erik Barnouw, *The Image Empire: A History of Broadcasting in the United States from 1953* (New York: Oxford University Press, 1970); Erik Barnouw, *Tube of Plenty: The Evolution of American Television* (New York: Oxford University Press, 1975); Philip T. Rosen, *The Modern Stentors: Radio Broadcasters and the Federal Government, 1920–1934* (Westport, CT: Greenwood Press, 1980).

4. Susan Douglas began the job of writing an alternative history of radio, but her trailblazing book stopped just as the political debate over broadcasting was getting underway. See Susan J. Douglas, *Inventing American Broadcasting, 1899–1922* (Baltimore, MD: Johns Hopkins University Press, 1987). See also: Susan Smulyan, *Selling Radio: The Commercialization of American Broadcasting 1920–1934* (Washington, DC: Smithsonian Institution Press, 1994).

5. "American Broadcasting," *The B.B.C. Yearbook 1932* (London: British Broadcasting Corporation, 1932), p. 47.

6. George Gilder, *Life After Television* (New York: Norton, 1992).

7. Among mainstream communication scholars my work garnered respect but did not really affect their perception of communication or what they were doing. It was at best a footnote. Among the dominant trends in cultural studies, too, my work was an anomaly. (See, for example, Thomas Streeter, *Selling the Air: A Critique of the Policy of Commercial Broadcasting in the United States* (Chicago: University of Chicago Press, 1996), p. 63. In his provocative book, Streeter acknowledges my work, accepts the veracity of the research, and then ignores it as he makes his argument.) There the tendency was to accept the commercial media system as a given and to assess issues of representation, subversive audience interpretations, and other such matters. Cultural studies, in the 1990s at least, seemed to emphasize locating unconventional opposition to the dominant discourse, but, for reasons I did not comprehend, showed little interest in organized opposition to the system that produced the dominant discourse, or to the system writ large. It appeared more interested in people as consumers or individuals than as citizens or as participants in organized social movements.

8. Chibber has written a highly acclaimed book. See Vivek Chibber, *Locked in Place: State-Building and Late Industrialization in India* (Princeton, NJ: Princeton University Press, 2003).

9. I also discovered that in the area of policy studies there was research that complemented the notion of critical junctures as

well. John Kingdon was especially useful in this regard. See John W. Kingdon, *Agendas, Alternatives, and Public Policies* (2nd ed.) (New York: Longman, 2002). See also: Deborah Stone, *Policy Paradox: The Art of Political Decision Making* (rev. ed.) (New York: Norton, 2001).

10. Some of this research is only coming into general distribution now, though Schiller has been doing the research for two decades. See Dan Schiller, "The Hidden History of U.S. Public Service Telecommunications, 1919–1956," *Info*, Vol. 9, Nos. 2/3 (2007). See also: Dan Schiller, "Telecommunications and the Cooperative Commonwealth: The Challenge from Below and Its Containment, 1894–1919," unpublished manuscript, 2003, part of longer book project, http://leep.lis.uiuc.edu/publish/dschille/Telecommunications_ And_The_Cooperative_Commonwealth.pdf. The forthcoming book by Schiller has a working title of *The Hidden History of U.S. Telecommunications*.

11. William E. Ames, *A History of the National-Intelligencer* (Chapel Hill: University of North Carolina Press, 1972).

12. Linda Lawson, *Truth in Publishing: Federal Regulation of the Press's Business Practices, 1880–1920* (Carbondale: Southern Illinois University Press, 1993).

13. See Richard B. Du Boff, "The Rise of Communications Regulation: The Telegraph Industry, 1844–1880," *Journal of Communication*, Vol. 34, No. 2 (Summer 1984): pp. 52–66; Richard B. Du Boff, "The Telegraph and the Structure of Markets in the United States, 1845–1890." In *Research in Economic History: A Research Annual*, Vol. 8, edited by Paul Uselding (Greenwich, CT: JAI Press Inc., 1983), pp. 253–77; Richard B. Du Boff, "The Telegraph in Nineteenth-Century America: Technology and Monopoly," *Comparative Studies in Society and History*, Vol. 26, No. 4 (October 1984): pp. 571–86.

14. Richard B. Kielbowicz, *News in the Mail: The Press, Post Office, and Public Information, 1700–1860s* (Westport, CT: Greenwood Press, 1989). Kielbowicz has established himself as the singular expert on the relationship of the post office to the press system. See also: Richard B. Kielbowicz, "Postal Subsidies for the Press and the Business of Mass Culture, 1880–1920," *Business History Review* (Autumn 1990): pp. 451–88; Richard B. Kielbowicz, "Origins of the Second-Class Mail Category and the Business of Policymaking, 1863–1879," *Journalism Monographs* (April 1986): pp. 1–26; Richard B. Kielbowicz and Linda Lawson, "Protecting

the Small-Town Press: Community, Social Policy, and Postal Privileges, 1845–1970," *Canadian Review of American Studies* (Spring 1988): pp. 23–45; Richard B. Kielbowicz and Linda Lawson, "Reduced-Rate Postage for Nonprofit Organizations: A Policy History, Critique, and Proposal," *Harvard Journal of Law and Public Policy* (Spring 1988): pp. 347–406; Richard B. Kielbowicz, "Cost Accounting in the Service of Policy Reform: Postal Rate Making, 1875–1926," *Social Science Quarterly* (June 1994): pp. 284–99. Much of this research highlights the important role postal policies played in spurring a vibrant political culture and encouraging popular political movements. For a provocative piece that argues that lowered postal rates in 1885 were foundational to the emergence and success of the populist movement, see: Wayne E. Fuller, "The Populists and the Post Office," *Agricultural History*, Vol. 65, No. 1 (1991): 1–16. What emerges from the work of these scholars is that debates over postal rates and policies were understood as a matter of tremendous importance to popular political movements and organizations.

    15. Michael E. Kinsley, *Outer Space and Inner Sanctums: Government, Business, and Satellite Communication* (New York: John Wiley & Sons, 1976); Dallas Smythe, *Counterclockwise: Perspectives on Communication*, edited by Thomas Guback (Boulder, CO: Westview, 1994), ch. 10; Charles Tate, ed., *Cable Television in the Cities* (Washington, DC: The Urban Institute, 1971); Ralph Lee Smith, *The Wired Nation: Cable TV: The Electronic Communications Highway* (New York: Harper & Row, 1972); Nancy Jeruale, with Richard M. Neustadt and Nicholas P. Miller, eds., *CTIC Cablebooks, Volume 2: A Guide for Local Policy* (Arlington, VA: The Cable Television Information Center, 1982).

    16. Robert W. McChesney, "Telecon: Corporate Robbery on the Information Superhighway," *In These Times*, July 10, 1995, pp. 1, 14–17; Robert W. McChesney, "The Digital TV Heist," *In These Times*, May 12–25 1997, pp. 20–24; Robert W. McChesney, "Digital Highway Robbery," *The Nation*, April 21, 1997, pp. 22–24, http://www.thenation.com/issue/970421/0421mcch.htm; Robert W. McChesney, "From Pacifica to the Atlantic," *The Nation*, October 11, 1999, p. 9, http://www.thenation.com/issue/991011/1011mcchesney.shtml; Robert W. McChesney, "Oligopoly: The Big Media Game Has Fewer and Fewer Players," *The Progressive*, November 1999, pp. 1, 20–24, http://www.progressive.org/mcc1199.htm; Robert W. McChesney, "Rich Media, Poor Democracy," *In These*

Times, November 14, 1999, pp. 15–17; Robert W. McChesney, "The New Global Media: It's a Small World of Big Conglomerates," *The Nation,* November 29, 1999, pp. 11–15, http://www.thenation .com/issue/991129/1129mcchesney.shtml; Robert W. McChesney "Antitrust and the Media—I," *The Nation,* May 22, 2000, pp. 4–5, http://www.thenation.com/issue/000522/0522mcchesney.shtml; Robert W. McChesney, "Blame the System," *Mother Jones,* December 1998, pp. 12–13, http://www.motherjones.com/mother_jones/ ND98/backtalk.html.

17. There were scores of newspaper op-eds, usually run through *The Progressive'*s op-ed project, the *Capital-Times* of Madison, or *Newsday.* For more centrist articles, see Robert W. McChesney, "The Costs of Commercialization," *Quill,* April 2000, pp. 9–11; Mark Crispin Miller and Robert W. McChesney, "Monopoly Game: Why America Is Sick of Media Mergers," *The New Republic,* October 4, 1999, pp. 14–17, http://www.thenewrepublic.com/ archive/1099/100499/miller100499.html; Robert W. McChesney, "America, I Do Mind Dying: Public Broadcasting in Troubled Times," *Current,* August 14, 1995, pp. 16–17, 19, http://www.current .org/why/why514m.html.

18. Herman and McChesney, *The Global Media;* Robert W. McChesney, *Corporate Media and the Threat to Democracy.* Open Media Series, No. 1 (New York: Seven Stories Press, 1997).

19. See McChesney, *Corporate Media and the Threat to Democracy;* see also: Edward S. Herman, *The Myth of the Liberal Media* (New York: Peter Lang, 1999). More recently: Eric Alterman, *What Liberal Media?: The Truth About Bias and the News* (New York: Basic Books, 2003). In *The Problem of the Media* (2004), I provided a systematic critique of the "liberal media" argument.

20. Mark Crispin Miller, "The Crushing Power of Big Publishing," *The Nation,* March 17, 1997, pp. 11–18; Mark Crispin Miller, "Who Controls the Music?" *The Nation,* August 25/September 1, 1997, pp. 11–16; Mark Crispin Miller, "Free the Media," *The Nation,* June 3, 1996, pp. 9–15; Mark Crispin Miller, "CBS-Viacom Nuptials," *The Nation,* October 4, 1999, pp. 3–7; Mark Crispin Miller, "TV: The Nature of the Beast," *The Nation,* June 8, 1998, pp. 11–13.

21. His classic work from this period is Danny Schechter, *The More You Watch, The Less You Know* (New York: Seven Stories Press, 1999). See also: Danny Schechter, *Embedded: Weapons of Mass Deception: How the Media Failed to Cover the Iraq War* (New York:

Prometheus Books, 2003); Danny Schechter, *Media Wars: News at a Time of Terror* (Lanham, MD: Rowman & Littlefield, 2003); Danny Schechter, *News Dissector: Passions, Pieces, Polemics 1960–2000* (New York: Akashic Books, 2001); Danny Schechter, *When News Lies: Media Complicity and the Iraq War* (New York: Select Books, 2006); Danny Schechter, *The Death of Media and the Fight to Save Democracy* (Hoboken, NJ: Melville House, 2005).

22. John Nichols and Robert W. McChesney, *It's the Media, Stupid!* (New York: Seven Stories Press, 2000); Robert W. McChesney and John Nichols, *Our Media, Not Theirs: The Democratic Struggle Against Corporate Media* (New York: Seven Stories Press, 2002); John Nichols and Robert W. McChesney, *Tragedy and Farce: How the American Media Sell Wars, Spin Elections, and Destroy Democracy* (New York: The New Press, 2005); John Nichols and Robert W. McChesney, "FAIR Turns 20," *The Nation*, October 23, 2006, p. 7; John Nichols and Robert W. McChesney, "Bush's War on the Press," *The Nation*, December 5, 2005, pp. 9–10, http://www.thenation.com/doc/20051205/nichoils; John Nichols and Robert W. McChesney, "The 'Liberal Media'? What a Myth," *Chicago Sun-Times*, November 13, 2005, p. B1; Robert W. McChesney, John Nichols, and Ben Scott, "Congress Tunes In," *The Nation*, May 23, 2005, http://thenation.com/doc.mhtml?i=20050523&s=scott; John Nichols and Robert W. McChesney, "FCC: It Could Get Worse," *The Nation*, February 21, 2005, http://www.commondreams.org/views05/0204-29.htm; Robert W. McChesney and John Nichols, "Up in Flames: The Public Revolts Against Monopoly Media," *The Nation*, November 17, 2003, pp. 11–14, http://www.thenation.com/doc.mhtml?i=20031117&s=mcchesney; John Nichols and Robert W. McChesney, "The Battle Over Media Ownership Is Far from Over," Common Dreams.org, July 7, 2003, http://commondreams.org/views03/0707-01.htm; John Nichols and Robert W. McChesney, "Standing Up to the FCC," *The Nation*, June 23, 2003, pp. 5, 22; John Nichols and Robert W. McChesney, "Whose Media?" Tom Paine.com, June 20, 2003, http://tompaine.com/feature2.cfm/ID/8165; Robert W. McChesney and John Nichols, "Reclaiming the Media," Common Dreams.org, June 16, 2003, http://commondreams.org/views03/0616-02.htm; John Nichols and Robert W. McChesney, "Media Monopoly vs. Democracy," Tom Paine.com, May 20, 2003, http://www.tompaine.com/feature2.cfm/ID/7851; John Nichols and Robert W. McChesney, "FCC: Public Be Damned," *The Nation*, June 2, 2003, pp. 5–6, http://

thenation.com/doc.mhtml?i=20030602&s=nichols; Robert W. McChesney and John Nichols, "The FCC and Media Ownership," *Adbusters*, No. 47 (May–June 2003); Robert W. McChesney and John Nichols, "Holding the Line at the FCC," *The Progressive*, April 2003, pp. 26–29, http://www.progressive.org/april03/mcc0403 .html; Robert W. McChesney and John Nichols, "Our Media, Not Theirs: Building the U.S. Media Reform Movement," *In These Times*, April 14, 2003, pp. 18–21; Robert W. McChesney and John Nichols, "Media Democracy's Moment," *The Nation*, February 24, 2003, pp. 16–20, http://www.thenation.com/doc.mhtml?i= 20030224&s=mcchesney; John Nichols and Robert W. McChesney, "On the Verge in Vermont: Media Reform Movement Nears Critical Mass," *Extra!* July–August 2002, pp. 26–27, http://www .fair.org/extra/0207/vermont.html; John Nichols and Robert W. McChesney, "Turning the Tide: It's Time to Fight the Enronization of the Media," *In These Times*, April 15, 2002, pp. 16–17, http:// www.inthesetimes.com/issue/26/10/feature3.shtml; John Nichols and Robert W. McChesney, "Only One Source for News Hurts All," *Capital Times*, February 26, 2002, http://captimes.com/opinion/ column/nichols/21196.php; Robert W. McChesney and John Nichols, "The Making of a Movement," *The Nation*, January 7, 2002, pp. 11–17, http://www.thenation.com/doc.mhtml?i=20020107& s=mcchesney; Robert W. McChesney and John Nichols, "Platform for Media Reform," *MEDIAFile*, Vol. 20, No. 1 (January/February 2001), http://www.media-alliance.org/mediafile/20-1/mcchesne y.html; John Nichols and Robert W. McChesney, "The Evjue Challenge: Speaking Truth to Media Power," *Extra!* Vol. 12, No. 3 (May/June 1999): pp. 24–25; Robert W. McChesney, Mark Crispin Miller, and John Nichols, "Media and Democracy," *The Nation*, November 3, 1997, pp. 6–7.

23. See, for recent examples, the speeches by Geena Davis and Jane Fonda at plenary sessions of the National Conference for Media Reform in Memphis, Tennessee, on January 13 and 14, , respectively. Although Davis and Fonda both are celebrities, they are each active with specific media activist efforts built on a strong and well-researched feminist critique of media. Fonda co-founded the Women's Media Center in 2006, http://www.womensmediacenter .com/home.html, and Davis founded See Jane, http://seejane.org/. For the video or audio recordings of their conference speeches, go to www.freepress.net/conference.

24. When the media reform movement exploded after 2002 a

crucial element was the "media justice" movement, and this activism was influenced by the critical race theorists and feminists
in understanding the systematic underrepresentation and
misrepresentation of women and people of color.

25. What was successful in the academy for postmodern research did not always translate well outside the seminar room. I attended a conference in the fall of 1997 on how intellectuals could
work with nonacademics to advance a more democratic global
communication system. The organizers wanted to tap into the cultural studies current that was then so prevalent on campuses. The
"star" postmodernist at the conference, who spoke at the plenary,
distributed a think piece outlining her thoughts on the subject. The
conclusion read as follows:

> In an era of pervasive intertextuality, the politics appropriate to
> democracy may demand a continual critical cognizance—both of
> radical contingency of social worlds and the expressive activity
> involved in articulating its parameters. If we acknowledge
> politics to be cultural activity, then its practices will demand
> appropriate access to materiality of both means and mediums
> of expressive communication. A radical democratic politics,
> then, may involve more than simply a libertarian celebration
> of regimes of freedom for appropriation. Postcolonial circum-
> stances cut across the grain of postmodern practices and urge
> upon us a heightened sensitivity to the differential relations
> of others and their relationship to the dominant practices of
> othering—an ethics of contingency. Such a politics must enunci-
> ate an ambivalence with respect to proprietary claims and retain
> an ironic awareness of the historical contingencies of alignments
> between authority and alterity. We need to avoid hypostatizing
> difference in our attention to alterity if we are to promote a poli-
> tics sensitive to the ongoing production of meaning and emer-
> gent registers of cultural difference in global democracies.

It is fair to say that just about everyone in the room, academics
and nonacademics alike, were at a loss to understand her point. To
my knowledge, this was her last venture into the public arena. What
became clear was that a good portion of the postmodern work, even
that with a stated concern for political struggles and social justice,
lost much salience once it had to engage with people outside a narrow sliver of the academy. When I saw just how irrelevant and

pretentious much of this work was to the people I was talking to off-campus—including the dispossessed whom this work often claimed to represent—I lost much of my interest in engaging with it.

26. For four classic examples from the mid-1990s, see: John H. McManus, *Market-Driven Journalism: Let the Citizen Beware?* (Thousand Oaks, CA: Sage Publications, 1994); Penn Kimball, *Downsizing the News: Network Cutbacks in the Nation's Capital* (Washington, DC: Woodrow Wilson Center, 1994); James D. Squires, *Read All About It! The Corporate Takeover of America's Newspapers* (New York: Random House, 1995); Doug Underwood, *When MBAs Rule the Newsroom: How Marketers and Managers Are Reshaping Today's Media* (New York: Columbia University Press, 1993).

27. Jay Rosen, *What Are Journalists For?* (New Haven, CT: Yale University Press, 2001).

28. See Robert W. McChesney, "The Internet and U.S. Communication Policymaking in Historical and Critical Perspective," *Journal of Communication*, Vol. 46, No. 1 (Winter 1996): pp. 98–124.

29. This is research that Ben Scott has been doing at the University of Illinois, and is the basis of his dissertation: Ben Scott, "Labor's New Deal for Journalism: The Newspaper Guild in the 1930s" (University of Illinois, 2007).

30. Inger L. Stole, *Advertising on Trial: Consumer Activism and Corporate Public Relations in the 1930s* (Urbana: University of Illinois Press, 2006). See also: Charles F. McGovern, *Sold American: Consumption and Citizenship, 1890–1945* (Chapel Hill: University of North Carolina Press, 2006); Kathy M. Newman, *Radio Active: Advertising and Consumer Activism, 1935–1947* (Berkeley: University of California Press, 2004).

31. Elizabeth Fones-Wolf, *Waves of Opposition: Labor and the Struggle for Democratic Radio* (Urbana: University of Illinois Press, 2006); Victor Pickard, "Media Democracy Deferred: Critical Junctures in U.S. Communications Policy, 1945–1949" (Ph.D. Dissertation, University of Illinois, 2008). See also: Gerald Horne, *Class Struggle in Hollywood: Moguls, Mobsters, Stars, Reds, and Trade Unions* (Austin: University of Texas Press, 2001).

32. Richard R. John, *Spreading the News: The American Postal System from Franklin to Morse* (Cambridge, MA: Harvard University Press, 1995).

33. See Robert A. Hackett and Yuezhi Zhao, eds., *Democratizing Global Media: One World, Many Struggles* (Lanham, MD: Rowman & Littlefield, 2005); Robert A. Hackett and William K. Carroll, *Remak-*

ing Media: The Struggle to Democratize Public Communication (New York: Routledge, 2006).

34. Robert W. McChesney, *The Problem of the Media: U.S. Communication Politics in the 21st Century* (New York: Monthly Review Press, 2004); Paul Starr, *The Creation of the Media: Political Origins of Modern Communications* (New York: Basic Books, 2004). See also: Timothy E. Cook, *Governing with the News: The News Media as a Political Institution* (Chicago: University of Chicago Press, 1998). A compatible argument can be found in Bruce Bimber, *Information and American Democracy: Technology in the Evolution of Political Power* (New York: Cambridge University Press, 2003). For a related history that influenced me a great deal in graduate school, see Daniel Czitrom, *Media and the American Mind: From Morse to McLuhan* (Chapel Hill: University of North Carolina Press, 1983).

35. Paul Starr, "Democratic Theory and the History of Communications," paper presented at Back to the Future Conference, Annenberg School for Communication, University of Pennsylvania, December 1, 2006.

36. Mark Lloyd, *Prologue to a Farce: Democracy and Communication in America* (Urbana: University of Illinois Press, 2007).

37. This is the text of the First Amendment: "Congress shall make no law respecting an establishment of religion, or prohibiting the free exercise thereof; or abridging the freedom of speech, or of the press; or the right of the people peaceably to assemble, and to petition the government for a redress of grievances."

38. C. Edwin Baker, "The Independent Significance of the Press Clause Under Existing Law," presentation to the Reclaiming the First Amendment: Constitutional Theories of Media Reform conference, Hofstra University, Hempstead, New York, January 19, 2007.

39. A classic example is: Potter Stewart, "Or of the Press," 26 *Hastings Law Journal* 631 (1975). See also: Gerald Gunther and Kathleen M. Sullivan, "Freedom of the Press." In *Constitutional Law, 13th edition* (Westbury, NY: The Foundation Press, 1997), pp. 1420–60; Geoffrey R. Stone et al., "Freedom of the Press." In *Constitutional Law, 5th edition* (New York: Aspen Publishers, 2005), pp. 1442–83.

40. Whenever I write about freedom of the press issues and the Constitution I find myself invoking the name Ed Baker, because his work provides the foundation on which I stand. It is ironic that

a law professor is doing so much cutting-edge communication research. His latest book is another example of his enormous talent: C. Edwin Baker, *Media Concentration and Democracy: Why Ownership Matters* (New York: Cambridge University Press, 2006).

41. Robert W. McChesney, "Constant Retreat: The American Civil Liberties Union and the Debate Over the Meaning of Free Speech for Radio Broadcasting in the 1930s." In *Free Speech Yearbook, Volume 26*, edited by Stephen A. Smith (Carbondale: Southern Illinois University Press, 1988), pp. 40–59.

42. Thomas I. Emerson, *Toward a General Theory of the First Amendment* (New York: Random House, 1966).

43. In what follows do not mistake my position on the Founders and Madison and Jefferson. They are not deities. Although I find their writings on freedom of the press enlightened and extraordinary, they were complex figures and far from perfect, even if viewed from the vantage point of their own historical period. I discuss the antidemocratic aspects of Madison's thought in *Rich Media, Poor Democracy*. A recent talk by my colleague Pedro Cabán delved into the racism and white supremacy of the Founders. Pedro Cabán, Comments for the February 9, 2007 Forum, "Disempowering Racial Oppression, Discontinuing Chief Illiniwek and Other Forms of Racial 'Entertainment,'" University of Illinois at Urbana-Champaign, February 9, 2007.

44. A good deal of important historical work on the Constitution has been done in recent years. See, for example: Akhil Reed Amar, *America's Constitution: A Biography* (New York: Random House, 2005).

45. John Durham Peters, "The Marketplace of Ideas: A History of the Concept." In Andrew Calabrese and Colin Sparks, eds., *Toward a Political Economy of Culture: Capitalism and Communication in the Twenty-First Century* (Boulder, CO: Rowman & Littlefield, 2004), pp. 65–82.

46. John Nichols and Robert W. McChesney, *Tragedy and Farce: How the American Media Sell Wars, Spin Elections and Destroy Democracy* (New York: The New Press, 2005). Here's another quote from Madison: "to the press alone, checquered as it is with abuses, the world is indebted for all the triumphs which have been gained by reason and humanity over error and oppression." Cited in Ralph Ketcham, *James Madison: A Biography* (Charlottesville: University of Virginia Press, 1990), p. 401.

47. *Papers of Thomas Jefferson*, Vol. 11: 48–49, http://press-pubs.uchicago.edu/founders/print_documents/amendI_speechs8.html.

48. I discuss this at some length in Robert W. McChesney, *The Problem of the Media* (New York: Monthly Review Press), ch. 1.

49. This is discussed in Mark Lloyd, *Prologue to a Farce: Communication and Democracy in America* (Urbana: University of Illinois Press, 2007), pp. 30–31.

50. As Mark Lloyd makes clear in *Prologue to a Farce*, the nature of capitalism in the United States in the founding period through much of the nineteenth century was quite unlike what we think of as capitalism today. For starters, the vast majority of people were neither employers nor employees. They were self-employed farmers, trades people, mechanics, and so on. And corporations barely existed. In this environment, the idea that private media were regarded as large, profit-generating corporate entities was nonexistent and would be for a good century. American history from this period is filled with ringing denunciations of the emerging corporate sector from leading figures, both on economic and political grounds. As Lloyd demonstrates, Lincoln made a series of criticisms of corporations, and even capitalism, which were not entirely dissimilar to what Karl Marx was writing at the same time in England. In November 1864, for example, as the postwar era was on the horizon, Lincoln wrote: "I see in the near future a crisis approaching that unnerves me and causes me to tremble for the safety of my country. As a result of the war, corporations have been enthroned and an era of corruption in high places will follow, and the money power of the country will endeavor to prolong its reign by working upon the prejudices of the people until all wealth is aggregated into a few hands and the Republic is destroyed." (See Lloyd, *Prologue to a Farce*, pp. 60–61, 294.)

51. See, for example: Eric Burns, *Infamous Scribblers: The Founding Fathers and the Rowdy Beginnings of American Journalism* (New York: Public Affairs, 2006).

52. For some sense of the crucial role of the press in the development of participatory democracy in the United States, see Sean Wilentz, *The Rise of American Democracy: Jefferson to Lincoln* (New York: Norton, 2005).

53. My point in this discussion is not to reify the Constitution. It

is not a flawless document. See Sanford Levinson, *Our Undemo-cratic Constitution: Where the Constitution Goes Wrong (and How We the People Can Correct It)* (New York: Oxford University Press, 2006); Bruce Ackerman, *The Failure of the Founding Fathers: Jefferson, Madison, and the Rise of Presidential Democracy* (Cambridge, MA: Belknap Press of Harvard University Press, 2005). Even if I thought the Founders explicitly conceived of the First Amendment as requiring a corporate-run, commercial media system regardless of the consequences for self-government, my argument in this book would remain the same. Fortunately, I believe there is power-ful evidence to suggest that the Constitution can and should be in-terpreted in the manner I suggest. One of the great strengths of the Founders, especially Madison and Jefferson, was their bedrock understanding of the role of a free press in self-government, and their understanding of what this entailed in an institutional sense. It is one of the great contributions of American politics to the world.

54. *Associated Press v. United States*, 326 U.S. 1 (1945), http://caselaw.lp.findlaw.com/scripts/getcase.pl?court=US&vol=326&invol=1.

55. *New York Times Co. v. United States*, 403 U.S. 713 (1971), http://www.law.cornell.edu/supct/html/historics/USSC_CR_0403_0713_ZC.html.

56. *New York Times Co. v. United States*, 403 U.S. 713 (1971), http://www.law.cornell.edu/supct/html/historics/USSC_CR_0403_0713_ZC3.html.

57. Madison added that "War is in fact the true nurse of execu-tive aggrandizement. In war, a physical force is to be created; and it is the executive will, which is to direct it. In war, the public trea-suries are to be unlocked; and it is the executive hand which is to dispense them. In war, the honors and emoluments of office are to be multiplied; and it is the executive patronage under which they are to be enjoyed; and it is the executive brow they are to encircle. The strongest passions and most dangerous weaknesses of the human breast; ambition, avarice, vanity, the honorable or venal love of fame, are all in conspiracy against the desire and duty of peace." Cited in John Nichols, ed., *Against the Beast: A Documen-tary History of American Opposition to Empires* (New York: Nation Books, 2005), p. 14.

It is striking that the two themes that Jefferson and Madison highlighted as central duties of the press—to assist the poor in stopping the rich from exploiting them and plundering the country; and to prevent militarism from destroying freedom—remain arguably the two most important concerns about media today.

58. I am hardly a lone wolf in making this argument. For some recent research I have found very helpful in developing my own thoughts, see Laura Stein, *Speech Rights in America: The First Amendment, Democracy, and the Media* (Urbana: University of Illinois Press, 2006); David S. Allen, *Democracy, Inc.: The Press and Law in the Corporate Rationalization of the Public Sphere* (Urbana: University of Illinois Press, 2005).

59. This figure is derived by the staff of Commissioner Michael Copps in consultation with various experts and based upon evaluating the amounts raised during recent spectrum auctions. See "Remarks of Commissioner Michael J. Copps," National Conference on Media Reform, Memphis Tennessee, January 12, 2007.

60. See James H. Snider, *The Citizen's Guide to the Airwaves* (Washington, DC: New America Foundation, 2003), p. 40.

61. Bruce Kushnick has made an initial attempt to uncover how telecommunication firms bilked the U.S. public of enormous government subsidies to build out a nonexistent infrastructure. His title tells how much he determined the public paid to get little or nothing in return: Bruce Kushnick, *The $200 Billion Broadband Scandal* (New York: New Network Institute, 2006), http://www.newnetworks.com/broadbandscandals.htm.

62. Personal correspondence with Toby Miller, January 21, 2007.

63. For a discussion of the time when the tax-exempt status of advertising was under serious review by Congress, see Inger L. Stole, "The Advertising Industry Goes to War with America: Critics and the Fight over the Excess Profits Tax During the Second World War." In Charles R. Taylor, editor, *Proceedings of the 2001 Conference of the American Academy of Advertising.* (New York: American Academy of Advertising, 2001).

64. Associated Press, "Gannett's Profit Rises in Quarter, Helped by Political Ads at TV Stations," *New York Times*, February 3, 2007, p. B4. Moreover, as political advertising has increased, the amount of actual coverage of political campaigns on the public airwaves has decreased. See Dennis Chaptman, "Study: Political Ad Time Trumps Election Coverage on the Tube," November 21, 2006, http://www.news.wisc.edu/13213.html.

65. Copyright is one subsidy where there is some debate over whether the government policy constitutes a subsidy. As one researcher for an industry-subsidized think tank e-mailed me in 2007: "There are no doubt numbers on the value of copyrighted works, but I'd see that more as value created BY the copyright holders, and protected by law, rather than a subsidy." (his emphasis)

66. The U.S. government historically has worked to expand and protect markets for U.S. media firms overseas. See, for example: Ian Jarvie, *Hollywood's Overseas Campaign: The North Atlantic Movie Trade, 1920–1950* (New York: Cambridge University Press, 1992); John Trumpdour, *Selling Hollywood to the World: U.S. and European Struggles for Mastery of the Global Film Industry, 1920–1950* (New York: Cambridge University Press, 2002).

67. This is a hint to any young scholars out there, and a clear example of where political economic analysis requires accounting skills.

68. For a detailed investigation of this "irony" of deregulation, see Robert Britt Horwitz, *The Irony of Regulatory Reform: The Deregulation of American Telecommunications* (New York: Oxford University Press, 1989.)

69. See, for a recent example, "Net Discrimination," *Wall Street Journal*, January 2, 2007, p. A22.

70. Sandra Braman has extended this argument, contending that the nature of the modern state has been transformed in the past few decades from a bureaucratic, welfare state to an "information state," with information policymaking at its heart. Her argument will be a subject of debate and study in the field in the coming years. See Sandra Braman, *Change of State: Information, Policy, Power* (Cambridge, MA: MIT Press, 2006).

71. It is why the problem of minority broadcast ownership is so vexing. Although minorities make up a significant percentage of American citizens, they account for a much smaller portion of the investment capital. That is the relevant pool for being an owner of a broadcast station, barring policies to funnel capital to prospective minority owners. See Joelle Tessler, "Diversity Debate Shapes Media Ownership Rules," *CQ Weekly*, January 29, 2007.

72. Amy Schatz, "Industry Braces for Net-Neutrality Fallout," *Wall Street Journal*, January 2, 2007, p. A3.

73. Comments of Edward Markey, National Conference on Media Reform, Memphis, Tennessee, January 13, 2007.

74. Kate Ackley, "AT&T Takes Shape as Lobbying Giant," *Roll Call*, February 20, 2007.

75. See Common Cause, *Wolves in Sheep's Clothing: Telecom Industry Front Groups and Astroturf* (Washington, DC: Common Cause, 2006), http://www.commoncause.org/site/pp.asp?c=dkLNK1MQIwG&b=1499059.

The classic text on this practice is Sheldon Rampton and John Stauber, *Toxic Sludge Is Good for You: Lies, Damn Lies and the Public Relations Industry* (Monroe, Maine: Common Courage Press, 1995). For two recent examples of this practice by communication firms, see the website for Verizon's Consumers for Tech Choice, which organizes popular support for Verison's positions in Massachusetts, http://www.consumersfortechchoice.org/. Note that the name Verizon cannot even be located on the website. In Illinois, AT&T created TV4US to do its bidding surreptitiously. See Anna Marie Kukec, " 'Astroturf' Groups Represent Industries, Not Members," *Daily Herald*, February 11, 2007, http://www.dailyherald.com/business/story.asp?id=280048.

More broadly, in view of what is at stake in terms of government subsidies and licenses, the industry lobbying effort is no surprise. They spend this amount because, like Roth and Corleone, they are fighting with each other for the biggest slice of the pie, though, as we will see in Chapter 4, some portion of that is now taking into consideration Leona Helmsley's little people. (During billionaire Leona Helmsley's trail for tax evasion in the 1980s, her former housekeeper testified that Helmsley stated: "We don't pay taxes. Only the little people pay taxes." Quoted in *New York Times*, July 12, 1989, http://www.bartleby.com/66/43/27743.html.)

76. See Jeff Chester, *Digital Destiny: New Media and the Future of Democracy* (New York: The New Press, 2007).

77. Benjamin Compaine has been one of the few defenders of the policymaking status quo. He argues that the policymaking process is as democratic as it could possibly be, because the various large lobbies duking it out behind closed doors prevent excessive corruption from resulting. But Compaine's standards for democracy might jar anyone with an education in elementary political theory; in the same article he terms corporations "extremely democratic" institutions because they must adhere to shareholders. See Benjamin Compaine, "The Myths of Encroaching Global Media Ownership," OpenDenmocracy.net, November 8, 2001,

http://www.opendemocracy.net/media-globalmediaownership/
article_87.jsp.

78. Robert W. McChesney, "Free Speech and Democracy: Louis
G. Caldwell, the American Bar Association, and the Debate over
the Free Speech Implications of Broadcast Regulation, 1928–1938,"
American Journal of Legal History, Vol. XXXV (October 1991): pp.
351–92.

79. Viewed this way the framing of debates around media looking exclusively or primarily at "media concentration" is wide of
the mark, at times even a red herring. Even if concentration in a
media sector is not increasing, or may even be in decline, that does
not mean all is well in the world. Media concentration tends to be
a bad thing, but it is far from the only thing that matters in media.
To the "immaculate conception" crowd, once it is shown that concentration is not growing at dramatic rates, the conclusion is invariably that the system works just fine, thank you, and critics
should shut up and shop. The real issue is, Why do we create and
subsidize media systems built around profit-maximization and
advertising in the manner that we do? I am reminded of the Chinese student dissidents in the late 1980s, when they protested the
meetings of Chinese government leaders with elected heads-of-
state. "Who elected you?" they would chant. That is the question
to be asked about the WGNs and AT&Ts in our world: "Who
elected you?"

80. I approached the top telecommunication or media researchers at each of the four "free market" think tanks in 2007,
asking if they could help me determine the size of the subsidy in a
number of specific areas. I thought this might be an area of interest
because these think tanks tended to be so adamantly opposed to
government subsidies and welfare that they might be interested in
determining the extent of such practices. I received gracious and
thoughtful replies in three cases; in each response, I was informed
that this was an area they knew nothing about and they knew no
one who was working on the subject. The other think tank did not
respond, and on none of the websites did I find any research remotely close to this topic. It is worth noting that some economists
raised concerns about the "rents" AT&T received as a result of its
monopoly status back in the 1960s and 1970s. The point then was
more to open up the telecommunications market to other firms
than to consider what the public might rightfully demand in exchange for those rents.

81. Robert W. McChesney, "Theses on Media Deregulation," *Media, Culture & Society*, Vol. 25, No. 1 (2003): pp. 125–33.

82. Steven Pinker, *The Language Instinct: How the Mind Creates Language* (New York: William Morrow, 1994).

83. This point is discussed in Spencer Wells, *The Journey of Man: A Genetic Odyssey* (New York: Random House, 2003). Jared Diamond makes this point in Jared Diamond, *The Third Chimpanzee: The Evolution and Future of the Human Animal* (New York: Harper-Collins, 1992). See also: Richard G. Klein and Blake Edgar, *The Dawn of Human Culture: A Bold New Theory on What Sparked the "Big Bang" of Human Consciousness* (New York: John Wiley & Sons, 2002).

84. Marcel Mazoyer and Laurence Roudart, *A History of World Agriculture: From the Neolithic Age to the Current Crisis* (New York: Monthly Review Press, 2006).

85. Wayne M. Senner, ed., *The Origins of Writing* (Lincoln: University of Nebraska Press, 1989); Stephen D. Houston, ed., *The First Writing: Script Invention as History and Process* (Cambridge: Cambridge University Press, 2004).

86. The classic works are Elizabeth L. Eisenstein, *The Printing Press as an Agent of Change: Communications and Cultural Transformations in Early Modern Europe* (Cambridge: Cambridge University Press, 1979); Elizabeth L. Eisenstein, *The Printing Revolution in Early Modern Europe* (Cambridge: Cambridge University Press, 1983); Adrian Johns, *The Nature of the Book: Print and Knowledge in the Making* (Chicago: University of Chicago Press, 1998).

87. Jared Diamond, *Guns, Germs, and Steel: The Fate of Human Societies* (New York: Norton, 1997).

88. Cited in Diamond, *Guns, Germs, and Steel*, p. 235.

89. Greg Ruggiero, *Microradio Broadcasting: (Low) Power to the People* (New York: Seven Stories Press, 1999).

90. National Public Radio, to its discredit, supported the NAB position. In the future, we hope that NPR's national leadership will take a more collegial approach to alternative forms of noncommercial radio broadcasting. See: John Anderson, "A Can of Worms: Pirate Radio and Public Intransigence on the Public Airwaves" (Unpublished M.A. thesis, University of Wisconsin-Madison, 2004).

91. See Robert W. McChesney, "Kennard, the Public, and the FCC," *The Nation*, May 14, 2001, pp. 17–20, http://radio.hampshire.edu/kennard.pdf.

92. There was a fourth episode, too, that in retrospect was quite revealing. I was part of an exchange on the OpenDemocracy website on the subject of global media ownership with a number of people including Benjamin Compaine, from fall 2001 through spring 2002. What was striking in the exchange was Compaine's unwillingness to engage with the issues and his resort to boilerplate industry PR and occasional ad hominem attacks. At the time, I thought it was simply a reflection of Compaine's debating style. I can now see that it reflected a real inability of industry to defend its privileges and performance when confronted with the five truths in the light of day. The arguments Compaine was making might have sounded convincing a decade or two earlier, but they had less traction with the American people by 2002. Compaine, and, by extension, the communication firms, had nothing to say to them that addressed their concerns. See: http://www.opendemocracy .net/media-globalmediaownership/debate.jsp, for an index of all the entries.

93. Sanders had done a town meeting on the problem of bias in news many years earlier with Jeff Cohen of FAIR, but it did not have a policy emphasis.

94. John Nichols and Robert W. McChesney, "On the Verge in Vermont: Media Reform Movement Nears Critical Mass," *Extra!* July–August 2002, pp. 26–27, http://www.fair.org/extra/0207/ vermont.html.

95. Both Sanders and Brown were elected to the U.S. Senate from the respective states in 2006.

4: Moment of Truth

1. Nick Penniman, now the publisher of the *Washington Monthly*, and FAIR's Janine Jackson were also present.

2. A longer discussion of Nelson's views can be found in Robert W. McChesney and John Nichols, *Our Media, Not Theirs* (New York: Seven Stories Press, 2002).

3. Robert W. McChesney, "The Escalating War Against Corporate Media," *Monthly Review*, Vol. 55, No. 10 (March 2004): pp. 1–29, http://www.monthlyreview.org/0304mcchesney.htm; Robert W. McChesney, "Media Policy Goes to Main Street: The Uprising of 2003," *Communication Review*, Vol. 7, pp. 223–58. See also: Ben

Scott, "The Politics and Policy of Media Ownership," *American University Law Review*, Vol. 53 (2004): pp. 645–77, http://www.wcl.american.edu/journal/lawrev/53/scott.pdf?rd=1.

4. Much is made of the threat of mobs and the fears we should have of people physically assembling. Every bit as important—indeed, in my view more important—are the positive aspects of human assembly, politically and psychologically. We are truly social beings. For an extraordinary account of this, see Barbara Ehrenreich, *Dancing in the Streets: A History of Collective Joy* (New York: Metropolitan Books, 2006).

5. The moral of the story: If you treat people like they are morons, they are more likely to act in a manner you might consider moronic. If you treat people with respect, and as sensitive and intelligent, they are more likely to surprise you and be sensitive and intelligent.

6. This revolution is most definitely not being televised.

7. See Project for Excellence in Journalism, "State of the Media 2006: An Annual Report on American Journalism," at: http://www.stateofthenewsmedia.org/2006/index.asp.

8. For a complete listing, see McChesney, *The Problem of the Media*, pp. 348–49.

9. Both the NRA and the PTC backed away from their stand on media ownership after the 2003 fight, apparently under heavy pressure from the Bush administration.

10. See L. Brent Bozell III, "Merchants of Cool Not So Hot," syndicated column, March 5, 2001, http://www.townhall.com/columnists/BrentBozellIII/2001/03/05/merchants_of_cool_not_so_hot; L. Brent Bozell III, "Are Liberals Ruining the Liberal Media?" syndicated column, January 25, 2000, http://www.mediaresearch.org/BozellColumns/newscolumn/2000/col20000125.asp.

11. "ANA '84: Washington Update, Cost Concerns," *Brodcasting*, November 19, 1984, p. 66.

12. Critique along these lines has been limited, though it will likely increase if the movement continues to grow and enjoy success. For a discussion of examples from 2005, see Nichols and McChesney, *Tragedy & Farce*, ch. 6. For a more recent example, see Cliff Kincaid, "Special Report: The Plan to Silence Conservatives," *American Daily*, January 15, 2007, http://www.americandaily.com/article/17246.

13. Barry Goldwater's famous line from the 1964 Republican

convention in San Francisco: "I would remind you that extremism in the defense of liberty is no vice. And let me remind
you also that moderation in the pursuit of justice is no virtue,"
http://www.washingtonpost.com/wp-srv/politics/daily/
may98/goldwaterspeech.htm.

14. Likewise, the cultural conservatism so prevalent since the
1980s and often religious in nature, has also proven fraught with
contradictions. It decries the loose morality of our times, yet it en-
dorses pro-market and pro-commercial policies that produce a
"greed is good, shop 'til you drop" mentality that is significantly
responsible for the crisis that concerns religious and cultural conservatives. As a movement with a significant working-class base, it
supports pro-business policies that go directly against working-
class interests. This can work for a while, but at some point it provides too much stress to hold. For a devastating presentation of
this contradiction, see Benjamin R. Barber, *Consumed: How Markets
Corrupt Children, Infantilize Adults, and Swallow Citizens Whole* (New
York: Norton, 2007).

15. "Richard Viguerie Blast Bush," *The Hotline*, January 23, 2007,
http://hotlineblog.nationaljournal.com/archives/2007/01/richard_
vigueri.html#more. See also: Richard A. Viguerie, "Bush's Base
Betrayal," *Washington Post*, May 21, 2006, p. B1, http://www
.washingtonpost.com/wp-dyn/content/article/2006/05/19/
AR2006051901770_pf.html; Richard A. Viguerie, *Conservatives Be-
trayed: How George W. Bush and Other Big Government Republicans
Hijacked the Conservative Cause* (Los Angeles: Bonus Books, 2006).

16. One academic who has also worked in the corridors of Washington e-mailed me: "Mark Cooper has almost single-handedly
done all of the media policy research that made a difference in the
dirty world of policy-making for the last twenty years. He not only
did this in media and telecom, he inexplicably also did this in energy policy. It is a testament to the ossification of academe that he
is not better known and his impact on the field isn't stronger."

17. Williams has since left Illinois and is now helping launch a
program in media studies, with a Ph.D. program on the horizon,
at the University of Virginia.

18. What was necessary to clinch the deal would be resources,
and there was only so much that schools could reach into their
own wallets to cover. The Ford Foundation assumed a leadership
role and, independent of COMPASS, earmarked funding for media policy research. It coordinated its funding through the Social

Science Research Council, which had a staff dedicated to the area. This is still in nascent stages; funders are notoriously conservative, so their widespread participation will come after a handful of brave pioneers blaze the trail and demonstrate its value.

19. "Administration Agitprop," *Washington Post*, January 8, 2005.

20. David D. Kirkpatrick, "TV Host Says U.S. Paid Him to Back Policy," *New York Times*, January 8, 2005; Christopher Cooper and Brian Steinberg, "Bush Draws Fire over Fee Paid to Columnist to Promote Policy," *Wall Street Journal*, January 10, 2005.

21. Joe Strupp, "Congresswoman Asks for Probe after 'Gannon' Quits WH Reporting Post," *Editor & Publisher*, February 9, 2005.

22. "Manhandled Media," *Houston Chronicle*, November 19, 2005; Matea Gold, "Former CPB Head Tomlinson Reportedly Broke Rules, Ethics Code," *Los Angeles Times*, November, 15, 2005.

23. "The Public Helps Public Broadcasting Regain Funds," Associated Press, June 24, 2005; Charlie McCollum, "House Restores Public TV Funding, but Fight Continues," *San Jose Mercury-News*, June 24, 2005.

24. Joe Strupp, "Media Vows to Pry Open Closed Doors in Washington," *Editor & Publisher*, June 3, 2004.

25. Andrea K. Walker, "Sinclair Claims Buzz from Kerry Program Boosted Its Ratings," *Baltimore Sun*, November 5, 2004.

26. http://www.fair.org/activism/cbs-niger.html; Stewart Pinkerton, "Redstone Vows 'Appropriate' Consequences for CBS News," forbes.com, September 23, 2004. For the position of the CBS News producer responsible for the Bush National Guard story, see Mary Mapes, *Truth and Duty: The Press, the President, and the Privilege of Power* (New York: St. Martin's Press, 2005).

27. J. Hoberman, "Lights, Camera, Exploitation: That's Our Bush! The President's Re-Election Campaign Kicks Off with a Shameless 9-11 Docudrama," *Village Voice*, August 27–September 2, 2003.

28. Jesse McKinley, "9/11 Miniseries Is Criticized as Inaccurate and Biased," *New York Times*, September 6, 2006; Ruth Marcus, "ABC's 'Path' Not Taken," *Washington Post*, September 13, 2006.

29. "AT&T and Domestic Spying," *New York Times*, April 17, 2006.

30. These episodes are covered in detail in John Nichols and Robert W. McChesney, *Tragedy & Farce: How the American Media Sell Wars, Spin Elections, and Destroy Democracy* (New York: The New Press, 2005), ch. 5.

31. Helen Kennedy, "Murdoch Hosts Fundraiser for Hillary, then McCain," *New York Daily News"* July 18, 2006.

32. S. Derek Turner, *Broadband Reality Check II: The Truth Behind America's Digital Decline* (New York: Free Press, 2006), p. 22, figure 16.

33. Robert W. McChesney and John Podesta, "Let There Be Wi-Fi," *Washington Monthly*, January–February 2006, http://www.washingtonmonthly.com/features/2006/0601.podesta.html.

34. Comments of Edward Markey, National Conference on Media Reform, Memphis, Tennessee, January 13, 2007.

35. For a discussion of how AT&T came to dominate the South through dubious political influence, not providing good service in the market, see: Kenneth Lipartito, *The Bell System and Regional Business: The Telephone in the South, 1877–1920* (Baltimore, MD: Johns Hopkins University Press, 1989).

36. In December 1999, I was on a panel of four or five experts for a CNN panel discussion on what to expect in media in the coming millennium. It was part of Time Warner–owned CNN's "Millennium" special television series, this one titled "Media and the 21st Century." It was hosted by Jeff Greenfield and Walter Isaacson, and aired on January 2, 2000. Among the other panelists was Time Warner CEO Gerald Levin. Early on I disputed Levin's claim that the Internet eliminated any concerns about media concentration, lousy journalism, and hyper-commercialism. Levin had personally built Time Warner's massive cable empire, and was moving into broadband service provision with a vengeance. Levin said in no uncertain terms that the Internet was completely uncensored, Time Warner had no control over what websites a user visited, and that was the genius of the Internet. So, in effect, my concerns were no longer warranted because people now had access to countless alternatives. In short, though he probably didn't realize it at the time, Levin presented Net Neutrality as being indistinguishable from the Internet, and as the basis of a legitimate media system.

37. Much of this background material on Net Neutrality was drawn from an internal Free Press memo written by Ben Scott, at times verbatim because Scott put the matter so clearly. Scott led the campaign in Washington on this issue and is my mentor on the subject.

38. Kent Gibbons, "Five Questions for Jeff Chester," *MultiChan-*

nel News, February 5, 2007, http://www.multichannel.com/article/
CA6413144.html?display=Opinion.

39. J. Scott Christianson, "Telecom Bill Tunes Out Customers Needs," *Columbia* (Mo.) *Tribune,*" February 6, 2007, http://www.columbiatribune.com/2007/Feb/20070206Commoo2.asp.

40. Comments of Edward Markey, National Conference on Media Reform, Memphis, Tennessee, January 13, 2007.

41. Quoted in PBS Bill Moyers special, "The Net at Risk," broadcast in October 2006, http://www.pbs.org/moyers/moyerson america/print/netatrisk_transcript_print.html.

42. See Daniel W. Reilly, "The Telecom Slayers," Salon.com, October 2, 2006, http://www.salon.com/tech/feature/2006/10/02/slayers/index_np.html.

43. "Protecting Internet Democracy," *New York Times*, January 3, 2007.

44. I need to keep his identity confidential for the purposes of his job, but I can acknowledge that he is not a Bears fan.

45. Quoted in: Charles Babington "Neutrality on the Net Gets High '08 Profile: Tech Issue Gains Traction in Election," *Washington Post*, February 20, 2007, p. D1, http://www.washingtonpost.com/wp-dyn/content/article/2007/02/19/AR2007021900934.html.

46. Jim Puzzanghera, "FCC Lawyer Says TV Study Was Hushed," *Los Angeles Times*, September 15, 2006; Jeremy Pelofsky, "U.S. FCC Chief Seeks Probe into Draft Media Studies," Reuters, September 20, 2006; Robert W. McChesney, "FCC Scandal Explodes with Second Revelation of Suppressed Media Ownership Research," Common Dreams website, September 19, 2006, http://www.commondreams.org/views06/0919-27.htm.

47. John Eggerton, "FCC Releases, Withholds Ownership Documents," *Broadcasting & Cable*, January 7, 2007.

48. Eric Klinenberg, *Fighting for Air: The Battle to Control America's Media* (New York: Metropolitan Books, 2007).

49. This point is discussed at length in Nichols and McChesney, *Tragedy & Farce*, ch. 6.

50. A reference guide to all the groups working in the media reform movement can be found at http://www.freepress.net/content/orgs.

51. See, for example: "A Clear, Bubbling Passion for Watchdog Journalism," *Seattle Times*, January 18, 2007, http://seattletimes

.nwsource.com/html/editorialsopinion/2003529572_confed18.ht
ml?syndication=rss; Jessica Clark and Tracy Van Slyke, "Fighting
the Media's 'Plantation Mentality,'" *In These Times*, January 18,
2007, http://www.inthesetimes.com/site/main/article/2999/.

52. For a summary of the pre-conference, see: Social Science Research Council, *A Research Agenda for Media Policy in 2007: A Report
on the Media Policy Research Pre-conference, Memphis Tennessee, January 11, 2007* (SSRC, 2007), http://www.ssrc.org/programs/media/
publications/mediaresearchpre-conferencereport0107.pdf.

53. http://ijoc.org/.

54. Sonia Livingstone and Peter Lunt, "Representing Citizens
and Consumers in Media and Communications Regulation." In
The Politics of Consumption/The Consumption of Politics, *The
Annals of the American Academy of Political and Social Science* (2007).

55. See, for example: John Nichols, "Newspapers . . . and
After?" *The Nation*, January 29, 2007, pp. 11–18.

56. Toby Miller, "Hollywood, Cultural Policy Citadel." In Mike
Wayne, ed., *Understanding Film: Marxist Perspectives* (London:
Pluto Press, 2005), pp. 182–93; Toby Miller and Richard Maxwell,
"Film and Globalization." In Oliver Boyd-Barrett, ed., *Communica-
tions Media, Globalization and Empire* (Eastleigh, England: John
Libbey Publishing, 2006), pp. 33–52; Toby Miller, Nitin Govil, John
McMurria, Richard Maxwell, and Ting Wang, *Global Hollywood 2*
(London: British Film Institute; Berkeley and Los Angeles: Univer-
sity of California Press, 2005); Toby Miller, "Global Hollywood
2010," *International Journal of Communication* 1: Feature 1-4, http://
ijoc.org/ojs/index.php/ijoc/article/view/52/24.

57. Dean Baker's brother, Randy Baker, an attorney who has
been active in media issues, is presently conducting research to develop the plan in greater detail.

58. See, for excellent examples: S. Derek Turner and Mark
Cooper, *Out of the Picture: Minority and Female TV Station Ownership
in the United States: Current Status, Comparative Statistical Analysis
and the Effects of FCC Policy and Media Consolidation* (New York:
Free Press and The Donald McGannon Center for Communications Research, Fordham University, October 2006). Available at:
http://www.freepress.net/docs/out_of_the_picture.pdf; S. Derek
Turner, *Broadband Reality Check II: The Truth Behind America's Digital
Decline* (New York: Free Press, 2006). Available at: www.freepress
.net/docs/bbrc2-final.pdf; S. Derek Turner, *Universal Service and
Convergence: USF Policy for the 21st Century* (New York: Free Press,

2006) Presented at the 34th Research Conference on Communication, Information and Internet Policy, Arlington, Virginia. Available at: http://web.si.umich.edu/tprc/papers/2006/646/Turner_tprc_revised.pdf; Mark Cooper et. al., *The Case Against Media Consolidation: Evidence on Concentration, Localism and Diversity* (New York: The Donald McGannon Center for Communications Research, January 2007). A summary and links to individual chapters is available at: http://www.stopbigmedia.com/=compendium; Peter DiCola, *Do Radio Companies Offer More Variety When They Exceed the Local Ownership Cap?* (Washington, DC: Future of Music Coalition; October 2006); Peter DiCola, *False Premises, False Promises: A Quantitative History of Ownership Consolidation in the Radio Industry* (Washington, DC: Future of Music Coalition, 2006), http://www.futureofmusic.org/research/radiostudy06.cfm.

59. For a thoughtful proposal from scholars and public interest advocates to reform data collection at the FCC, see: Philip M. Napoli and Joe Karaganis, *Toward a Federal Data Agenda for Communications Policymaking* (New York: Social Science Research Council, 2007), http://www.ssrc.org/programs/media/publications/Toward%20a%20Federal%20Data%20Agenda%20for%20-Communications%20Policymaking.pdf.

60. Keynote address of Jonathan Adelstein, Pre-Conference on Media Research, sponsored by the Social Science Research Council and Free Press, Memphis, Tennessee, January 11, 2007.

61. For a discussion of this, and striking data, see Project for Excellence in Journalism, "State of the Media 2006: An Annual Report on American Journalism," at: http://www.stateofthenewsmedia.org/2006/index.asp.

62. Wolfgang Donsbach, "The Identity of Communication Research," *Journal of Communication*, Vol. 56 (2006): pp. 437–48.

63. Interestingly, these are areas that get far more attention as a rule in communication departments outside the United States. As ICA president Sonia Livingstone, a professor at the London School of Economics and Political Science, wrote to me upon reading this section of my manuscript: "I am less sure about ongoing U.S. research, but I am clear that this is, exactly, the research agenda for many of us in Europe. Indeed, it reads like a run down of what's going on in my department right now." Sonia Livingstone e-mail to the author, February 23, 2007.

64. Elizabeth Fones-Wolf, *Waves of Opposition*.

65. For a provocative discussion of this, see Michael Perelman, *Railroading Economics: The Creation of Free Market Mythology* (New York: Monthly Review Press, 2006).

66. Joseph E. Stiglitz and Bruce Greenwald, *Towards a New Paradigm in Monetary Economics* (Cambridge, MA: Cambridge University Press, 2003); Joseph E. Stiglitz, *Economics of the Public Sector* (New York: Norton, 1988); Joseph E. Stiglitz, *New Developments in the Analysis of Market Structure: Proceedings of a Conference Held by the International Economic Association in Ottawa, Canada* (Cambridge, MA: MIT Press, 1986); Joseph E. Stiglitz, *The Economic Role of the State* (Malden, MA: Blackwell Publishing, 1989). See also, for example: Colin F. Camerer and Ernst Fehr, "When Does 'Economic Man' Dominate Social Behavior?" *Science*, January 6, 2006, pp. 47–52. There are classic texts that make these points as well, and they are well worth reading: Tibor Scitovsky, *Welfare and Competition* (Homewood, IL: R.D. Irwin, 1971); K. William Kapp, *The Social Cost of Private Enterprise* (Cambridge, MA: Harvard University Press, 1950); E.J. Mishan, *The Costs of Economic Growth* (London: Staples Press, 1968); E.J. Mishan, *Cost-Benefit Analysis* (Westport, CT: Praeger, 1973); E.J. Mishan, *21 Popular Economic Fallacies* (Middlesex, England: Pelican Books, 1971); E.J. Mishan, *Economics for Social Decisions: Elements of Cost-Benefit Analysis* (Westport, CT: Praeger, 1973); E.J. Mishan, *Introduction to Political Economy* (London: Hutchinson, 1982); E.J. Mishan, *Technology & Growth: The Price We Pay* (Westport, CT: Praeger, 1973); E.J. Mishan, *Economic Myths and the Mythology of Economics* (Brighton, England: Wheatsheaf Books, 1986); Francis M. Bator, *The Question of Government Spending: Public Needs and Private Wants* (New York: Harper & Brothers, 1960).

67. For some examples, see: N. Gregory Mankiw, "A Quick Refresher Course in Macroeconomics," *Journal of Economic Literature*, Vol. 28, No. 4 (December 1990): pp. 1645–60; N. Gregory Mankiw, "The Reincarnation of Keynesian Economics," *European Economic Review*, Vol. 36, Nos. 2–3 (April 1992): pp. 559–65; Robert J. Gordon, "What Is New-Keynesian Economics?" *Journal of Economic Literature*, Vol. 28, No. 3 (September 1990): pp. 1115–71; Bruce Greenwald and Joseph Stiglitz, "New and Old Keynesians," *Journal of Economic Perspectives*, Vol. 7, No. 1 (Winter 1993): pp. 23–44; James Tobin, "Price Flexibility and Output Stability: An Old Keynesian View," *Journal of Economic Perspectives*, Vol. 7, No. 1 (Winter 1993): pp. 45–65; Janet L. Yellen, "Efficiency Wage Models of Un-

employment," *American Economic Review*, Vol. 74, No. 2 (May 1984): pp. 200–205; George A. Akerlof and Janet L. Yellen, "A Near-Rational Model of the Business Cycle, with Wage and Price Inertia," *Quarterly Journal of Economics*, Vol. 100 (Supplement): pp. 823–38; Lawrence H. Summers, "Relative Wages, Efficiency Wages, and Keynesian Unemployment," *American Economic Review*, Vol. 78, No. 2 (May 1988): pp. 383–88.

68. For some good examples, see: Joel Waldfogel, "Preference Externalities: An Empirical Study of Who Benefits Whom in Differentiated-Product Markets," *RAND Journal of Economics*, Vol. 34, No. 3 (Autumn 2003): pp. 557–68; Lisa M. George and Joel Waldfogel, "The *New York Times* and the Market for Local Newspapers," *American Economic Review*, Vol. 96, No. 1: (March 2006): pp. 435–47; Simon P. Anderson and Stephen Coate, "Market Provision of Broadcasting: A Welfare Analysis," *Review of Economic Studies*, Vol. 72, No. 4 (October 2005): pp. 947–72, October 2005; James T. Hamilton, *All the News That's Fit to Sell: How the Market Transforms Information into News* (Princeton, NJ: Princeton University Press, 2004); Carl Shapiro and Hal R. Varian, *Information Rules: A Strategic Guide for the Network Economy* (Cambridge, MA: Harvard Business School Press, 1998).

Three introductory texts that lay out basic propositions and which point to the considerable research still to be done are: Gillian Doyle, *Understanding Media Economics* (London: Sage Publications, 2002); Alan B. Albarran, *Media Economics: Understanding Markets, Industries and Concepts* (2nd ed.) (Ames: Iowa State University Press, 2002); Colin Hoskins, Stuart McFadyen, and Adam Finn, *Media Economics: Applying Economics to New and Traditional Media* (Thousand Oaks, CA: Sage Publications, 2004).

69. See Eileen R. Meehan, *Why TV Is Not Our Fault: Television Programming, Viewers, and Who's Really in Control* (Lanham, MD: Rowman & Littlefield, 2005). I discuss this point at some length in *The Problem of the Media*.

70. See, for example: Associated Press, "Materialism Is Growing Obsession for Today's Youth," *The Capital Times*, January 23, 2007, p. A5. I take this point up below in my discussion of the Internet.

71. Inger L. Stole, "Philanthropy as Public Relations: A Historical and Economic Assessment of Cause-Related Marketing," Association for Education in Journalism and Mass Communication, Annual Conference, Toronto, Canada, August 2004.

72. I am reminded of the comments of *New Republic* editor

Bruce Bliven in the 1930s. He found broadcast advertising so "obnoxious" that he wished "the radio had never been invented." Cited in McChesney, *Telecommunications, Mass Media, and Democracy*, p. 105.

73. Dee Juliet B. Schor, *Born to Buy: The Commercialized Child and the New Consumer Culture* (New York: Scribner, 2004); Jeff Chester, *Digital Destiny: New Media and the Future of Democracy* (New York: The New Press, 2007), ch. 7.

74. See, for example: Jack Goldsmith and Tim Wu, *Who Controls the Internet? Illusions of a Borderless World* (New York: Oxford University Press, 2006); Yochai Benkler, *The Wealth of Networks: How Social Production Transforms Markets and Freedom* (New Haven, CT: Yale University Press, 2006); Lawrence Lessig, *Code: And Other Laws of Cyberspace* (New York: Basic Books, 1999); Lawrence Lessig, *Free Culture: How Big Media Uses Technology and the Law to Lock Down Culture and Control Creativity* (New York: Penguin Press, 2004); Lawrence Lessig, *The Future of Ideas: The Fate of the Commons in a Connected World* (New York: Random House, 2001).

75. One very important scholar of telecommunications who has addressed the Internet directly is Milton Mueller. See: Milton L. Mueller, *Ruling the Root: Internet Governance and the Taming of Cyberspace* (Cambridge, MA: MIT Press, 2004); Milton L. Mueller, *Telephone Companies in Paradise: A Case Study in Telecommunications Deregulation* (New Brunswick, NJ: Transaction Publishers, 1993); Milton L. Mueller, *Competition, Interconnection, and Monopoly in the Making of the American Telephone System* (Lanham, MD: AEI Press, 1998); Milton L. Mueller, *Telecom Policy and Digital Convergence* (Hong Kong: City University Press, 1997); Milton L. Mueller, *China in the Information Age: Telecommunications and the Dilemmas of Reform* (Washington, DC: Center for Strategic and International Studies, 1996); Milton L. Mueller, *International Telecommunications in Hong Kong: The Case for Liberalization* (2nd ed.) (Hong Kong: The Chinese University Press, 1992).

76. Richard Hoffman, "When It Comes to Broadband, U.S. Plays Follow the Leader," *Information Week*, February 15, 2007, final.pdfhttp://www.informationweek.com/story/showArticle.j html?articleID=197006038. This piece draws from: S. Derek Turner, *Broadband Reality Check II: The Truth Behind Americas Digital Decline* (New York: Free Press, 2006). Available at: www.freepress.net/docs/bbrc2-final.pdf.

77. Michael Calabrese e-mail to the author, February 9, 2007.

78. Tim Wu, "Wireless Network Neutrality," Social Science Research Network working paper, January 2007, http://papers.ssrn.com/sol3/papers.cfm?abstract_id=962027; for Milton Mueller's work, go to: http://blog.internetgovernance.org/blog.

79. See J.H. Snider, *The Citizen's Guide to the Airwaves* (Washington, DC: New America Foundation, 2003), p. 28.

80. For an official explanation of IRAC, go to: http://www.ntia.doc.gov/osmhome/iracdefn.html. J.H. Snider notes that: "There was a movement in the late 80's and early 90's to open up the IRAC process but it faded away. However, it may have been instrumental in fostering the 1994 and 1995 auctions of government spectrum for PCS." Personal communication, J.H. Snider to the author, January 29, 2007.

81. To be precise, the new term used is "Sensitive, but not classified."

82. Personal communication, Jim Snider to the author, January 29, 2007.

83. J.H. Snider, "Public Needs to Know How Government Runs Its Airwaves," *San Francisco Daily Journal*, May 10, 2006, http://www.newamerica.net/publications/articles/2006/public_needs_to_know_how_government_runs_its_airwaves.

84. For a good review of trends in the music industry, see David J. Parks, *Conglomerate Rock: The Music Industry's Quest to Divide Music and Conquer Wallets* (Lanham, MD: Lexington Books, 2007).

85. See, for example: Michael Perelman, *Steal This Idea: Intellectual Property Rights and the Corporate Confiscation of Creativity* (New York: Palgrave, 2002); Siva Vaidhyanathan, *Copyrights and Copywrongs: The Rise of Intellectual Property and How It Threatens Creativity* (New York: NYU Press, 2003); Siva Vaidhyanathan, *The Anarchist in the Library: How the Clash Between Freedom and Control Is Hacking the Real World and Crashing the System* (New York: Basic Books, 2004); Ronald Bettig, *Copyrighting Culture: The Political Economy of Intellectual Property* (Boulder, CO: Westview Press, 1996); Ronald Bettig and Jeanne L. Hall, *Big Media, Big Money: Cultural Texts and Political Economics* (Lanham, MD: Rowman & Littlefield, 2003); Kembrew McLeod, *Freedom of Expression: Overzealous Copyright Bozos and Other Enemies of Creativity* (New York: Doubleday, 2005).

86. For another discussion of this, with some hard data, see

Tom Fenton, *Bad News: The Decline of Reporting, the Business of News, and the Danger to Us All* (New York: Regan Books, 2005).

87. Overholser is working on developing a variety of structural policy measures. See Geneva Overholser, "On Behalf of Journalism: A Manifesto for Change," paper published by the Annenberg Public Policy Center, University of Pennsylvania, 2006, http://www.annenbergpublicpolicycenter.org/Overholser/20061011_Jo urnStudy.pdf. For background, see Geneva Overholser and Kathleen Hall Jamieson, eds., *The Press* (New York: Oxford University Press, 2005).

88. W. Lance Bennett, Regina G. Lawrence, and Steven Livingston, *When the Press Fails: Political Power and the News Media from Iraq to Katrina* (Chicago: University of Chicago Press, 2007).

89. As Geneva Overholser wrote to me: "I used to feel that there was hope in addressing corporate governance. I was part of a group of former editors pressing for such measures as more retired journalists on boards, committees to audit journalism and the like. I think it's too late for that now, the crisis is too advanced. We need more sweeping reform proposals that might provide dramatic change to address the magnitude of this crisis." Geneva Overholser e-mail to the author, February 26, 2007.

90. James Rainey, "Scion Offers Ideas for *Times*: In an Opinion Piece to Run Sunday, Harry Chandler Proposes Community Ownership," *Los Angeles Times*, November 11, 2006; Harry B. Chandler, "A Chandler's advice for the *L.A. Times*: The Newspaper Can Only Thrive if Its Owners and Editors Make Drastic Changes," *Los Angeles Times*, November 12, 2006.

91. A recent study by the Government Accountability Office puts the present and future of public television in bleak terms barring major policy intervention. See: U.S. Government Accounting Office, *Telecommunications: Issues Related to the Structure and Funding of Public Television* (Washington, DC: U.S. Government Accounting Office, January 2007), http://www.gao.gov/new.items/d07150.pdf.

92. Monroe E. Price, *Media and Sovereignty: The Global Information Revolution and Its Challenge to State Power* (Cambridge, MA: MIT Press, 2002); Nancy Morris and Silvio Waisbord, eds., *Media and Globalization: Why the State Matters* (Lanham, MD: Rowman & Littlefield, 2001).

93. See, for example, Peter S. Grant and Chris Wood, *Blockbusters and Trade Wars: Popular Culture in a Globalized World* (Van-

couver: Douglas & McIntyre, 2004); Damien Geradin and David Luff, eds., *The WTO and Global Convergence in Telecommunications and Audio-Visual Services* (New York: Cambridge University Press, 2004).

94. See, for example, Peter Drahos and John Braithwaite, *Information Feudalism: Who Owns the Knowledge Economy?* (New York: The New Press, 2002).

95. For an example of the sort of communication research that can be indirectly affected by the recognition that we are in a critical juncture, consider Diana C. Mutz's thoughtful new book, *Hearing the Other Side: Deliberative versus Participatory Democracy* (New York: Cambridge University Press, 2006). Mutz is concerned with the issue of whether and how people engage with political views opposed to their own. Although the book is less about media than interpersonal and group communication, it assumes a certain type of media with a certain type of media content. It is a given, not a variable. What if we hold the power to dramatically transform the nature of the media system and the nature of media content? Then she might need to reconsider and reframe her argument and her research.

96. This was done by the broadcast reform movement in the early 1930s. They made the control of radio the national debate topic one year. See McChesney, *Telecommunications, Mass Media, and Democracy.*

97. Bill Moyers, "For America's Sake," *The Nation*, January 22, 2007.

98. Pierre Bourdieu, "A Reasoned Utopia and Economic Fatalism," *New Left Review*, No. 227 (1998): pp. 125–30.

Index